An Administrator's Perspective from North East

An Administrator's Perspective from North East

Aalok Shrivastava

GYAN

ISBN: 978-81-212-6151-7

Published, 2022

Published by

Gyan Publishing House
5, Ansari Road
Daryaganj, New Delhi-110002
Phone: 011-47034999, 9811692060
www.gyanbooks.com
E-mail: books@gyanbooks.com

Printed at: Gyan Press, Delhi.

Cover Photo
Tosar Lake (13,000 ft.) North Sikkim
Courtesy Sikkim Tourism
Back Cover
Author

Aabhar (Acknowledgement)

To amalgamate feelings, expressions and experiences of a long career in a book form is not easy. While a few of my write ups belong to yesteryears, I have tried my level best to do adequate justice to contemporary social and political developments, leaving at the end, some scope for indulgence in poetry. Needless to say, my late child was a better master of creative writing.

I may also mention that during and immediately after Covid period, attempting a book in constrained circumstances was not a cakewalk.

In this endeavour, I would like to heartily acknowledge the contribution of following:-

Jayshree, my spouse for supporting me wholeheartedly.

Editors of Sikkim Express, Indian Bureaucracy.com, Indian Century.in, Outlook, Social Action, Indian Dominion, Indian Mountaineer, Akshar Parv and Grihswamini for permitting me to reprint my published articles.

Sarvasri Sonam Wangdi, former C.S., Sikkim, Prof. Santosh Rath, Prof. Soumendra Jain, Prof. Himanshu Ranjan, my erstwhile colleagues M.G. Kiran, V.B. Pathak, Bhawani Rai, Robin Chacha, Surendra Bhaiya and Dinesh Singh.

Dr. Jitendra Nath of Radiant Consultant for initial processing & printing works.

Sarvasri B.P. Garg, Amit Garg, Javed Sultan and Imran, DTP person of Gyan Publishing House, N. Delhi for a professional and impressive work.

Lastly, Sarvasri Rajesh Ranjan, Vishwamitra Kumar, Archit and Anand for their remarkable role during various stages of this book. If some names have been left out, I would express my regrets.

Aalok Shrivastava, IAS, (R)
Ex-Chief Secretary, Govt. of Sikkim
alok.secyskm@gmail.com
9434086959

C-104, Apex Athena,
Sector 75, Noida

Contents

(A) CHANGING LIFESTYLES

1

Modernization of Indian Consumer Goods Tradition[1]

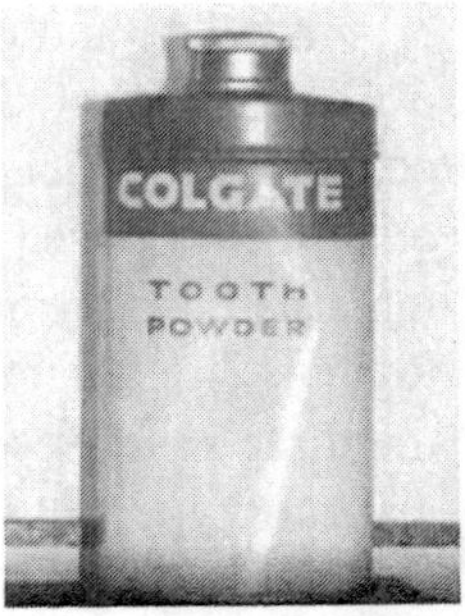

Consumer goods are the goods purchased and utilized by consumers rather than by producers or manufacturers who produce goods, such as, clothing, food stuff, beverages, footwear, P.O.L. products etc. In a way, goods of daily use would come under this domain. Discipline of Economics looks at these as any tangible commodity that takes care of day to day wants and needs.

When we say so, we basically mean three categories of consumer goods: durable goods, non-durable goods and consumer services. Instances of consumer goods could be, automobiles, furnitures, home appliances, telephones, now Cell phones etc. While haircut or beauty parlour services and small equipment and automobile maintenance could come under the ambit of consumer services.

Ever since the British began consolidation and Independence of the country followed suit, a sea change was seen in the psyche of Indian consumers, their taste, habit and preferences. It was not only spread of education leading to hike in standards of living but rising contact with the West became an important turning point. While M.N. Srinivas, Father of Indian Sociology called these processes as 'Sanskritisation and Westernization'. Yogendra Singh, another Sociology pioneer used the expression 'Modernization of Indian Traditions'.

On the other hand, James Duesenberry, an economist spoke of 'Demonstration Effect' on the part of deprived sections who would follow the "haves", irrespective of flow of cash pattern to them. These theorisations, reflecting a certain aspect of social change, can not be delinked from upward looking consumer behaviour.

Per kind courtesy Sri Kuchey, a friend from Jammu & Kashmir, an Internet video aptly links a beautiful Lata Mangeshkar song from a 1956 film Shirin Farhad- "Gujra Hua Zamana, aata Nahin Dubara" (A bygone era will not return) to the variety of consumer products used since Independence. Beginning wrongly with a black & white T.V. and obsolete dialing phone, it ends with a Prestige pressure cooker. In a time span of 3.9 minutes, twenty nine consumer products have been featured. Had it begun by focusing on stove (opposed to coal chulha) and slowly shifting to a lamp, lantern and a Petromax, in that order, perhaps that may have been logical. Fire, afterall is needed everyday for cooking food, one of the three basic necessities. Two stove versions shown are also of pressure type, not the 'battiwala', the precursor, apart from being affordable.

As first item to break the day was usually tooth powder, very rightly Colgate powder has been featured. But to see Prudent paste advertised by the actor Ashok Kumar instead of hugely popular Colgate paste is rather surprising. A Favre Leuba type of time piece has been correctly included, as apart from head of family no one could afford a watch (perhaps HMT) those days and this vital product not only showed time, it was also used for setting loud alarm for the wee hours when either someone had to "revise" lessons prior to an examination or had to catch an early morning train.

The useful Geep torch would be a necessity as twenty four hour power supply was an unthinkable proposition at one point of time. No doubt, batteries were needed for making it functional, so, Eveready battery has been rightly placed in the galaxy. Lux bath soap, advertised by Heroines, namely Sadhna and Zeenat Aman was certainly not a luxury item in a tropical and humid country like India. Incidently, this was a popular product promoted by the heroines and that Shahruk Khan was the sole hero to have figured in its campaign. Sitting topless in a tub, he is shown surrounded by the heroines, who were his 'predecessors' in the advertisement. The 501 washing soap and Surf, one misses over here very much.

Display of omnipresent Dalda is definitely an eye catcher. Its wide use in every house could never be doubted. However, it would have been alright if it's close competitor Rath was also included. It is not that people purposely used either of these to raise their cholesterol level but actually not everyone could afford 'Ghee' even on occasions, namely worships, festivals or weddings. One very much also feels ommision of acute necessities, such as, Atlas and Hero cycles.

In the next category of semi-luxuries : radio, bulky 'Dhobi' iron, Ponds and Afghan creams have been correctly roped in. But surprising, exclusion of market leaders: Tata, Bata, Philip's, Murphy, Binaca, Lakme, Fair & Lovely etc. could not be understood. Also over here, ever in demand transistors, vernacular dailies viz, Times of India, Hindustan Times, Indian Express, Navbharat Times and magazines, Viz, Illustarted Weekly of India, Readers Digest, Dharmyug, Nandan, Manohar Kahaniyan, etc. can not possibly be excluded. It's good that Filmfare got a place.

Further, not to be missed, old model non-digital telephones of four colours have been displayed, which was called for. O yes, the caption "Remember messing up the last number meant that one had to dial again all the five or six numbers", certainly brings a smile. From the comparative angle, present day landline or cell sets are very convenient and user friendly light weight devices. But left in 'auto gear' these also disturb peace, distract, hide, divert, toss, encourage untruth and jealousy, create misunderstanding etc, apart from being indispensable to office management, law & order duties, natural disaster management and E-learning in tense Covid

times. At the same time, when it comes to making fake call and certifi-cate centres, printing counter-feit currency, kidnappings, smuggling and aiding frauds and committing Bank & Cyber crimes, Cell phones are unfortunately on the forefront.

One should be failing if the office aid and the then luxury goods spectrum was left out. Courtesy the video, its thrilling to remember type writers, V.C.P.'s, V.C.R's, floppies, C.D.'s, Vespa Scooter, Rajdoot Motor Cycle, Isola camera and Fabina & Bombay Dyeing suiting, advertised respectively by Rajesh Khanna and Amitabh Bachchan. Recalling days of injurious Charminar and Panama cigarettes was not necessary. Ideally the video should end with Ambassador and Fiat cars even when old reliable Lambretta scooter was ommitted.

Closing the chapter with Prestige not Hawkins cooker may raise questions than giving answers in respect of our economy which turned liberal from umpteen pressures of 'Inspector Raj' in 1991.

To conclude, my purpose was to analyze the process of change in the consumer goods sector from 1947 onwards. To what extent, the same was achieved, it is for the learned readers to assess and judge.

Most of the new developments, are no doubt time and money saving devices. But these are meant mainly for grown up students and the adults. These should not be found in the hands of children for obvious reasons.

Fast electronic waste and polythene disposal mechanism coupled with harmless recycling must not be ignored at this crucial juncture. Also a word of caution pertaining to their use and adoption should be to have clarity and integrity as regards our intent and ultimate output. Not to be cowed down by "Free" or "heavily discounted" offers, one should work positively in the overall interest of the society.

2

Communication Through The Ages In India[2]

A look at the facsimile of a Post Card launched after the World wars carries a special value to me as an essential item of University days and formative years of service. Why so ? For want of a telephone connection (a sort of luxury those days) it was not possible to talk home.

Last when I saw a Post Card, famous Ashoka pillar emblem was replaced by a sketch of a tiger. The Post Card was a low cost affordable medium which was open on both sides, perhaps to ensure a flair for transparency. Not only one could scribble main welfare message in short, same was also expected to convey felt emotions of the moment. There would be no worry or hurry in respect of a reply. That would be forthcoming within a week to ten days. One was used to waiting, unlike at present, when patience is unheard of. Heaven was not going to fall in between, I would console myself. If someone came from home and delivered home made cookies or pickle, a treat will be arranged with friends.

A different kind of joy would be noticed on the faces of both sender and receiver, when the Postman or 'Dakiya' in his Khaki dress would ring his cycle bell. His on and off arrival was greeted with cool water/home made cold drink or tea, depending upon weather, if he had ample time. He would be entitled to a tip (bakshish) if a Money Order was brought. At the University hostel, it was a different ball game with the urban Dakiya. Slips for M.O. will be left on hostel table a day in advance, actual currency would arrive only the next day.

INLAND LETTER CARD (Antardeshi)

Later Postcards were supplemented not replaced by a light blue coloured Inland Letter Card to ensure privacy of the news/ message. Though it was a closed or shut object, yet fun loving mischievous relatives or friends would manage to sneak into from sides, to find out the juicy content or teary eyed expressions of a lover or a spouse vis a vis a beloved or a husband, physically separated but determined to maintain an emotional bond.

ENVELOPES & REGISTERED POST

With a view, perhaps to fortify the contents of Inland Letter Card, Envelops hit the scene. Not only they ensured a cover and safety, there would be no limit on number of pages. Of course one was required to pay extra as per added weight. To cut short time and ensure delivery, envelopes could be also sent under a 'Certificate Of Posting' or through Registered Post. An authentic receipt issued after acceptance at the counter would become a valid proof of despatch/evidence.

Now Speed Post facility at an increased cost has taken us much ahead. Its movement can be also tracked from time to time, so as to check delays in delivery.

TELEGRAMS

Telegrams facilitated through a wireless Walkie Talkie soon emerged. A code would ensure saving of expenditure. It had restriction on words and the facility would be limited to short messages concerning birth of a baby, successes, weddings, death, get well messages etc. Meaning thereby, it conveyed Joy's and Sorrows of life. When I used the facility by paying only a paltry sum of Rs Two and Fifty Paise in May, 1984 upon getting selected into the Civil Services, my inner joy won't know any bounds.

But somehow the news of arrival of a Telegram in any house was generally linked to a bad omen or sudden expiry of a dear departed. I too suffered once on this count as name of my eldest deceased Bhabhi (sister in law) was not indicated in the telegram. So suspense and anxiety prevailed during the course of a long train journey over twenty four hours.

MONEY ORDERS TO ELECTRONIC TRANSFER OF MONEY KEPT IN SAVINGS BANK ACCOUNT

The chain won't be complete unless we also discuss the necessity and efficacy of Money Orders. It was most important means for survival of families and students staying away from home. For fast transactions, Telegraphic M.O. could be also availed of. At the bottom of M.O. form, one could write brief messages addressed to the receiver. It would be routinely torn off and handed over to the receiver. Nonetheless, the Postman had to be given a tip on such happy occasions. Both of these facilities now have been dispensed with in view of rapid expansion of net banking operations.

Electronic transfer of money from one branch to another (on written request of account holder) within the same bank as also to a branch of another bank has become a fast reality through Real Time Gross Settlement (RTGS) and National Electronic Fund Transfer (NEFT). Both of these facilities are maintained at the level of R.B.I. and maximum limit is Rs. ten lakhs at a time. Transfer is almost free of cost within half an hour in respect of Inter Bank transfer while same may be by the end of the day in regard to the transfer to a branch of another bank. Now literate and net savvy customers have a wide choice for Personal, Mobile and Corporate banking operations.

A poor illiterate person may, however, has to suffer as he /she has to pay a certain amount as "commission" to other well versed persons. Latter exploit, take undue advantages, such as, withdrawal of another person's money, cloning of A.T.M. cards, etc.

STATICS & DYNAMICS OF PHONES

Role played in regard to transition from a static (being called landline) to a cordless and subsequently to Cell phone cannot be undermined. One and all are either in possession of a set or two or are familiar with its pros and cons. Gone are the days of "Talk Less, Work More". Unnecessary and compulsive speaking/chatting, that too every now and then has, unfortunately become order of the day. People no longer excuse themselves to take a call when some meeting or important discussion is in progress. Most of immature lots consider it their birth right to respond to a call immediately. Afterall, missed call facility too can be utilized later.

Apart from encouraging undesirable flight of temper and causing noise pollution for no rhyme or reason, access to a Cell can cajole also and upset or hurt a person in a matter of minutes. No need to carry a bad memory home. In about a decade or so, use of mobile has become a source of national pass time, if not endless self centered refreshment or entertainment. All users must make it a point to use the device in a peaceful setting sparingly and make maximum use when a law and order, accident and natural calamity challenge is being confronted. Sharing of input without verification and confirmation, nevertheless, has to be avoided.

REVOLUTION THROUGH INTERNET, E-MAILS, WHATSAPP ETC.

With the advent of Internet in the seventies and its further fine tuning in the eighties and introduction of WhatsApp in 2008, the communication scenario began changing rapidly. USA, China and

India have maximum number of internet users and its stupendous growth is bound to see more changes on earth.

Further innovations in form of Video calls, SignalApp and Telegram-App are also spreading very fast. With such multiple choices, human beings especially in developing world often are under the wrong impression that it is the right time to relish the freebies. But are we aware that anything free always comes with a concealed cost ?

Our immovable assets, art objects, plot of land, flat, vehicles and some other physical possessions will be at risk if we get too friendly while showing our concern and make a commitment without consulting experienced family friends or well wishers. It is desirable to be a good listener and move slowly.

End To End Encryption: A Myth ?

There is nothing like it, as claimed by the service providers of social media outlets. The most widely used "Free Search Engine", according to a source quoted by a popular Hindi T.V. Channel keeps a two Biga bite record on each user. Whatever you disclose even in good faith is kept in a profile form in a safe place. Your assets, in addition, in different forms or data generated, itself becomes a product to be used by the goody goody service provider to earn profit out of advertisements.

The most widely used Google believes in 'delivering googlies'. According to same source, in 2019 alone, the estimated income of Google was $ 11 Lakh 81 thousand Crores, of which, $ 9 Lakh 86 thousand Crores was generated out of digital advertisements.

Injurious Impact of Smart Phones

Widespread use of smart phones by our countrymen (thanks to E-Learning imposed during Covid waves) increases the addiction level of youngsters in addition to causing gradual damage to their mental faculty. Not only these attractive hand held 'toys' are kept very close to brain, these have to be changed frequently as if a dress is to be bought quarterly, if not on a monthly or weekly basis. We need to introspect ourselves as to which direction or path is correct.

In the beginning of new millennium one had to pay a paltry sum for Internet connection but same would be probably peanut compared to mine of informations that could be downloaded or uploaded. Later cost/tariff vanished completely and thus actual exploitation of innocent but greedy Indians harping for higher education and employment abroad, began. Many websites, addresses, portals would turn out to be fake affairs.

Now gears are getting reversed. More and more foreigners are also getting duped by Indian self-proclaimed agents. The National Capital Territory zone, unfortunately specializes in these frauds, more so, they seem to have mushroomed with the connivance of former employees of banks and similar financial institutions as also some policemen during and after two Lockdown periods. Passport, Visa, bank account, fixed deposit, insurance, EMI detail and what not, are not easily known but disclosed voluntarily by ever eager Indians having a desire to become millionaires overnight. Warnings issued from time to time by the Government and authorized agencies mostly fall on deaf ears.

Safety & Precautionary Devices

As a safety device, all transactions, loan advances, credit debit exercises must have confirmation copies to be conveyed through a closed or sealed envelope. Signature on same by the authorized person has to be insisted upon for the reasons of safety and authenticity. The usual alibi or pretext of absence of an authorized signatory or a computer generated slip/statement receipt should not be accepted under any circumstance. It's the question of one's life time hard earned savings which may be linked to the future well being of the offspring or the "will" in favour of deserving nominees but only after one has ensured a decent accommodation for the self and spouse.

One may have digressed sufficiently but same was intended to be in public interest. It is felt that need for unhindered communication will arise even if Space Tourism gathers momentum or colonies are planned at Moon or Mars planet.

Adequate care and precaution should be our hallmark.

With each passing day, urge to learn afresh and saving for the sake of giving (not lending) should also be our motto. Appropriate concluding line may be:

"TAKE VACCINE BUT DO NOT GIVE UP MASK, THE MASK OF SAFETY."

3

Travel By A City Bus

A wait of half an hour near RML Hospital, Delhi appeared longer than an hour. Even when I was fasting for over twelve hours, having finished Yoga, I was not feeling tired. On a Saturday or holidays, as per my old habits that die hard, I neither use official conveyance nor a three wheeler. Rather, to mingle with the common man and elicit his candid and often cruel critique, I would prefer hopping into a DTC or Blue line bus or occasionally use Metro, introduced from 2001. This day my endurance was bound to be tested.

It was a pleasure to see an infant playing in the lap of her mother at the bus stop. Giving her company was a boy slightly older, seated close to a heap of ground nut. An old lady wearing a white Sari was doing brisk business by selling seasonal fruits. People of myriad faces, heights and dimensions would throng the bus stop. In no time, they would attempt to catch the barely stopping buses. Some would succeed, others would be left behind to admire the beauty of the swanky bus stop, conveying the message "Commonwealth Games only 1000 days away". On the contrary, the diagonally opposite bus stop still welcomed Monsoir Sarkozy, the French President even after a month of his official visit to India.

My wait having the correct dose of patience, tolerance and perseverance finally paid off when I saw a D. T. C. bus. It slowed down but no one showed any inclination to hop in as it turned out to be a 'Mudrika', normally plying on the Ring road. I too resisted the temptation to get in as it would have left me half way. The next bus became a sort of "mirage in the desert". But it was a Railway Special, not a bus following normal routes. The third time I was NOT unlucky. I almost got into a Blue Line, till I realised that a large, green, hi-tech DTC bus plying on 740 route stopped right behind. I made no mistake.

I was happy to see a moving screen, proclaiming that the gigantic bus charged normal fares of Rs. 3, 5, 7 and 10. My entry took longer as the automatic gate would not open easily. I thought that only a few were waiting for long. I was shaken virtually on noticing a group of giggling young, teen aged girls getting hurriedly into the already fully occupied bus. Prior to introducing this service the City Government had vowed at last to follow the capacity mode. "But it is Delhi, Yahan Sab Chalta Hai", remarked an old, haggard Sardarjee, duly supporting his ailing wife, struggling to sip juice from a plastic bottle.

The five girls: Aishwarya, Kareena, Priyanka, Bipasha and Katrina missed no time in occupying whatever space was available. None had monthly student pass (Rs. 12 & 50 Paise a month) nor they showed any intention to buy a ticket. Within five minutes, two of them, Kareena and Katrina, donning latest midi and frock respectively, managed window seats upon grabbing a God sent opportunity. At Eleven Statue Point, when two senior citizens inquired about a locality, situated much ahead, these 'bright' teenagers, guided as if that was close to the next stop. They were naturally 'advised' to rush through. Needless to say, none of the divas, could, however, escape the vigilant Conductor. Buying five tickets was the natural corollary.

The other three' muskeeters' were busy gossiping and giggling to glory. Variety of talks were resorted to: studies, make up, Gol-gappas, strict Mummies, encouraging Papas, T.V. serials, the latest SRK, Saif and John Abraham movies, tourism up in sky and Cricket Down Under. Aishwarya, sporting a pair of blue embroidered Jeans with a contrasting 'Top', generally will speak less, nodd and smile more and would not argue. Bipasha, wearing a bright flashy skirt, was a confirmed chatterbox, not only in drawing fellow passenger's attention but also in pulling her friends apart. She would make fun of every body and display the tantrums of a Jhansi Ki Raani. Priyanka was neither proactive nor subdued. She appeared studious, urbane and fun loving in her figure hugging red Corduroys.

Looking at these 'dramas', time frittered away. Bus had entered Chankyapuri by now. I was glued to this comfortable setting even while standing for half an hour. The young eves would not allow any passenger to move or exit easily. Rather, they would be advised to promptly use the rear gate, something vehemently opposed to by the Conductor. I managed a lead, nevertheless, much to the discomfiture of Bipasha, who gazed and stared, while posing to be thoroughly engrossed in reading a romantic Mill & Boons novel.

They say, even a dog has his way. This writer, therefore, had to assert upon being pushed by an elderly ' oversized' couple. The girls too had to relent. Before the bus screeched to a halt at Malcha Marg, Aishwarya initiated a soothing melody. Priyanka, Kareena and Katrina, all followed suit. But Bipasha won't budge. No one was looking at her, so she began looking outside, blowing a whistle.

It was time for me to get down at Railway colony on S.P. Marg. The door once again took time to open. To my satisfaction, the elderly couple got a seat at last and thereby, perhaps, decided to enjoy further the 'comforts' of the swanky bus.

The common feeling of adoration on the part of passengers for the amenities being extended in form of hi-tech buses, extension of Metro, separate bus corridor, new flyovers, underpasses etc. on the eve of 2010 Commonwealth Games sounded nice and awesome but a large majority of country's population was deprived of these.

Soon after getting off, I jumped over a piece of stone kept precariously near the bus stop. Afterall, I was wearing a brand new blue track suit, belonging to Ankoor, my teenaged son doing B. A. in Political Science at Venkateshwar college. I was in a mood to display some semblance of youth even on the eve of my golden jubilee.

When after break fast, I sat down finally on my desk at 14, Panchsheel Marg, a streak of smile would come over my face time and again, reminding me vividly of the giggling girls of 740, instrumental in providing a free, fearless and fabulous entertainment.

4

Flying May Be Safest, But Is It Safe To Fly Nowadays ?[3]

Who does not like travelling and tourism , more so, in the post -Covid era ? Depending upon one's paying capacity and with a view to save time, one may prefer a flight or a Mail/Express train if desired place is not connected by air. Flying, afterall, all over the World is considered safest way to travel.

We have to prepare for an air journey sufficiently ahead of time. But, perhaps, all know how frustrating it can be if something goes wrong.

On the ground, one is given reasons, such as, aircraft has not arrived, weather is bad, or there is a technical flaw etc.Reasons connected to manpower constraints are generally not disclosed.

Upon check in and security clearance, one should be sure to fly but sometimes, donot be surprised if you are informed in the departure area that "You have reported late". So despite your request and pleadings, you are denied boarding.

While waiting for the next flight (if there is one) you gather that some "important" person or possibly a "person with deep pocket" was adjusted at the last moment against your bonafide seat.You may not know, it happens due to old and nefarious practice of over booking by the private airlines.It has been learnt that those providing security at the airport too are hand in glove on many occasions.

Either you are made to pay an unreasonable amount or depending upon your convincing powers, you are issued a fresh boarding card to be accepted back. It is also a mystery, as to how only your luggage is identified and off loaded within a few minutes of being declared "ineligible" for the first flight.

Once inside the aircraft, one is not sure of take off immediately. Even after being hurriedly pushed into the bus, donot be surprised if a VIP looking hefty man or woman keeps everyone waiting and flight takes off after their settling in.Usual drafted apology message is read out in an anglicized accent by the host or hostess.

FEEL LUCKY IF YOU ARE OFFERED WATER WITHOUT ASKING.

Checking of Aircraft Is Mandatory

While IT IS MANDATORY to thoroughly check an aircraft before being declared "Air Worthy", in the past few weeks, Indigo and Spicejet have inconvenienced and risked the passengers by reporting the following:

- Smoke is coming out from the engine,
- Wings have suffered some damage,
- Overhead hand baggage container has suddenly opened,
- Window panes have developed cracks,or
- Even the front window has some issue.

Due to such reasons, aircrafts have to return or get diverted to another nearest airport or pray for emergency landing in a country that does not allow her air space for use by us.

In the event of last named episode, another aircraft comes after hours of wait or sometimes next day. But it may happen at the cost of other passengers who may get deprived of their planes taking off in time resulting into disruption of their schedules or appointments.

Another sad experience one faces is the practice of private carriers to close the aircraft gate much ahead of scheduled take off time.When questioned, they never forget to defend themselves. It happens due to two reasons:

- Either they follow instruction from 'Top' to give preference to a big destination ahead of time, or
- The airlines has no inclination to pay the halt charges of the crew.

Latter may be the main excuse due to heavy losses suffered by the private carriers in the recent past.

This writer was compelled to miss two such flights from two North East airports as also once due to supposed overbooking or preference to a heavyweight passenger as described in para 3. INDIGO, the concerned airline and head of CISF were approached ,however, no opportunity was given to lodge a formal complain, forget about looking into the inconvenience caused or tendering an apology.

VIEWS OF MINISTRY OF CIVIL AVIATION

On hearing or taking suo motto cognizance of aforesaid facts, the standard replies of the Ministry are :

> 'passenger safety is paramount', spot checks will be conducted or already conducted, suitable direction has been given to the concerned airline to avoid technical snags, go for operation of only 50% of the flights, better audit of aircrafts by engineers will follow, etc.

REACTION OF D.G.C.A.

Aviation watchdog in India is Director General, Civil Aviation. Its head is supposed to be a technically qualified Aeronautical engineer of sufficient seniority.

Sadly over the years, non technical Civil Servants of Joint Secretary rank are heading this vital organisation. Whatever they say or observe ,therefore, is based on technical inputs of their aeronautical or mechanical engineer colleagues. Hence, one can imagine the end result. Distortion in communication is most likely.

Instead of concentrating on technical issues already described, it has been reported that even foreign airlines that had come to India had reported fifteen technical snags in the last eighteen days.Specific details about such snags, however, are never disclosed.

DGCA has also the audacity to say that that there is No Need To Panic as none of the events that have been reported/ discussed " had the potential to cause havoc".

REMEDIAL MEASURES

Even though the DGCA has promised to go for trouble shooting, ordering replacement of defective valves and to undertake a two month long Special Audit of the airlines, it may be premature to say that Indian aviation sector is safe and that snags reported are of Routine Nature.

CAN IT BE BELIEVED ?

Hold your breath and think seriously before booking air tickets of private carriers. Only what has been described may not put you to risk. There may be some other reasons also for flight disruptions and sudden and abrupt cancellations.

Pilots, Air Traffic Controllers, Despatchers together with ground duty men, all are bound to work according to a defined system and all need to be monitored and reviewed regularly.

Passenger rights and obligations are generally well explained in manuals and displayed instructions. But only a person who feels the pinch (not always) can assess the actual gap between the Cup and the Lip.

Last but not the least, due to changing lifestyles on our part, we need to follow also "Plane Appropriate Behaviour", rather than rushing in and out of an aircraft as if one is having a bus or train ride. Senior and ailing passengers too deserve a special treatment.

INFECTION FROM MONKEY POX

The W.H.O. after taking cognisance of over 20,000 cases of Monkey Pox in 75 countries has rightly declared a PUBLIC HEALTH EMERGENCY OF INTERNATIONAL CONCERN. This viral Zoonosis disease was already prevalent in many countries of Africa. Symptoms reportedly last for two to four weeks.

We need to take adequate care against this fresh epidemic which may come through air, sea or ground routes. We should be guided by effective prevention and control measures undertaken during three waves of Covid-19. At present, it may not appear that Contagious but one cannot predict what may be turn of events in future.

Apart from developing a dedicated vaccine for the new viral infection, all state governments must exercise State of Alert from now onwards at all the borders and save the population from another harrowing experience.

5

Social Media and Freedom of Speech[4]

Freedom of speech and expression in some form or the other has prevailed in every community and country right from the 5th Century B. C. In modern era, before discussing the characteristic features of some of the modern democracies that have guaranteed such a right, it may be appropriate to explain the basic concepts and nuances. We may also flag the name of ten countries wherein no freedom of speech and expression exists even at present and that every information has to flow through state agencies. These countries are: North Korea, Cuba, Libya, Syria, Myanmar, Turkmenistan, Uzbekistan, Belarus, Equatorial Guinea and Eritrea.

Freedom of Speech

It is guaranteed in U.SA. by the first amendment to country's Constitution. In France, freedom of speech is guaranteed by the Declaration of the Rights of Man and of the citizen of 1789. It came into being immediately after the French Revolution.

Further, Right to freedom of expression has been also recognized as a human right in the Universal Declaration of Human Rights and International Human Rights Law by the U.N.O. Many countries have enacted legislations that protect free speech. But certain restrictions have been also provided in matters of national security or public order, depending upon background and circumstances.

In India, Article 19 (1)(a) of the Constitution provides for freedom of expression to the fellow citizens. It states:

> "Everyone has the right to freedom of opinion and expression, this right includes freedom to hold opinions without interference and to seek, receive and impart information and ideas through ANY media and regardless of frontiers."
>
> It can be in form of written texts, word of mouth or any other form of communication. Further the mode can be through pictures, movies, broadcasting or electronic means.

(1) FREEDOMS AVAILABLE TO CITIZENS ARE:

- (a) freedom of speech and expression,
- (b) freedom to assemble peacefully and without arms,
- (c) freedom to form associations and unions,
- (d) freedom to move freely throughout the territory of India,
- (e) freedom to reside and settle in any part of the territory of India and
- (f) to practice any profession, or to carry on any occupation, trade or business.

Thus people everywhere can freely express themselves and also engage in public life without fear or discrimination.

Freedom of expression like other Fundamental Rights provided by the Indian Constitution is not Absolute.

IT CAN BE RESTRICTED.

One has seen and experienced it during the days of Emergency (1975-77).

The common limitations or boundaries to such freedom may relate to libel, slander, obscenity, pornography, sedition, right to privacy and dignity etc.

Social Media

According to Wikipedia, "Social Media are interactive digital channels that facilitate the creation and sharing of information, ideas, interests and other forms of expression through virtual communities and networks."

By this free medium one can contact, convey and know the latest developments in regard to kith and kin, friends and well wishers, contemporaries and elders. Socially relevant causes can be also espoused and awareness about an idea or innovation can be also generated. Not only one can learn something new but can also hone up skills and expertise.

FORMS OF SOCIAL MEDIA

Various forms of this Internet based means of communication are: blogs, micro blogs, social networking sites, photo and hobby sharing sites, video hosting sites and an opportunity to have access to Instant Messaging etc.

When so many social media sites are available on the Net, one should take time and adequate care in selecting the right one.

According to one rough estimate, globally people spend an average of two hours and 24 minutes everyday on Social Media. It gradually influences their ideas and thinking process.

Facebook has 2.9 Billion active users in a month, YouTube has 2.3 Billion, WhatsApp 2 Billion and Facebook Messenger & WeChat, 1.3 Billion each.

Controversies To Be Avoided

Freedom of expression does not mean that we should have ill will or an intention to harm others without any rhyme or reason. With rapid development and reach of technology or the evolution of digital age this freedom can, rather has become controversial.

Advent of Internet, Mobile Telephony and now Social Media definitely are extending further precious rights of man for free communication of ideas and opinions. Social media being under individual control is having a profound effect on its users. One reacts instantly and immediately without waiting to verify or confirm an episode or event or without looking into the authenticity of its source. Very few people think about the adverse repercussion, a comment or observation may have.

Sometimes one sees same incidents or episodes, such as, C.A.A. and NRC protests, Kisan stirs, Shaheen Bagh dharna, Use of Bulldozers in removing encroachments, Jahangirpuri, Prayagraj and Kanpur disturbances, Nupur Sharma's statements, Kanhaiya Lal's beheading, Umesh Kolhe's murder, Indian Justice system etc. making rounds and rounds in different languages.

On many occasions there is miscommunication or wrong targeting or an urge to generalise an issue based on one incident. It may misguide the common man leading to unnecessary flare up.

Not only one comments casually but also one feigns ignorence about a legal framework or defined redressal mechanism, if caught on wrong foot.

MERITS OF SOCIAL MEDIA

In absence of authentic literature on this subject, an attempt has been made to cull out information available on internet and attempt an analysis.

(a) Social Media can assist in pursuing good causes and practices by faciltating contact with like minded individuals. It can give a boost to voluntary donation and charity work,

(b) One can connect easily with people one may desire from anywhere in country or World through this medium,

(c) Through this fast medium we can get upto date data and information which may be faster than television and much sooner than waiting for a newspaper or a magazine,

(d) It may prove a bonanza to education and health sectors. Who may not desire latest developments in human resource development and medical science ? Tele-medicine can be further boosted and fine tuned.

(e) For a business person it may prove helpful in advertisement, sale promotion, large audience for products with least possible investment and possibly risks,

(f) Any one can use it to create select groups of people having common interest or hobby which may lessen normal tensions associated with ageing/ illness,

(g) Its an advantage situation for all types of political parties. It has been proved so in many general, assembly and bye elections in India,

(h) Social media is a good source of entertainment and a voluntary means to pass time.

We can share & exchange images and videos and access to some rare things may be also possible without undertaking a visit,

(i) Above all, social media can boost creativity and intelligence and herald positive or fast forward thinking as well.

DEMERITS

(a) It may, rather, is leading to many health issues, such as, damage to sleep cells leading to sleep disorder, depression, loneliness, headache, short temperedness and anxiety,

(b) As it is a distraction in many ways, with passage of time, it may impact one's future and career prospects,

(c) One may have the false feeling that it helps in unwinding and killing time but in reality it may have adverse effects over youth and students,

(d) Users of social media do become victims of forgeries and on line scams operated mostly with connivance of former bank employees,

(e) Hacking is becoming very common on social media especially on sought after sites, such as, Facebook, Tiktok, Whatsapp and Twitter,

(f) It reduces face to face communication skills which may result into anxiety, suspicion and lack of confidence, at times,

(g) After getting addicted to it, growth of children suffers. They get cut off from real world or society and may suffer from adjustment problems in a normal social gathering,

(h) For the grown ups life may become sedentary for many hours during day as also night. Inclination to walk, talk or playing games may wither away gradually,

(i) As majority of users have false social media accounts with a view to tease or get sarcastic pleasure, after sending photos and visuals, they become traceless. One can imagine the mental agony on the part of receivers,

(j) Social media may lead to creation and dissemination of FAKE NEWS. Some people and organizations may create something on a hot or burning issue and post, which can neither be verified nor confirmed,

(k) Sometimes disrespectful and harmful comments may be also conveyed, especially in hurried up stage. At times, a person may not mean it but by the time realisation comes, damage is done.

TO SUM UP

Roots of social media have become deeper than imagined. It has the potential to become a competitor to the traditional print and electronic media. It is much faster apart from having a wide coverage. People who have no desire to write and comment get carried away. Emotions may override rational thinking. Some may have made fortunes also out of loopholes, one may not notice so quickly.

But anything which has a tendency to go astray may have negative repercussion and prove harmful to society at large in intent and content. Also unwanted Trial attempted through this medium may prove counter productive, one day.

There is immediate need to apply brakes to regulate the flow by coming out with viable and implementable measures subsequent to wide ranging discussions with all stake holders. One can not put the clock back. As thinking and well meaning beings one has to move ahead.

A bill to regulate digital media outlets has been listed for the upcoming Monsoon Session of the Parliament. It is a welcome step to make media outlets liable for violations that apply to print media. Values of freedom of expression are propsed to be upheld. Shall we hope that firm message will also go to the rumour mongers and fake news spreaders ?

(B) HEALTH IS WEALTH

6

Exercise & Yoga Help, Mindset & Life Style Too Need Changes[5]

We get only one life. We should, therefore, endeavour to and lead a life free from worries, tension and stress.

These may be part and parcel of our life cycle. But how we manage, contain and regulate them is the issue that needs to be flagged at the outset.

Generally it is seen, felt and observed that we tend to succumb to various pressures rather easily. But rich experience of two year of Corona period put us to Litmus tests. And during the third wave, armed with two doses of Vaccine we performed better. Though fourth wave has begun knocking, we seem to be better equipped.

Life, being a precious gift of nature, its each and every moment may have to be understood and analysed carefully, as far as possible, prior to feeling, experiencing and relishing.

At the same time, it is also said and generally believed that life is never a 'Bed of Roses', but that should not mean that it is only or completely full of thorns.

Difficulties need to be faced boldly, disputes should be resolved amicably and approaching hurdles should be minimised or removed without hurting anybody.

Perhaps all anger is foolish but at the heat of moment we tend to forget the same. So, same has to be controlled, as far as possible to rekindle freshness and energy.

How do we do it ?

Recent distress situations have shown that there is no substitute for sincerity and honesty and that hard and careful work with adequate application of mind mainly helps.

Light Exercise & Yoga Regime

With International Yoga Day approaching soon, stressed or depressed lots should not get trapped by certain self appointed or proclaimed greedy masters and instructors.

Yogic Postures

Need of the hour is to correctly understand and follow the Essence of our Shastras and Puranas.

The time tested Yogasana techniques, one of the six systems of Vedic philosophy propounded by Maharshi Patanjali, should be followed in letter and spirit.

Meditative postures, such as, Padmasana and Vajrasana, Relaxing ones, namely, Shavasana, Makarasana, Naukasana, Halasana, Bhujangasana, Shalbhasana, Tadasana etc. and the ultimate, Surya Namaskar (not exceeding 20 postures in all) may not only lead to gradual reduction of side effects of Allopathic medication, these also may enable us to display a pleasing face, cool temperament, strong determination, better patience and what not ?

Past Being Vast, Should Not Come In Between

Let us Attempt to Ignore and forget the past and develop an optimistic but achievable Vision For Furure.

Shall we not reclaim and relish the Joy of Waking Up Early like the innocent birds, such as, Sparrows or Cocks and attempt the suggested Yogic exercises. Done with discipline and care, it should end with a bout of meditation and Breathing exercises. One may soon realize that energy and exhilaration has entered the life.

By following such a routine, let us help each other in Minimizing if not Eradicating sorrows of life.

Cue From One's Own Life

To illustrate further, Could I take liberty to turn Auto-biographical ?

In April 2007, my physical Angiography showed seventy percent and thirty percent blockage in two portions of my heart. I was, prescribed Open Heart Surgery (OHS) by the owner of a Bye Pass "Factory".

I took some time off, consulted relatives, friends and a handful of experienced and trustworthy Cardiologists. Soon I sensed something, began listening to my Inner Voice and resumed morning & evening walks with a fresh resolve.

I padded the same with an useful course on Coronary Yoga at RML hospital. Followed it up with regulalated diet, timely medicines and restricted work, based on prescription of a Senior Cardiology Professor of AIIMS.

I also experienced a deficiency of one of vital Vitamins in between. For a while, not only lost appetite but also symptoms of disturbed mind and sleep. But I wo'nt give up and surrender.

Regular Yoga and exercise coupled with correct intake of vegetarian food, bereft of spice and curtailed oil content at a fixed time became Order Of The Day.

Also an Inner Command to change lifestyle HELPED me in the ultimate analysis when chips appeared down.

I gradually resumed kicking, thinking, interacting and writing.

Now I attempt to Share and Disseminate my frugal knowledge to the understanding and optimistic lots in my own way.

To sum up, a person may be capable of Reaching a "Take Off Stage" but for attempting "Self Actualization", not only Wishes and desires have to be contained and curtailed but I and You have to learn to become a sort of Contented Human Being, Not a Sanyasi.

Om Shanti.

7

Illnesses Caused Both By Self & Medical Negligence[6]

April 26, 2022

A person is expected to take responsibility of his own health. Spouse or immediate relative or paid attendant may lessen the pressure but in actual desperate situations, Self Help and inner strength come to rescue. There has to be a desire to live, instead of resigning to fate.

Despite rise in allocation for health both at the state and central levels, sizeable sums are spent for treatment of common ailments, Blood Pressure, Diabetes, Ulcer, Backache, Migraine, Arthritis, Cancer, Constipation and so on. But till recently, we were giving scant attention to Menstrual hygiene and Psychiatric check up.

As a result, according to Dr. Paramjit Rana (Total Health, 2002), our digestive, respiratory, nervous, cardiovascular, excretory, reproductive and musculo-skeletal systems continue getting impacted from time to time.

Contemporary Situation

While remarkable advances keep happening in the domain of Science & Technology and new wonder drugs, namely Vaccines for treatment of Covid-19 (including Nasal) get developed in a record time, diseases don't also reduce. Corona pandemic has shown that modern man, having drifted away from nature has invited many ills in his day today life.

Not only do we breathe polluted air,water and food stuff, especially vegetables, fruits and milk & milk products, we and our children also have a lust for Junk food. Thus, many of the contemporary diseases are of our own making. Some of them are contracted even in hospitals and public places as during three waves of Corona.

State of unnecessary anxiety leading to depression was generally unheard of, say, thirty years ago.

What Needs To Be Done ?

We should believe, rather make it a habit to leave the comfort of bed if not before the Sun rises, at least within a few minutes of that. Remembering the Almighty may be a person's choice but washing face & eyes gently ,followed by two glasses of water for easy bowel movement should be a daily routine. Next may follow the essential ritual of cleaning our teeth, to be succeeded by morning walk, light exercise or Yoga.

Students are expected to study before sunrise to build their memory power, a habit disappearing fast.

Some may like to take warm or cool water baths, depending upon weather prior to having a feel of fresh air.

On holidays there is no harm in getting up late but the same should not be later than 8 a.m. or else valuable time to recapitulate the immediate assignments may be lost.

In many houses growing up children are found glued to computers till early morning leading to inordinate delay in getting up. Parents often feel helpless.

Why A Doctor Is Needed ?

A question may arise if we all act in an orderly manner, do we need a Doctor ?

Doctor-patient relationship is both a matter of service and contract .When approached, the former owes a duty to explain the facts relating to an ailment and its cure mechanism.As one of the oldest professions, there is no better service than medical profession to serve the sick, injured or suffering.

Moral values as also professional ethics guide and regulate the relationship in which there should be no scope for caste, race, religion or social standing based discrimination.

If there are duties laid out for a Code of Conduct for the doctors, patients and their attendants are also expected to behave in an orderly manner and give due regard to the practitioner.

However, it is also a fact that free or subsidized treatment in a welfare set up mostly misguides the patients, leading to arguments and assaults at times at Government run clinics.It goes without saying that health centers in towns often work beyond their carrying capacity, but picture is reverse at PHCs or PHSCs, which have perpetual issues relating to availability of doctors, paramedics, medicines and emergency transport. Situation, however, seems to have improved with the implementation of N.R.H.M. in many states.

An annual health check up has become necessary if the reality of a definite rise of life span to 64 years is some indication.

If we look at the health status in British India, the situation was pathetic not only due to negligence of our rulers but also due to our own Carelessness. It's a different matter that owing to our own intake of relatively pure and uncontaminated food or food supplements, visits to doctors or natural healers would be once in a blue moon.

Domestic remedies or Grand mother's formula tried first were expected to work, if not to work wonders.

Though diseases may be of many types, specialized medical intervention may work if diagnosis is correct and by an experienced hand.

It is also important that the workload of a Specialist should not exceed his carrying capacity even if demand may be on a higher side.

Apart from expecting a miracle from a Physician or a Surgeon, many of us get misguided also due to internet inputs as also unsolicited opinions of fellow friends or relatives.

Avoid Self Medication

Self medication or self-dropping of a few doses may appear to be tempting at a certain stage of recovery but it may not be an opportune time to give up.

Very often we are fond of not only talking of side effects but also feeling the same if some other ailment strikes.One needs to remember that at this stage, a qualified and hygienic test is very much called for.

That brings us to the question of Self measuring of blood pressure or blood sugar. It is felt that in emergencies these can be resorted to but once something unusual comes to notice, treatment thereof, should be the responsibility of the Physician.

Also the conduct or considerate approach of a doctor should be to listen to the issues patiently, rather than prescribing something, based on usual practice.

All said and done, if a patient has a recent Biochemical or Haematological report, the same should be believed rather than insisting on another report as per physician's own choice. Many illnesses get aggravated due to it. Some may lose their life also if the element of seriousness gets overlooked due to the Rush factor.

There can be arguments and counter arguments on the issue of medical negligence but investment in terms of both faith and money cannot be undermined.

Another issue that needs attention is that we tend to rush to a Speciality or a Referral set up upon hearing its name from others, mostly based on their experiences. But element of abnormality in anatomy differs from person to person. Long and undesirable wait in such places, therefore, often leads to loss of life.

Accident Cases

Cases of accidents too throng every hospital anytime.It may be remembered that sometimes, an accident happens due to our own mistakes or oversight. Blaming a doctor for any negligence due to loss of crucial Golden Hour should not be fair. How we carry an injured person from a busy road or an isolated place subsequent to a fall, is very important.

Adequate and timely First Aid prevents blood loss and boosts the level of confidence of the victim which may facilitate recovery.

Delivery Cases

Further, in such cases, it should be the duty of a Gynaecologist to encourage and mentally prepare a patient for a non-caesarian section, as far as possible. If the same is needed even late at night it should be ensured. Those belonging to poor and marginal sections should get preference.

As such, rarely wealthy persons check into a Government facility for delivery.So logically speaking, deliveries should be a flawless exercise and ambulances have to be in a state of readiness rather than being utilized for non medical purposes or for bringing supplies.

There is no end to talking about this essential human duty. It is never an intention of the doctors or nurses to wilfully cause a situation but these may also happen, sometimes ,due to our own oversight or negligence.

Blaming the Angels in white uniforms is not desirable.

We need to also take adequate care and responsibility according to changes in weather.No therapy can ensure a total cure.We should attempt to use best of all the therapies.

When conditions, such as, Heart attack, detachment of Retina or apparent loss of sight, irregularity in Kidney functioning, delivery cases, accidents needing orthopaedic attention and other emergencies occur, there is no alternative to Allopathy.Doctors not only have to be Trusted, but they, should also express Regrets if an act of negligence or callousness has caused a loss of life.

While doctors should not forget their Hippocratic Oath, the attendants should also show a restrained behaviour in hospitals, as acts of misbehaviour and attack on doctors are increasing.

To sum up, it may be appropriate to quote Dr. P.D. Shenoy, a distinguished Civil Servant of Karnataka from his masterly book "Medical Negligence" (2013).

I quote

"…………medical profession has been a noble profession. Relationship between a patient and his family doctor was one of trust and confidence on the part of patient and one of care and concern on part of doctor. Disappearance of the concept of family doctor and growth of super speciality hospitals has totally changed the old relationship, based on long term association and trust."

Unquote.

8

Polluted Water, Fruits, Milk and Vegetables adding to Covid Woes[7]

August 3, 2021

Five natural key elements, including air and water are indispensable not only for human beings but all living beings. In all the metros and a few "Smart" cities, human beings are being compelled to breath polluted air with a profound Air Quality Index (AQI), mostly ranging from 200 to 300 (Poor quality). The difference becomes distinct during Lock Down (L.D.) and non-L.D. periods.

In environment conscious Delhi, it has varied from 105 in April 2020 beginning to 418 (severe) on December 22, 2020. Besides, the urban dwellers are made to consume "clean looking" polluted water, either through pipes or sourced from ground.

Another burning issue is spurious supply of chemically made milk and milk products.

Lowering of water Table from 7 to 23 meters in some areas of National Capital Region is not only a cause of serious concern but all along the banks of major rivers in many states.

Land, per se, may look fertile and may also yield bumper crops, but very few of these areas are free from poisonous and hazardous substances causing diseases, such as Cancer.

Depressing Milk and Vegetable Scenario

Added to issues flagged, is another aspect of non-visible pollution entering human body, through duplicate medicines, "chemical" milk and milk products and green, sparkling and healthy looking vegetables.

As per standard norms, any vegetable is not supposed to contain more than 0.1 PPM of Lead but in some vegetables grown in Trans Yamuna area of Delhi, PPM upto the extent of 28.06 has been found by a Study. Similarly, prevalence of 3.42 PPM of Cadmium has been found which should not exceed 0.1 PPM normally.

Common man is also taken for granted by flood of chemical milk supply and products, such as, Paneer, Ghee, Curd etc. Due to their high demand, forgery and element of deceit is never ruled out.

To cater to the N.C.R., hill towns of J&K, H.P., Uttarakhand, West Bengal, Sikkim and states of North East as also major upcoming urban conglomerates, vegetables are not only being propped up by chemical fertilisers but their cultivation is mostly carried out in polluted and slushy plots whose soil health is a matter of doubt.

Gradually, therefore, slow poison penetrates our body from sources hinted, causing varied complications and short and long run diseases.

Setbacks to Early Fruits

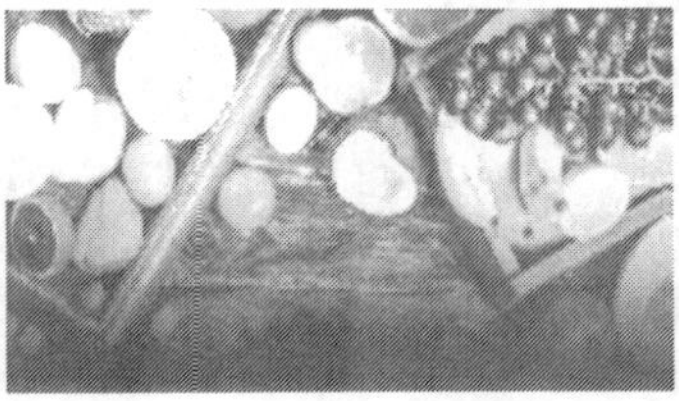

One is already sadly facing the old process of speeding up the ripening through carbide in respect of Banana, round the year available fruit. Such a nefarious practice gathers momentum when it comes to Mangoes also during its peak season from May to August. On top of it, the havoc played by Covid pertaining to Alphonso, Chausa, Dushery variety of mangoes for two years in succession, should not be undermined. Apart from severe and shocking losses to the growers since April, 2020, the consumers in general too have suffered. Such a state is expected in 2022-23 also.

Is Alert and Vigilant Consumer A Misnomer?

In addition to two fruits, a certain foul play may be going on without the knowledge of now "vigilant and empowered" consumers when it comes to milk and milk products, Lichies, Papayas, Oranges, Kharbuja and Pineapples.The mere fact that some milk products, Lichies and a certain type of Oranges have relatively short season or shelf life, their availability in the market of any specification, beyond a certain period, raises genuine suspicion.

REMEDIAL ACTION

Recent plantation drive in Yamuna Bank and Chilla areas of Khadar region of Trans Yamuna Delhi could be considered a good start to check growth of sprawling, illegal vegetable cultivation in an area, polluted heavily by contaminated water.

Herein, two pertinent questions, never the less, could be posed:

***Has any Study been carried out about the impact of such vegetables already consumed by lakhs of people during a decade or so ?

***Secondly, Is there any cess or tax being realised from the growers who have pocketed lakhs of Rupees by way of profit from their prised produce, going to the extent of over Rs 3 to 4 Crores annually?

According to a recent Vernacular daily report, about 22 Bighas of land were being utilised in the Trans Yamuna area. Now that total land use has been scaled down by the green measures adopted by the N.C.T. Forest Department, corresponding, 'illegal' profits, naturally, may have boomeranged. The said report, quoting an authentic study, indicates further that the turn over from such vegetable cultivation could be doubled to Rs 8 Crores annually, once Yamuna water is cleaned up finally (?) atleast, along Delhi stretch.

CLEAN YAMUNA, ULTIMATE SOLUTION

No wonder, a chorus of voices are coming from the environmentalists and NOT from "Immune" field officers of the Government that there has to be a ban on contaminated vegetable cultivation till the whole of Yamuna passing through Delhi is declared not only clean but also same is declared fit for human consumption.

Over the years, sadly, as such, owing to rise in the level of both air and water pollution together with high incidence of chemical fertilisers, both productivity and production have declined considerably. In view thereof, temporary barricading and plantation, may be of non-endemic species along some areas of river bank, could be only a temporary solution to a permanent problem.

LIVELIHOOD EQUALLY IMPORTANT

Not only clean environment "sky wise" with atleast 150 AQI, actual potable water, genuine milk products and essential fruits have to be the Need of the Hour during the ongoing Covid Wave, providing safety and security to the livelihood of the vegetable and other growers is also to be given paramount importance.It is in view of fast deteriorating inflation scenario, rural and urban unemployment (CMIE reports) and overall crime rates.

FREAK WEATHER IMPACT

With a view to have an appropriate understanding in the midst of freak weather all over World, resulting into landslides and flash floods even in hard rock high altitude terrains of Kargil, Amarnath, Kinnaur, Sirmaur, etc. coupled with flash floods and massive soil erosion in dry areas, such as, Jammu or pockets of Rajasthan, there is no harm in mentioning that concerned technical and development officers are having gala time in Bihar, J&K, Uttarakhand, Kerala, U.P., M.P, Maharastra, etc.

Annual Overflow Scenario and Rainwater Harvesting

When it comes to the annual "Overflow Scenario" in Assam and Bihar, it has not only become a fashion but established practice to utter "The Upsurge is being caused by the neighbouring countries".

And show of vested interests goes on, year after years.

Last but not the least, the highly useful practice of inculcating RAIN WATER HARVESTING habit or making it mandatory for passing maps and plans of urban houses appears to have been conveniently forgotten by one and all.

We tend to remember it only during high level seminars and conferences organised by Government Departments and Multi lateral UN organisations, held mostly in Five Star settings.

To Conclude, Shall we say that

High Covid ridden "happening" country of India on the eve of 3rd Wave and 75th Anniversary of Independence is destined to suffer both in Ati-Bristi (Excess Rain) and Ana-Bristi (paucity of rain) situations ?

Who is not aware of pollutants and malpractices concerning air, water, drugs, milk, fruits and vegetables ?

But how many of us are willing to come forward, identify, fix responsibility and Bell the Cat ?

WHO WILL TAKE CARE ?

9

Await COVID-19 Third Wave, Face Uncertain Weather[8]

October 3, 2021

As Covid-19 is expected to make a comeback in October, are we ready to pull up our sleeves or willing to commit mistakes of the Second Wave? We have seen the worst between first week of April to third week of May in 2021 but we tend to forget these despite having a massive setback in view of a record 4 lakh 14 thousand 188 confirmed cases on 7th May, 3023 deaths and 34 lakh plus active cases were also recorded. While Maharashtra, Karnataka, Kerala, U.P., T. N. and West Bengal were top six states, Delhi at 10th position had one of the highest positivity rates at 36% on 22nd April which came down to 23.3% on 8th May. Top ten states had accounted for over 27 lakh cases. In retrospect, there is a felt need to check and cross-check such crucial figures. WHO has already expressed concern over the general practice of wrong reporting.

VACCINATIONS:NEED & WASTAGE PREVENTION

Despite all claimed and actual reports, apart from need for vaccine, wastage prevention should have been also focused. At the peak period, both Pfizer and Moderna should have been permitted along with Sputnik. As such, allowing Sputnik was an exercise in lip service.

Human elements, such as, social stigma and avoidance faced by the healthcare workers, both from neighbours and family members shall also have to be addressed swiftly.

Ironically, Kerala leading in terms of impressive coverage with least vaccin wastage, is still leading in terms of 24 hour cases. Further, as regards need, requirements are mostly put on higher side. Such as, Delhi highlighted the need for 26 million more doses by first week of May. Later, State was also found guilty of inflating the requirement of Oxygen cylinders. Sensing or assessing correctly, dedicated former Union Health Minister went on record that WITH the then daily Vaccin administration figures of 17 lakhs a day, our country was going to take THREE YEARS TO COVER ADULT POPULATION ONLY. (Who knew that speaking such a bitter truth was going to COST his job?)

On the other hand, Manish Sisodia, the Deputy C.M. of Delhi had alleged that 6.5 crore doses were exported to 93 countries when they were badly required domestically. The Health Minister had also honestly confessed that S.I.I, Pune was in a position to produce 6 crore doses per month as against an unimpressive performance of Bharat Biotech, Hyderabad at barely 2 crore doses per month. Thus, combined daily production of two drug manufacturers would come to roughly 26 lakh doses only.

Insult to Injury

To add insult to injury, mind boggling or astonishing surge took place in a fortnight at this juncture. High figures disclosed officially by the Health Minister were self explanatory- 'Assam had a fortnightly SPIKE of staggering 294%, Kerala 178%, W. Bengal 143%, Pudducherry 116%, and Tamil Nadu 104%.'

Even the tiny and safe state of Sikkim recorded over 200 cases daily from 5th to 9th May, 2021. Maharashtra which was unfortunately the "Leader" for a long time, surprisingly showed a marginal decline of 0.4%.

International Comment

Coming to International assessment if not soothsaying, WHO Senior Scientist Mrs Swaminathan further warned that the Corona variant of B. 1. 617 spreading in India was more contagious. The renowned LANCET Institute too expressed candidly that "Govt. of India did not ACT in time, so condition had deteriorated".

Rural Situation

When the Pandemic spread rapidly in rural areas also, almost everywhere, complaints of headache, bodyache, sleep loss, fever etc began surfacing. According to a report, fifty thousand cases were reported in Karnataka alone, of which atleast 50% were from Bengaluru. Incidently, earlier "major villains", viz, Mumbai, Pune and Nashik could exercise more control as opposed to situation there in during the first wave.

Weather Position

On the weather front, maximum temperature began hovering between 40 to 43 degrees with little bit of drizzle in between, making life more miserable.

It is generally believed that subsequent to a head shave off, hailstorms will have a field day. Rightly so, that is happening if the dry and wet weather trend since August is to be closely examined. In September 2020, it was an adverse and challenging scenario in respect of spread of Corona Virus. This September (wettest in 114 years), temperature has fallen rapidly due to unusually WET conditions. Nature God appears to be angry with slight variation, in almost all nooks and corners.

Emerging Vaccination Trend

On the one hand, the speed of Vaccination seems to have picked up momentum with 88. 96 crore vaccinations (roughly 44% of population). However, fresh or "reworked" GOAL of one Billion Jabs by early October MAY NOT BE REALISTIC. Also people with two doses number barely 23.97 crores. One must not forget that one is considered fully protected only after receiving the second dose.

Not only a nasal vaccine seems to be on the anvil but ZyCoV-D, a DNA vaccine being developed by Zydus Caddola is also about to go in for commercial production. It is also likely to be a precursor to first Dengue DNA vaccine. Meanwhile, reports are also being received about under reporting of Dengue, viral fever and Corona cases especially from Haryana, U.P., Delhi and Bihar. While 12 plus children are to be administered vaccines from 1st October, Illegal Corona jab drive also seems to be a thriving business for materialistic Indians in several places.

Grim Mortality and PR Scene

There is only a marginal decline in casualty figures in major states, such as, Maharashtra, Karnataka and Tamil Nadu (4,48, 000 Pan India as opposed to 6,75,000 in USA) and almost adamant phenomenon of positivity rate still being between 5 to 10%, especially in Kerala, Mizoram, Maharashtra, Tamil Nadu and Sikkim. In Mizoram, average daily number of over 1400 cases (highest 1846 being on 28th September) during 13 day period from 16 August to 30th September, defies all imagination. A more focussed drive by the Centre on a war footing may be urgently needed. Instead of an expected "fall", a non-abatement situation, is certain to give us less tension and anxiety.

Topsy Turvy Weather

Let us examine to what extent moody or topsy turvy weather has to contribute to the mess, together with our irresistible and unique, Back To "Social" temptation.

Indian Meteorological Department (IMD) opines that the atmospheric low pressure and depressions lead to heavy rain. Cyclones too are not ruled out. We already had three on East coast and one along the West coast during 2021, leading to tremendous loss of life and property. The latest one, Gulab, is predicted to make a turn around with Shaheen which may hit west coast as well.

The South West Monsoon which touched the coast of Kerala, three days late in June, and about four weeks behind schedule in Delhi area, was due to meet its natural end by 16 September. On the contrary, as per trends, its "withdrawal symptom" is unlikely to be noticed by 10th October. According to IMD, the withdrawal

process is going to be second most delayed in 41 years. The extended range model of IMD is hinting at a widespread rain till 7th of October and a "patchy" one till 14th October. Thus, the left over spirit of the Navratras, D. P, Vijay Dashmi, Diwali and Chhath will be further subdued. For Good?

Possibility or Certainty of Third Wave

As such, the common man is getting confused with expected

arrival of Third Wave soon, or its denial or slowing down or may be non-existence altogether, as winter picks up momentum, slowly.

Fear consciousness if not Psychosis is looming large side by side, since August especially in Haryana, U.P, NCR, Bihar etc due to onslaught of a strange viral kind of fever which has taken a toll of over 500(?), mainly children and more than 300 or so still struggling for their lives in the dilapidated hospitals and dispensaries. Hundreds of Dengue and viral fever cases are being added every week in Delhi, Ghaziabad and Noida. As an instance, 467 patients with respiratory issues and 337 with fever one day, turned up at a Health camp in NOIDA.

Having come across this unusual wrath of nature, one may genuinely ask:

"Is Global Warming worth its name or has it turned into Global Cooling?" Developments in the domain of weather forecasting indicate so.

From the Death Valley in USA to Greenland in Europe to the cold deserts of Siberia to warm ones of Sahara and Thar and from Indian to Pacific Ocean, its the same strange play of nature. Should we hope that in the wake of revival of QUAD or initiative of defence alliance of AUKUS, both targetted at China, something positive also comes out on weather front?

Unprecedented Rise in Natural Calamities

Over two years, there has been unprecedented spike in number of earthquakes, volcanoes, cyclones, hurricanes, floods, flash floods, cloud bursts, landslides, forest fires etc. Many of them may have occurred in non-identified vulnerable or susceptible zones.

In almost all the continents as also North Pole, its the same haywire situation or the erratic wrath of nature.

Nature seems to be annoyed as we are resorting more and more to unsustainable utilisation patterns by ignoring the minimum possible needs of future generations.

Is it a mad Rush or a calculated desire to Crush (Each Other)?

By ensuring long duration international co-operation and adoption of careful wait and watch strategy could be a sensible alternative, instead of planning and executing hurried and short term cut and paste solutions. Close on the wheels of P.M.'s address at UNGA setting up of a crack team of top scientists by the WHO to re-examine the origin of Corona virus could be considered a welcome step. However, it could have been resorted to, long ago. It is never too late.

To withdraw the mouse, A. Malthus, the renowned British Economist had said long Ago "When Man Fails, Nature Takes Over". Is it actually happening? Almost 20 lakhs Indians die of heart attacks every year but less than two lakhs Covid deaths during 2021 severely impacts our mental faculty and family stability. Let us introspect with due care and caution by forgetting our taste and preferences, to seek a viable answer for the good of entire human race.

10

COVID Prevention and Control: Introspection Need of the Hour[9]

September 7, 2021

After twenty months, do we remember painful, perturbing and unprecedented human tragedy of Coronavirus in Wuhan?

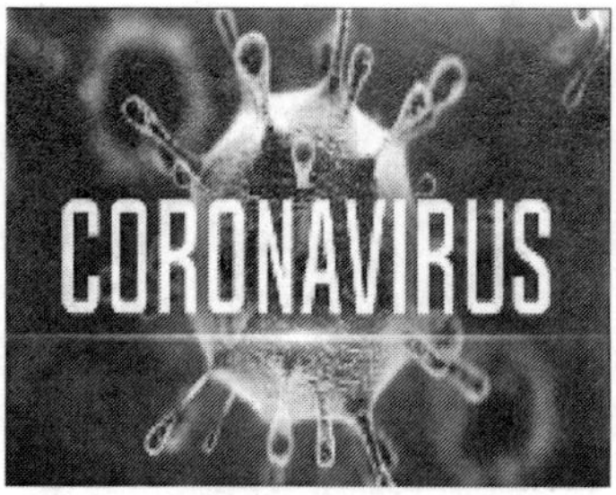

Within a month of its occurrence, genesis of Corona virus began in India when a medical student landed at Kerala. Next month, another Indian entered the fray in Delhi. Perhaps both survived, presumably with "normal" allopathic treatment. As time passed by, not only Homeopathic and Ayurvedic but Naturopathy were also tried.

GRACE OF GOD

It has been generally felt that there is nothing special about this ailment. However, it is an open secret that mostly those thronging the hospitals suffered and lost lives, while during the fag end of two waves, not only normal medicines prescribed for fever, headache, common cold, weakness, lack of appetite etc. began working, but also several lives were saved due to advice for "home hospitalisation".

No doubt, a person confined to bed like me, knew the effect of disease and how normal or lethal it could have been. Many suffered or died not merely because of wait in compound or corridor of a hospital or delay in actual treatment but also due to Unusual and Acute Anxiety in family or neighbourhood.

CLOSE TO REALITY

I do not wish to sound like a novice but may admit that in view of tough experience of self that standard prescription/combination of medicines Worked, as suggested by experienced friends and sufferers but in lesser measure by qualified doctors. They were either fully occupied (or even pretended so) during peak period but also would hardly show any inclination to get close to patients at home for fear of getting infected themselves.

VIRGIN TERRITORY

Since it was a 'virgin territory', doctors of more than one discipline, say, Physicians, Pulmonologists, Kidney & Liver Specialists, Intestine Experts, ENT Doctors, Opthalmologists etc got engaged. Some known docters would confess in private that the disease also puzzled them.

Not only they began treating (their primary duty) but: Commenting also on mutations and variants. A few may have added to their knowledge. Every now and then, new variants are discovered, these are considered more harmful and injurious than its predecessor. Currently, four groups, namely Alpha, Beta, Gamma and Delta have been identified. Latest one, C. 1. 2, detected in South Africa, is supposed to be more transmissible.

SYMPTOMS

In view of shocking news of death of over 130 persons and hospitalisation of 200 plus in Firozabad, Agra and Ghaziabad, reportedly due to Dengue fever, a doubt arose in respect of symptoms.

Thus following extremely significant issues may be flagged in Public Interest:

- One has to be told after routine tests, whether a particular ailment is actually a viral fever,
- OR is it a Flu unrelated to Covid-19 ?,
- Is it a fever with running nose & cough?,
- OR is it H1N1(Swine Flu)?
- Whether patient needs sufficient hydration and nutrition,
- Expected Duration of the ailment, and
- Patient should know whether treatment will have a standard norm.

Lucrative Industry ?

Peeping into past, one gathers that within no time, foundation stone for lucrative Corona "factories" was "laid". Not only a deadly disease was here to stay but a new "Sun Shine Industry" was also destined to thrive and sustain. Thanks to swift means of communication, not only disease spread faster, but dissemination of both positive and negative information, too became an easy proposition.

MANY EXPERTS IGNORED

But our country's experience of 18 months shows that many good, competent and experienced doctors, specialising in Epidemics and Sister Science were neither consulted at treatment stage nor were they involved in further research in between two lethal waves (a few, Pune based and elsewhere were interviewed). ICMR and NITI Aayog, however, were pushed beyond imagination.

Further, one is compelled to say that some Cardiologists, Pediatricians, Neuro surgeons etc too began speaking and giving advice and expert opinion in virtual seminars and never ending debates on mass media, possibly by ignoring their main vocations.

Needless to mention, they began guiding, if not influencing policy formulation and may be, later execution also.

6TH DECEMBER 2020, A TURNING POINT

No wonder, medicines ranging from Crocin, Paracetamol, HCQ, to Remdesivir etc. were prescribed till a specific vaccine came from Pfizer & Astra Zeneca.

One hopes that the process of development of vaccine during SARS-I has been taken into account before hitting the target now.

PRECURSORS

It may be pertinent to cite the example of Spanish Flu in 1918-20. As far as its spread is concerned, one may not get authentic documentation OR details of treatment.

As per grapevine, the vaccine for SARS-II pandemic was also expected not before October '20 or February '21.

How Come, It Was Preponed?

NEW INDUSTRY

It may not be inappropriate to say that with the swift passage of time in 2020, number of testing centres multiplied and new, rather ultra modern kits and instruments too were developed. No sooner than later, disease control became secondary while capital investment in this new "industry" became a primary factor, or a matter of cardinal interest.

China, France, Japan, U. S. etc. began taking lead even when sub-standard materials were discovered soon in supplies to various countries.

INDIA DID NOT LAG BEHIND

India too, seeing this golden opportunity in a Acute Crisis, took rapid strides and very soon imported medical items, such as, kits for medics and para medics, beds, ventilators, oxygen cylinders and many other hospital accessories entered and qualified for "Export" category.

But despite being away from worldwide Recession twice, India could not do much to take adequate advantage and revive its sagging or dragging economy to the "aimed" extent.

CONSTRAINTS

There may have been more than one factor responsible. Over population is one, unemployment and exodus of migrant workers and daily wagers was another (6% unemployment in July 2021 has gone upto 8.32% in August, as per CMIE). Inclement weather or variance of weather depending on "strange vagaries" of Monsoon could have also contributed. Efficacy and content of the raw materials and weak demand and supply chain/ linkages could have been also responsible.

On the other hand, vast technically qualified manpower, together with prevalence, if not complete dominance of I. T.. using or savvy manpower even in smaller places, May Have Acted as a catalyst or facilitator.

By our actions have we served the humanity as per expectations? WE NEED TO PRICK OUR MIND TO INTROSPECT, SRIOUSLY, FAILING WHICH PEOPLE OF NEXT GENERATION MAY NOT PARDON US.

BURNING QUESTIONS

Prior to Lifting The Cursor, Following Pertinent & Burning Questions & Possible/ Attempted Comments May Be Perused, Seriously in National Interest:

*Is Attending Mass Events even After Two doses Desirable?

No, Even if some Opine so.

*Second Wave Is Not Yet Over BUT Fears are in Air For Third Wave in Oct. 2021.

Who to Believe, school students, common workers, daily wagers or shop keepers may ask, as disease was likely to surge further.

- If cases Spike after Festive Season, why not to put them on Hold?

  Only marches/ processions of a particular collectivity shouldn't face a kind of unequal treatment, when everyone is supposed to be Equal before Law.
- Social Media generally acts contrary to social interest and gets, undue publicity even in the event of fake news. Looks like, only top courts can do needful and prevent further hatred & division of Social Framework.
- 39 Dists (down from 56) still have an alarming positivity rate of 10%, and 38 have 5 to 10%. On the contrary, Kerala's positivity rate has risen from 68 to 70%, when State is recording more than 31,000 daily cases for eight days with the exception of a day or two.

If one sees the 24 hour figures of 2nd Sept., of 47, 092 cases nationally, 32,803 were from Kerala. If Kerala cases are deducted, seven day average of national cases would be just 13,218 which is alright for a vast and densely populated country, such as, India.

REMEDY

As an immediate solution, complete Lockdown needs to be declared in a state like Kerala. Also war footing, measures, such as, deputation of ACS level officers in every problematic district may have to be ordered.

TO SUM UP

As major countries of E.U., who have vaccinated eligible adults and Israel which was starting Booster doses after finishing vaccination, had a 24 hour figure of over ten thousand on Wednesday, and now well contained Japan and Vietnam are also facing the pandemic. Again one can think about overall gravity of situation in India when elusive or imminent 3rd Wave actually hits. **We Must Not Take A Chance.**

11

Corona Vaccine: Fair Distribution and Reduced Pricing Matter[10]

24 December, 2021

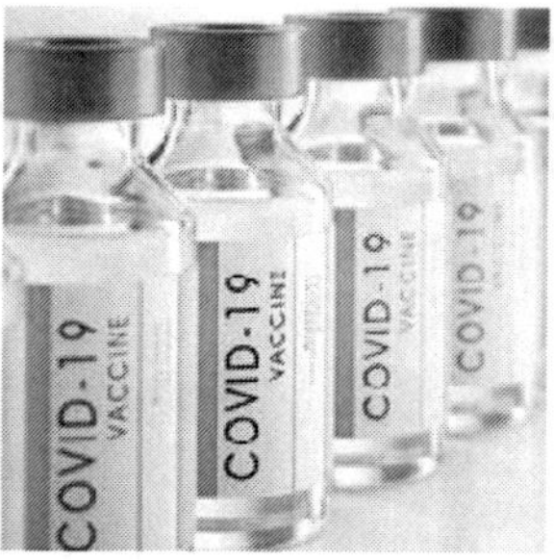

In view of the Air Quality Index in the NCT region hovering still around the 'severe' (above 400) category for almost five days, due to the wind being rather slow and the minimum temperature further going down, bone chilling experience is not only being felt, Omicron fears have also widened reach in U.K., France, Germany, Poland, Denmark, China (Fresh lock downs ordered) and the USA. In India also, states of Maharashtra, Delhi, Haryana, MP, UP, and Rajasthan began imposing night curfew and fresh curbs to check the rising spike. Mumbai and many towns of Maharashtra as also Delhi and Bengaluru might have further added to 350 number of cases by now. It is solely due to violating and flouting of norms becoming order of the day.

Clear Stand of World Heath Organisation

All this is happening when the Director General of WHO has warned that Vaccine Inequity must come to an end (to cater to left out conutries of African continent) or else it may lead to prolonging the Pandemic. He went on to add that the existing vaccines continue to provide significant protection against severe disease from Omicron variant. He has further indicated that the majority of hospitalisations and casualties were among un-vaccinated, not the un-boosted ones.

Morale Booster ?

The obvious and unfortunate comment is bound to boost the morale of the poor and politically fragile and shaken nations, many of whom are still deprived of even the first dose, despite many positive assurances from the UNO and GROUP of nations, such as, G-8, G-20 or could be ASEAN. Unfortunately in Nigeria, millions of doses had to be destroyed due to expiry factor.

Lust of Companies

But it may not fit in the schemes of the giant Vaccine manufacturers, such as, Pfizer, and Moderna of USA, supported otherwise in all respects by their "mother" country. Both the Indian ones, Sputnik kind and Chinese vaccines too have come up precisely due to State support.

Connivance Factor

According to the revelations in the media, due to well thought of manipulations of conmen, middlemen, hackers and lobbyists, not only funds were arranged on easy terms in advance but the manufacturers went on to determine terms and conditions, influence patent clauses and what not, such as, getting the title of co-inventor, which may ensure some additional benefits. Once on a loss making spree, these drug manufacturers as compared to actual Indian "leaders" in the field, swung back to profiteering, rather huge profit making situation, thanks to the Corona virus, its mutations and recent shift from Delta to Omicron variant. And who knows, what would be actually in store in 2022-23 ? Latter, as we now know, is much more stronger and spreading at an unprecedented speed.

It is, in addition, more transmissible but chances of hospitalisation too have reduced substantially on the positive side.

Explore Booster Doses and Mint Money

Also the point to be flagged is the rising rate of vaccination in most of the developed nations and introduction of Booster doses in some of them is also expected to make a difference. However, what should actually bother the humanity at large is tremendous or unthinkable profit making tilt or motive of the companies, being generated out of an outright tragic situation. If reports are to be believed, against the per dose cost of one Dollar, actual price at present stands at $ 25 to 30 or £20. Such a lust is never ending, rather bound to be endemic, forget about defying all expectations.

Inhuman, Beyond Thinking

Can we afford it in such an uncertain situation? Is it not inhuman, a beyond imagination phenomenon? Economic Opportunity should not mean that procurement may be easily facilitated to a rich minority while the majority who may find it difficult to afford and survive, should BE DESTINED TO SUFFER. A pathetic situation, nothing else. Also effective control and regular monitoring thereof, has to be ensured to obviate the possibility of any other outbreak.

Indian Situation

We, in India, are being talked about to enter a Community Transmission phase in view of rapid, unfortunate strides, already made by West Europe, South Africa and the USA. Neither, however, there is a need to panic nor the fear or apprehension should be underplayed. A re-assessment of critical gaps in the already fine tuned and upgraded hospital infrastructure and addition of ventilators and close by oxygen availability, should be very much on the cards.

Vaccine for the Left Outs

While doing so, the vital decision to introduce the boosters for the elderly and more needy as also introduction of vaccine for the children and teenagers, on the basis of UK's nod to Pfizer vaccine, also will have to be taken up on priority.

Fresh Steps by Israel

It may be close on the heels of an Israeli initiative to offer the fourth dose to the elderly above 60, those with compromised immune systems and the health workers. It was a part of the drive to ramp up the shots and outpace the spread of Omicron.

Somewhat Relieving South African News

Further, a South African study has just hinted at a reduced rate (80%)of hospitalisation among Omicron patients and that for the hospitalised ones, the risk of severe disease was reported to be roughly 30% lower. These may be, perhaps due to high population immunity now. While we need to draw lessons from it, one should not forget that the worst of the pandemic had not come to an end.

A Pill at Last?

We may wind up on a positive note to indicate that Drug and Food Administration of USA has authorised introduction of a Pfizer Pill, expected to be first at home treatment mechanism. It claims to have 90% efficacy in preventing hospitalisations and deaths of high risk patients.

12

One Hundred Crores Surpassed, Yet Miles to Cover[11]

October 26, 2021

The recent unbelievable, nevertheless, remarkable achievement on Covid vaccine front, speaks eloquently about India's acumen, capacity and potential.

Addressing the nation at 10 am on 22nd October, the Prime Minister said "It is not just a number but symbol of the country's ability and of a New India."

It happened against umpteen visible and invisible challenges, 289 days after the launch of our own Covishield and Covaxin. More under pressure, if not competition with Pfizer and Astra Zeneca vaccines. Latter were first introduced in UK, followed by USA in first fortnight of December, 2020. Launch was preponed due to some "other" claim related considerations.

HATS OFF TO HEALTH MINISTRY and CO-WIN

The vital figures compiled with due care and attention by the Co-WIN, under competent guidance of the Ministry of Health have to be believed, irrespective of initial controversies connected to reporting, by some of the major states.

There was a time when dip in daily vaccinations, supply bottlenecks and marked hesitancy among targetted people, including health personnel, emerged as major constraints, if not challenges.

Ministry of Health and Family Welfare

Having begun the daunting task on 16th January, 2021, India's dedicated campaign picked up rapid speed soon with rightly chosen first three frontline categories, as per risk and vulnerability considerations.

Nevertheless, same hobbled by mid-July. Against a "summit" of 5.8 million daily vaccinations in the last week of June, 2021 it dropped to 3.5 millions by 11th July.

LACK OF EXPECTED STIMULUS FROM STATES

Both the Centre and a few major, rather opposition ruled states should take moral responsibility for alleged tussle in procurement mechanism. To ensure smooth sailing to common man, the states, after having faced shortages, were advised to float global tenders even, but of no avail.

Centre had no option but to take command again by fresh takeover of purchase responsibility, offering free doses to all adults and assigning 75% of the supplies to the states. Further, owing to highest ever spate of over 4 lakh 14 thousand cases on 7th May, general psychology of patients and suspected ones was, in a way, put to a litmus test.

Seeing no other option, people began coming forward for vaccines. States were firmly directed to open new centers. With the passage of time, supply bottlenecks too were overcome. Encouraged by these positives, it was hoped that with daily administration of eight to ten million injections, the then target of vaccinating all the eligible adults could have been achieved by 31st December 2021. It was contrary to an assessment by the former

Health Minister, that is, only sometimes in 2023, revised national target was to be met.

STATISTICS AND BEYOND

We may be better than USA, UK, Brazil, Russia, Syria, Turkey, Iran, Malaysia, Singapore, Australia, New Zealand and even China, when it comes to statistics not jugglery. There are pockets in China, Mongolia and many European and Latin American countries which belied expectations in not only slowing down the rate of vaccinations but having seen resurgence once or twice in the recent past. In the meanwhile, guesswork or conjectures too began having a field day relating to the efficacy of less than six vaccines in the world market. Varying claims upto 77% in general, were made.

VACCINE EFFICACY

When UK, first country to start, officially noted or confirmed the effect of vaccines, ball began rolling again, if not according to myriad and confused "expectations".

Logically speaking, more and more of fulfilling of target, could have led to rapid fall in confirmed cases but in India, as compared to situation during the peak period of September 2020, things became worse and the gigantic figure of 4 lakhs 14 thousand and 188 on 7th May was unfortunately recorded.

Not only the number increased drastically, psychologically too people, especially from rich sections were more shaken and shattered vis-à-vis first wave. Panic ruled the roost all over. Each time, phone would ring, one was expecting a negative news in the consanguinal family. On the positive side, not to fail, bond of joint family got a fresh lease of life even in ultra modern USA.

AWEFUL, UNFAIR PATIENT CENTRED PRACTICES

The Oxygen Cylinder game, coupled with created shortage of beds for obvious monetary gains(sic) and rampant cheating in the name of Covid test (yes, this writer too was a victim) and issue of fake Corona positive certificates due to extreme agony and helplessness factor in every family, added fat to the burning fire. Many cases of wrong estimation, overall hike in prices and tariff, entry of hoteliers-cum-smugglers into the grim scene too began being sadly witnessed.

LACK OF DIGNITY IN DEATH

The number of serious and precarious cases as also deaths went on a swelling spree, more so, in Delhi, Surat, Bhopal, Prayagraj, Arrah, Bengaluru, Mumbai etc. Even disposal of dead bodies came under the spell of fear, further infection and who knows, intimidation in more than one place. While there was hardly any praise for concerted efforts made equally by the Indian states and the Centre in the international media, unwarranted pathetic saga of 1918-21 Spanish Flu time were recalled and recounted, rather shamelessly. Ganga Maa, her tributaries and some other river fronts, yet again, were at receiving end.

Even close relatives and so called upper caste persons got indirectly involved in cremation and burial rituals. It was an unimaginable scene that defied all logic, decency and religiosity.

The states of Bihar, UP, West Bengal, Gujarat, Maharashtra, MP, Delhi and lately Kerala had no regrets about wrong and misleading reporting on this count, which also included wide variation in figures maintained by Cremation and Cemetries vis-à -vis State Registrars of Births and Deaths.

The total number of deaths in the country at 454,269 so far with an average of 231 to 245 deaths per day since August may be still be a matter of deep concern. This figure was 431 to 480 in the preceding months. On 22nd Oct. all of a sudden it has recorded a high of 666 as against 16,326 confirmed daily cases, mainly because of statistical mismanagement of Kerala. A few months ago, Bihar had this dubious distinction.

LAXITY TO BE DETRIMENTAL

With impressive figures, such as, National Recovery Rate of 98. 17%, Positivity Rate of 1.19%, 173,594 Active cases, 33,548,605 Recoveries and 59,97,71,320 persons Tested As On date, things may look slightly comfortable at Present.

But A STATE OF EVER ALERT is necessary in view of once again casual style of the masses towards masks, handwash and social distancing.

Also Free mixing during the Onam and Durga Puja in Kerala and West Bengal respectively have already upsurged daily cases and mortality figures in these and some other urban centres.

FRESH ATTEMPTS AT CONTROL AND NORMALCY

From this kind of pathetic situation, bringing back the train of Covid control back to the main line was not an easy proposition.

Was it not herculean or daunting indeed ?

Not only fresh steps were taken, review mechanism at the PM level directly and also anchored by Health Minister and Secretary, Health were spruced up. These were tightened further, as per circumstance or need. There were, nevertheless, some villains in form of West Bengal, Maharashtra, Punjab, Tamil Nadu, Kerala or obliquely, Chhattisgarh, Bihar and Assam, who would not supply correct figures. Such a behaviour pattern added to creating confusion also in the number of casualties.

SAVE YOUR SKIN, BLAME THE OTHER PARTY

Coming to casualties, not only some of these states, but MP, Gujarat, Delhi, Andhra Pradesh etc., too began showing their non-cooperative attitude, even after not uttering a single word in a series of twenty two Reviews taken meticulously by the P. M. himself. One can imagine the task, challenge, impediment and overall headache of the Central Govt. under the circumstances.

FACTS SPEAK LANGUAGE OF COMPASSION, PATIENCE, TOLERANCE AND PERSEVERANCE

If the daily figure of 25 million Vaccinations on the birth Anniversary day of the P. M., followed by FASTEST RECORD ANYWHERE OF 100 CRORE FIRST DOSE VACCINES (102. 10 Crores on 23rd October) WAS FINALLY ACHIEVED BY BHARAT VARSH, MAXIMUM CREDIT WILL HAVE TO GO TO THE P. M., WHO ASSISTED BY A FEW ADVISORS & Health Ministry RIGHTLY LED FROM FRONT.

COULD WE CALL HIM A HUMAN ARMY COMMANDER-in-CHIEF ?

What USA, Brazil, UK, Canada, China, Russia etc could not do, we, allegedly "lethargic" Indians, bereft of a true National Character, have done. It was an example of true professionalism upon scoring over nations and reputed self proclaimed critics of Vaccine Diplomacy.

It has been learnt from NET sources that only Canada (71% 1st Dose vaccine coverage), China (70%) and USA (56%) were ahead of India. But despite having created a record at 9.47 am on 21st October, India could have a coverage % of 37. However, the point which may go in our favour is that India having second largest population of the world after China could attain this encouraging deadline within just 289 days.

IT SHALL ALWAYS GIVE AN UPPER HAND TO INDIA

And Govt. of India actually began vaccinating her suffering masses after supplying vaccines to as many as 89 countries, some receiving free of cost.

Instead of receiving accolades for her yeomen service at initial stages of the first wave, our humble and unassuming PM got unfortunate brickbats from leader of a superpower.

HAVING A COVID ALLEVIATION MISSION MODE OR A READY RECKONER BASED ROAD MAP

For Preparing a road map for future,

* First and foremost, correct figure of projected population of the country, District-wise will have to be arrived at, in active consultation with the Chief Census Commisioner and the State authorities,
* Thereafter, Day, Week and Month-wise realistic and very much achievable vaccine targets should be fixed,
* Number of functional Oxygen plants has to be made readily available in public domain,
* Simultaneous record of fully experienced Covid Medical Warriors to be kept Ready (As per WHO, One lakh 80 thousand health workers all over world had died doing Covid service till May 2021.)
* Quantification of vaccine wastage, preventing misuse of patient dedicated transport and state of alertness of Covid treatment exposed security personnel to be taken note of,
* A swift documentation of willing and non-willing factors and related issues (now better understood by the Collectors and the C.M.O.'s) is bound to be helpful.
* All the positive and adverse lessons learnt seriously, in the past may have to be given topmost priority, and
* A Covid & Sound Health Advisory Authority (CSHAA) may be planned and finalised for every state to assist the Chief Minister, Health Secretary, Education Secretary and DG, H.S, from now onwards.
* To make matters simple, may I suggest drafting

A Covid Prevention and Control Ready Reckoner (CPCRR)?

FROM INDIA WITH LOVE FOR NEEDY OF ASIA and AFRICA

(a) Gradual diversion of Covid vaccine to the friendly and "Other" countries on Actual Cost and Transportation basis may have to be planned, but only after meeting the domestic obligations.

(b) Sincere drive against the unhealthy practice of hoarding of vaxins shall have to be launched internationally. Sustained surplus on this count as also from "Reserved Stock" of all vaccine manufacturers should go from strictly humanistic perspective, to the poor countries of Asia & Africa.

(c) Exigency emerges from the fact that in many of them not even 5% vaccination of the first dose had been possible till then.

(d) The exalted or essential second dose is a FAR CRY.

(e) Is there any follow up or feedback on a Special Fund in this regard, announced by the high profile G-8 nations, atleast six months ago ?

SECOND DOSE COVERAGE IS TO AUGMENTED AT ONCE

In India, the unimpressive figure of 32. 02 crores (roughly 25% of current reported population of 139 Crores) in respect of persons vaccinated by two doses will have to be speeded up & enhanced substantially.

We may need 106 crore doses everyday to fully vaccinate the targetted population by 31st December 2021.

According to NET inputs, enough vaccine is available to administer to 40% of left over population. Further, last week 4,281,557 doses were administered each day. AT THIS RATE, IT MAY TAKE ANOTHER 64 DAYS (By 26th January, 2022), to administer enough doses for another 10% of population, adds the input further.

Giving 1.51 Crore vaccines daily, however, IS GOING TO BE DIFFICULT, keeping in view ONGOING PACE & ISSUES emanating from freak weather conditions (fresh spell of Rain likely to hit Nortern India as per IMD).

In view of the advice of WHO, Booster Dose may have to be administered ONLY AFTER prescribed gap between two doses. Consequently, vaccines for below 18 years and DNA based vaccines or the single dose being developed, shall have to wait.

Human Problems and Issues Should Have Human Remedies, based on a Regular But Focussed Feedback.

TO CONCLUDE

We appear to be on right track. Iron is hot. Let us strike with more vigour and vitality. We may feel elated, no doubt, but actual celebration should be after giving both the doses to all eligible offsprings of Bharat maata.

13

From Corona to Omicron, Apprehension or Fear Lingers on[12]

December 22, 2021

As we come close to the challenging, painful or excruciating phase of Covid dominated life, is it not the appropriate time to re-assess, re-prioritise, if Not merely to re plan?

Record Vaccinations

It is not for business, profit, loss or gain. Its going to be FOR OUR VERY SURVIVAL in the midst of an "object", we are yet to see but the one that has claimed millions of lives the world over, including 4.78 lakh deaths from 34,751,889 cases in India at a time when 88% of eligible population have reportedly received first dose of vaccination and 58% fully vaccinated (data of Ministery of Health) in eleven and a half months.

Renewed Worry

Cause of renewed worry and anxiety lies in the past devastating pandemics of Spanish Flu, MERSE I, II, III, SARS-I and may be, certain man triggered or natural calamities, our eyes could not see or ears could not hear or mind or senses could not comprehend or visualise.

Well it's a shift or change from the Coronotics or Corona phase to the Omicron. No sooner than later, we may be or could be seeing enhanced wrath of World wide Bio or Virus impact.

Adverse Effect All Over

Over the last two years from unfortunate genesis in Wuhan, China, it is now centered around Africa upon having traversed to Korea, Iran, Middle East, West Europe, USA and Latin America.

Even the latest variant has been so swiftly discovered in as many as 97 countries as per Internet, in the findings of WHO.

The World body in general and the British Prime Minister in particular have not only called for stepped up efforts but also deferring of Christmas and new year celebrations by two weeks to one month.

Anxiety and Losses

Virtually fed up by overall boredom as also unimaginable losses by tourism and producer goods enterprises, protests galore in most of Europe, USA and obliquely within our own relatively affordable labour market set up.

Over ninety one thousand Omicron cases in 24 hours in UK as compared to 28 millions vaccinated, leading so far to 1, 47, 000 casualties (44 in just 28 days), by any counts is an astounding and scaring figure.

As per reliable analysis, such a surge is three times more than the increase in cases at this time of the year 2020.

Shift to Sombre and Subdued

On the other hand, Christmas has already become a sombre and subdued affair and tiny tots and teenagers have been denied entry to schools in many countries, such as, France (92% fully vaccinated), Germany, Netherland, Belgium, Denmark, Portugal (maximum vaccinated in the world), Canada, Australia, New Zealand, China and Thailand.

Tightening of Curbs

Coming to tightening of measures and announcing fresh curbs, apart from UK and West Europe, while Switzerland and Wales are meaning business in their "fifth" and fresh wave, respectively, USA has declared that vaccines are critical for maintaining armed forces, so much so that more than one hundred marines have been removed, twenty thousand reprimanded and thousands have been discharged.

Vaccine Saga and India's Lead

Notwithstanding the massive surge in confirmed infected cases in India and neighbourhood, if one talks of edge of positives over negative, in less than a year, we had three vaccines and that has risen to eight.

The specific vaccine, developed by Pfizer was first administered in UK on 7th December 2020, followed by a week later by USA.

India, the largest vaccine manufacturer, though being leader in its research, naturally received bouquets and brickbats. Thus testing of 'local' Covishield and Covaxin vaccines spearheaded by the P.M. Narendra Modi himself became a sort of natural corollary and highlighted event.

Divide Between The Developed and Poor Africa

It is not that vaccines were not possible for Covid-19 or SARS-II, in the light of such a success during SARS – I, a decade ago which saw barely 747 deaths. From initial hitch to a gradual compromise as a life saving device, the vaccines manufactured by Pfizer, Oxford, Moderna and our own 'desi' Covaxin of Bharat Biotics could spread every-where and provided needed succor to the humanity. Approval by the WHO was delayed in respect of all.

The same humanity that benefited the developed world first (some like Canada procured more than their requirement), left in lurch, the poor, politically and economically shaken African nations.

Through the Waves

From First wave (March to July 2020 to Wave IA (September to November 2020) to Wave Two (April to July 2021) to alleged or claimed Wave Three between August to October 2021 and the fresh wave probably by change of name and overall impact-Beta to Delta to Omicron and its latest and supposedly more stronger variant has been a long, rather never ending saga.

EFFICACY FACTOR

When 70 to 75% of West Europe and USA have vaccinated their adult population by the first dose and a vastly populated India upto 55% (137.50 crores), fresh doubts have arisen whether the 34 to 40 % second dose vaccinated ones, would be able to withstand the onslaught of more devastating Omicron or its latest 'cousin'. It is also being keenly debated.

While Imperial College of London study does not show more strength in Omicron variant than the Delta one, a study of 400 samples in China has indicated that leading vaccines approved by the WHO are effective. Similar sentiments have been expressed by the Director, AIIMS, India when he has opined that Omicron is milder as compared to the previous Delta variant.

This disclosure has come at a time when fourty nine thousand Covid cases have been reported in India in just one week (lowest in 19 months).

Mind it, we are still talking of the most vulnerable front liners or the adult population upto 60 to 65 years of age. Unfortunately, the doses meant for the children and teenagers do get talked about but kept getting side tracked when we resort back to face to face education for a brief while as opposed to largely ineffective and time wasting E-learning process. Needless to say, in the vast educational hinterland of India, it has become a "Roller Coaster Ride".

Some children donot even know names of their schools, yet they manage to Clear two classes (standards) in succession, sitting at home. It is very unfortunate. To make matters worse, for the vital 9th to 12th classes, now there is no need to take examination. Such a dismal scenario has rightly led Delhi University to announce All India Entrance Tests for Specialised as also less sought after courses from academic year 2022-23. It goes without saying that these courses have been “attacked” by the high percentage BUG.

The country has to run and without careful and cautious handling of health and education sectors, we are certain to hit a bottom line.

Against such a backdrop, LET US NOT LOWER OUR GUARD AGAINST THE LATEST COVID VARIANT.

The prevailing insensitive, casual and careless attitude, coupled with getting back to re-socialisation in terms of unnecessary walks, tours, outings, festivals may once again prove very expensive.

In addition to the WHO, the NITI Aayog and now topmost Omicron specialists and analysts are predicting/sooth saying 8 to 10 lakh cases a day during the next wave as compared to 4.5 lakh cases a day during the Wave Two in intense and painful Summer of 2021.

It is not a guess or conjecture. Let us take it as a life saving device by forgetting for the time being the Booster dose or an upgraded version or the soon promised single dose or for that matter, a Nasal dose, being talked about almost for six months or may be more.

Over the four consecutive days, when minimum temperature is hovering between sub zero to 2.9 to 5 degree celcius in most of the northern India, average AQI of 324 to 332, is yet again in “very poor” category and the overall Omicron tally stands close to 180, Shall we not be more cautious and serious?

Not only pertaining to automobile pollution, dust control and waste management, for the life, per se, let us try to have adequate saving mechanism from the consistent bouts of revived anxiety and depression.

Already Sensex has tanked 1190 points amid Omicron worry and the annual and crucial World Economic Forum at Davos has postponed its meet from January until mid-2022.

LET US TRY TO REBUILD OUR NEST

14

CORONA AND CORONATICS: Are we Alive to Ethics and Morality Aspects ?[13]

August 31, 2021

Religion is supposed to be well established system of belief and practice. Our daily behaviour – whether good or bad, moral or otherwise, is influenced by such a time tested system.

One had been taught that religion was neither scientific nor unscientific. Instead, it is a non-scientific entity. Neither it can be proved nor can it be disproved. Looking at the ongoing struggle of the common man vis-à-vis never ending mutations and variants of the waves of Covid, Can we dare to state that unprecedented anxiety pertaining to Corona Auntie or Coronatic Uncle has taken the shape of a fresh OPIUM for the masses?

After all, poor and rich alike have been in a 'fix' situation, suffering and departing from Earth at a much faster pace.

Conceptual Part

While there has been a renewed inclination towards moral

education in schools and colleges due to gradual fall in values and while same keeps getting debated here and there, one should take note of steps already taken for moral education and ethics in schools run by the Christian Missionaries. It may or may not have led to conversions. One has no wish to support conversion in a secular set up but the early 'penetration factor' into the 'needy poor' minds by providing early access to health and education should be taken note of.

Ethics is a study of what is right and what is wrong with the human behaviour or a belief system about what is morally correct or acceptable. The fact remains that it is and should be an intrinsic part of our day-to-day primary and secondary socialisation patterns.

It should always matter as it may guide the action patterns of a group, while stressing upon respect, trust and rational behaviour vis-à-vis much wider groups.

A society is supposed to be a smooth sailing one if individual entities not only follow but also reciprocate the moral behaviour. Thus, what may be good or bad, could be also considered moral duty and obligation.

Need OR Greed ?

It is rightly believed that surge in greed element may lead to compromising one's moral or ethical standards. You tend to deviate from main line, at times. Gradually, there may be a competition between the meritorious and strenuous considerations. In the long run, we become victorious if we follow ultimate moral and ethical standards and stick to same till we depart.

Past and Present Icons

In the public life, even if there are multifarious challenges, threats and calamities of Corona, cyclone, flood or landslide kind, we need to follow brilliant examples of ever shining heroes and numerous basic need institutions who could keep public welfare away from profit motive.

To name a few, Mahatma Gandhi, J.L. Nehru, Dr. Rajendra Prasad, Sardar Patel, J.P., Dr. V. Kurien, Dr. APJ Kalam, Aziz Premji, Ratan Tata, Dr. Pramod Karan Sethi, Mother Teresa, Anna Hazare, Dr. Devi Shetty, Dr. R. K. Pachauri, AIIMS, Tata Memorial Hospital, C. M. C. Vellore, Shanker Netralaya, Chennai etc come to our mind, bereft of any doubt.

Integrity and Dignity, Key to Success

For want of simplicity and sincerity, how can one hope for integrity during the irritating course of Corona? Will self reflected dignity be possible ?

It may not be out of context but in overall human interest to politely ask a former super power Head of State as to where was the urgency to show undesirable interest in an European drugs firm, as early as June 2020 for ensuring supplies of a particular brand, when trends of Covid-19 were very much in mystery. It was different that his own country had been world leader in cases and casualties. Also his reckless remarks about the Indian P.M. were totally uncalled for.

Personal Hygiene and Treatment Protocol

There should be no harm in taking additional care of personal hygiene in the wake of seriousness of Covid situation. But a pertinent question may arise-If a soap or its liquid form can work, why should we need sanitizer ? If a Gamcha, Chunni or Hanky (as initially prescribed) come to our aid, why do we need a factory produced mask ? Breathing through a mask is a tough proposition. If Home Isolation or in a health facility by taking usually prescribed headache, cough and fever medicines can mostly save, is there a requirement for expensive beds, Oxygen Cylinders, ventilators and thus exposing yourself to the risk of organ extraction ?

OR when the Ayurveda or any other Indian system of medicine is showing the desired positive results in many cases, why not to keep trying them ?

E- LEARNING

Imposed E-learning, is leading to undermining physical exercise/running around by the school and college students is already showing a negative trend and anxiety syndrome. Apart from the need to buy expensive 'Smart Phone', there has been also rise in needed quantity.

Parents, especially single parents are compelled to run from pillar to post and at times, have to resort to loans or out of way means to meet growing demands of their sons and daughters. Side by side, it should not be forgotten that the regular use of electronic devices may also aggravate anxiety, apart from fresh personality and medical challenges, yet to be known.

IMPACT OF VACCINES

Introduction of now eight vaccines since first week of December, 2020 has not made much impact, rather, many cases keep resurfacing even after two doses. A cocktail of two vaccines, once considered risky, has been looked at afresh. In regard to two vaccines introduced in India, one cocktail has recently proved beneficial (effectiveness was claimed upto 77%). In normal course, both from clinical and moral angles, the identified health personnel of a PHC in U.P. could have been liable for penal action when a "mistake" was committed by them. Based on trial and error strategy, none of the researchers or the medical practitioners had something called prior experience, thus they need to be pardoned.

HOW TO FIX MORAL RESPONSIBILITY ?

However, fixing moral responsibility for fiddling with a case or spoiling it further or an ultimate demise may have to be made loud and clear in the mind of treating doctors. It is not that doctors and para medics or other front liners have not died or suffered for long, but it needs to be felt deeply by them that much more suffering is in store for thousands of relatives of the Covid dead.

If many of them were IMMORALLY mistreated by the chemists, traffic police, taxis, three wheelers, as also profit minded hospital staff, they are destined to face much more louder music one day. We need to take a cue from Western countries to improve things.

DEDICATED DOCTORS AND STAFF NEED ENCOURAGEMENT

Side by side, one has to laud and salute the untiring efforts made by many top and new doctors (for instance, Late Dr. K. K. Agarwal, Dr. R. Guleria, Dr. V. K. Paul, Dr. Arora, among others) and para medics as also Heads of Ministry of Health & F. W., AIIMS, ICMR, Niti Aayog, Ram Manohar Lohia Hospital, J. P. Trauma Centre, Sir Gangaram Hospital etc.

During the hour of acute crisis, especially during the second wave peak period of 4th April to 15th May '21, mental strength of patients and attendants had hit an all time low, so much so that unfortunate expressions, such as, Home Hospitalisation had to be coined and acted upon.

To avoid and get rid of desperate patients, especially in the "claimed" Oxygen cases, many private hospitals in Metro cities not only resorted to Immoral practices but some of them probably ought to have been reminded of their Hippocratus Oath and the GROUP ETHICAL practices, they have to follow during rest of their years.

TINGE OF MORALITY IN ANALYSING CORONA FIGURES

Malaise or connivance sets rolling from reporting daily cases, number of tests, positivity ratio, case fatality ratio, daily vaccinations, casualty figures etc.

Primarily owing to habit of taking a task merely as a routined one, mistakes are bound to happen at the cutting edge. Due to tremendous long hours leading to stress situations also, one may have a tendency to falter. Wrong reporting takes place also due to peer group differences and at times, undesirable pressures from superiors. The phenomenon of Cascading Effect may also take its toll. In addition, situations, such as Mahakumbh in Haridwar and fortcoming festivals force labs, companies, Government employees too to act and perform in immoral ways in a haste, by adding to number of tested individuals. Inquiry ordered in respect of malpractices of three labs in regard to Haridwar tragedy drags on and on. They still figure in the "official list".

We will later see how official Covid death figures have differed drastically from various registers maintained by Cremation grounds and Office of Registrar of Births & Deaths in many States. There were also a number of cases of creating confusion between normal deaths, accidental ones and Covid related deaths.

When it comes to worse, religious beliefs and faiths are not respected and unthinkable takes place- Dead People donot get the dignity they deserve, rather, many who should be cremated, get thrown into river or have to be buried on account of reasons of time, precaution or cash or perpetual fear of Dom Raja, who may not understand basics of Ethics and Morality. Why only to point fingers at an End of Social Strata and outright ostracised individual like him, when there are "sophisticated" players at work.

At a Bazar of a Ganga river bank in U.P. some people from so called upper caste have been also found removing Kafans, sheets, Gamchhas etc. from half cremated/half buried dead bodies and reselling them afresh. Such a highly immoral and unthinkable act may not happen in other societies.

Its Atrocious, its Mind Boggling in a country wherein family values steeped in customs, traditions, mores, folkways and ultimate religious beliefs are taught from the beginning to end.

STATISTICAL MISTAKES, MAGIC OR JUGGLERY ?

Talking of this vital index of Public Administration, Policy or Economics, the Centre For Global Development of USA, upon analyzing data from March '20 to June'21 has reported on 24th August that India's Corona death toll is upto TEN TIMES HIGHER than 4,15,000 fatalities reported by the authorities. Such a rise was partly "fuelled" by the Delta variant during April and May 2021. EASILY IT COULD BE THE WORST HUMANITARIAN DISASTER since 15th August, 1947.

Incidently, the official death toll of country as on date, that is, 4.36 Lakhs continues to be third highest, after 609,000 fatalities of USA and Brazil's 5,42,000.

SCOPE FOR DOUBT

While genuine doubts have been casted on country's death toll, time and again, also by the Courts, overstretched health services, lack of proper rest since the first wave, illness and deaths of immediate relatives could be also cited as contributing factors. These need to be considered.

Many large states have revised their Virus tolls in recent weeks, thus adding thousands of "Backlog" deaths. While major concern States of West Bengal and Assam are maintaining a safe silence since their Assembly elections, Bihar has divulged as many as 251,000 "Excess" deaths registered by Registrar of Births and

Deaths under Civil Registration System (CRS) pertaining to the period March '2021 to May '2021. It is 48.6 times, the official number of confirmed deaths (5163) in the state in the same time period.

Undoubtedly, it is a Highly Immoral Act on the part of the concerned persons, making it one of the largest deviations in Excess Mortality. The State Government had submitted earlier differing figures to Patna High Court at the level of Divisional Commissioner, Patna and Chief Secretary of the State.

FURTHER DATA ANALYSIS

Deviation in Mortality figures has been also reported by a major national daily in respect of other states, such as Kerala, Tamil Nadu, Andhra Pradesh, Telengana and Karnataka in one category and Maharashtra, Gujarat, Assam, H.P. and U.P. in the other. It has reflected a very wide range of undercount factors- as little as 0.42 times in Kerala (otherwise having highest number of 24 hour cases and highest Positivity Rate of 19.03 %) to 43 times in U.P. (based on available data of 24 districts).

GLOBAL MESS

Globally also, as per WHO, Covid-19 deaths may be as much as two-three times the official figures of 44.8 lakh deaths from 21.5 Crore cases.

Suppression of data has been reported from time to time from China, Russia, Brazil, UK, Italy, Peru, Mexico, South Africa and many poor countries of Africa. Thus, the persons involved in tabulating and analyzing such figures in other countries ALSO NEED TO BE TAKEN TO TASK for their act of misleading.

GOOD SAMARITANS AND ROAD AHEAD

A sizeable percentage of populace get perturbed after getting infected by Covid pandemic.

Moral or rational behaviour and response patterns may not emerge, many a time. Nevertheless, one comes across Good Samaritans in all professions, who not only forget their family and health for the sake of duty but sheer magnitude and population of the country and almost absence of a work culture lead to several road blocks. These need to be reviewed and success stories should be replicated for common good.

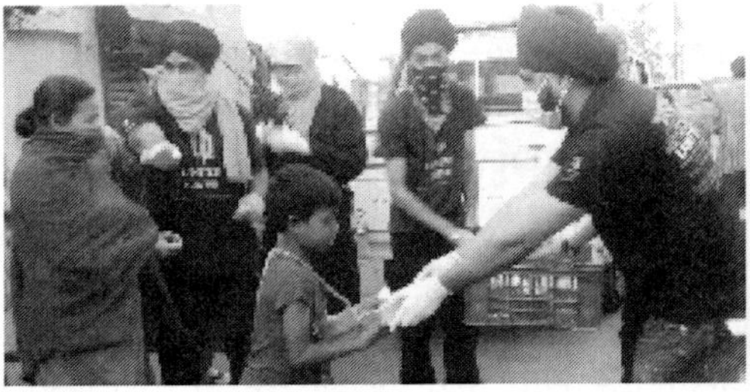

As regards issues of Ethics and morality, it can not be a positive scenario always, that too in a situation when profit makers refuse to budge. Rumour mongering and panic spreading should not have a place amidst us. When an usual kind of viral fever during a particular time of the year strikes, it has to be tackled, responsibly, in a human way.

LATEST VACCINE DEVELOPMENTS

Our sincere approach, reputation and character may help in winning over any epidemic. We have to keep trying by being in touch and correctly feeling the pulse of the people. While we spread the dictum of 'protecting yourself and your family safe at home', we should not be IMMUNE to the ongoing research on a Booster dose, 3rd dose or a Nasal one. Such a behaviour pattern will not only be most effective weapon but ethically and morally correct also. While one may take note of 32.64 Crore cases against 60.24 Crores vaccinated with ONE DOSE (49.5% Adults) and 50.5% of population yet to be vaccinated, one can IMAGINE the HERCULEAN TASK AHEAD IN 2022-23.

However, record One Crore JABS administered on 27th August may BOOST OUR MORALE.

(C) PROTECTION OF ENVIRONMENT

Author

15

Conserve Water As Mercury Shoots[14]

One of the most serious challenges that many nations of Asia and Africa face is that of water supply when it does not rain or when it is sparse. Situation becomes pathetic for humans, birds. plant life and animals from Sahara desert in Africa to Cholistan in Pakistan to Bikaner, Barmer, Jaisalmer and in some districts of south India. It is despite the fact that water constitutes more than 70% of the Earth's surface. But again entire water is also not safe from drinking point of view.

While thinking about this issue, one began running through a masterpiece- 'Everybody Loves A Good Drought' by P. Sainath.

Published in 1996,the comprehensive work based on drought situation in eight districts of four states is a sad saga of human tolerance. It begins with casual approach in selecting districts for well known DPAP scheme and goes on to explore how villagers are increasingly losing control over common water resources and destruction of traditional irrigation systems is gaining speed.

According to Sainath, the struggle over water resources not only operates within a village but in many ways also between villages, castes and classes. The account of water lords of Ramanathapuram, Tamil Nadu explains the crux of the problem. The lords used to own private wells sunk in public tank beds reflecting "sad example of creeping privatization of water resources."

Thanks to their political links each one of them would make Rs. 60,000 a month in a region having 6000 ancient tanks. As many would need major repairs, poor peasants in large numbers would be forced to migrate to more fertile and prosperous Thanjavur district. Lack of water would touch every aspect of life in drought prone areas from health and education to industry, the literacy drive to slow debt repayment.

Situation has only marginally changed in last twenty five years. As Water is basic necessity for sustaining life, many techniques have been devised to save water. Yet, most of us fail to understand importance of water. Slogans like "Save every drop of water" appear short period solutions.

If we continue with such a casual approach, by 2050, situation may become very alarming, according to a study.

Rural women still have to struggle for fetching water, mostly bare footed, by covering a distance of five to ten kms on a daily basis. In the process, they along with their children are exposed to several health hazards which remain mostly unattended. Animals living in arid zones suffer maximum as they lack the power of expression.

When we have a dry and painful spell, such as, from mid March onwards to July or August in the country, people face a combined impact of unbearable heat and restricted water supply. It severally affects life of the people, animals, aquatic life and birds living in dry and arid zones, apart from many other pockets which have lost forest cover over the years.

In view of the fact that the vital issue is ignored during and after rainy season, we have to encounter perpetual problems such as, Cauvery river water dispute between Tamil Nadu and Karnataka and one involving Yamuna river water between Haryana and Delhi governments.

There are many more rivers passing through more than one state especially in the North East but so far inter-state disputes have not surfaced on this count. Rather, to get maximum returns, long term schemes to inter link major rivers is being revived seriously.

Perpetual Water Crisis of Overgrown & Pampered Delhi

During summer months tremendous shortfall is noticed despite issuing of advisories to general public. The Haryana government consistently maintains that it releases adequate water as per existing agreement. They, on their part, also blame the Punjab Government for restricted supply.

As per latest information, Delhi gets 40% Yamuna water supply from Haryana and rest from Ganga river through U.P. and Bhakra Nangal from Punjab.

Old Habits Die Hard

Whatever may be the weather pattern or play of climate change or unreliable IMD forecasts, we, as consumers do not change our day to day habits in respect of our work concerning kitchen, washing clothes, shaving, brushing teeth, watering plants, crops, lawns etc.

Need For Water Conservation

If we think and act seriously, there is tremendous scope for water conservation in the individual performed activities, such as:

(a) Use of a bucket instead of shower to take bath,

(b) Tap water should not be running when soap is applied to body,

(c) Tap should be closed/shut while we brush teeth or shave or clean hand or wash clothes,

(d) Flushing of toilets unnecessarily must be avoided,

(e) Pour minimum water while mopping or cleaning cemented or tiled floors,

(f) Use of bucket and mug instead of pipes while washing vehicles. Latter damages/erodes pitch on roads very fast, especially in hilly terrain,

(g) Finish water left in a glass instead of throwing. (A few years ago through an appeal, Delhi Govt. used to ask school children to pour left over water of their bottles into flower pots) and

(h) Closing of taps properly after use.

Rainwater Harvesting (R.H.)

As far as collective or community level initiatives for conserving water are concerned, R.H. should now get the topmost priority.

Its origin dates back to 3rd Millenium B.C. in China. This technique aims to collect and store rain water which invariably runs off from top of roof, roads, open grounds etc.

By storing it near or under the house or into natural reservoirs or tanks, one can very well meet requirement of water in the lean and dry season without incurring huge expenditure.

Consistent replenishment of ground water is also possible apart from taking care of kitchen garden ,irrigation and industrial needs by suitable catchment, conveyance and storage components.

Treatment & Recharge Possible

Rainwater so collected can be treated with a few tablets of Chlorine for making it fit for human consumption. Rainwater harvesting tanks can come up above ground, these can be partly underground as also fully underground.

However, cleaning and disinfection is required to be carried out regularly in order to ensure quality of water.

Further, recharge of Dug wells and abandoned Tube wells in the plain areas is also possible by taking water from roof tops by providing drain pipes.

JAL JEEVAN MISSION

Launched by the Central Government in 2019, it aims to provide safe and adequate drinking water to 20 lakh individual household taps in rural areas by 2024 on nominal payment basis. Probably at last Government has realized that

"Unless a charge is levied, wastage can not be prevented".

As per updated information, 10 lakh connections have been already made available. It is a commendable achievement.

All the Gram Punchayats/rural communities are expected to plan, implement, manage, own, operate and maintain their In Village Water Supply Systems.

Drought prone zones and deserts will be focussed areas.

It also aims to develop human resource for plumbing, electrical, water quality management, water treatment and often neglected area of Catchment Protection. Augmentation of existing sources of water is also proposed to be taken up.

Before concluding, two key comments are called for:

(a) We had enough of old wine in new bottles. Now more robust and strict stand needs to be taken especially against those diverting or cutting water pipes and those indulging in corrupt practices during the execution of such schemes,

(b) Its a pity that after 76 years of Independence we will still need more than two years to provide potable tap water to all.

But Government of the day should not be blamed always.

What do you do when new households and hamlets very much add to the overall burden or responsibility, or when new roads and foot paths are laid ostensibly, due to lack of co-ordination between departments ?

16

Come September, Has It Not Come With A Bang? Remembering River Valley Civilisations[15]

September 21, 2021

Approaching early evening of life, one has to manage with curtailed sleep to find cool, soothing wind, blowing with tolerable drizzle, one September morning. It turns torrential soon, propelling me to think deeply about the vast amount of water that simply goes waste, almost every now and then.

Where are the tall and loud promises for treating million gallons of river polluted water or fresh guidelines for agonising dictum of Rain Water Harvesting?

September 2021 may turn out to be wettest in 141 years as per IMD, yet human sobbing or cribbing may not have any limits. One has read about four great River Valley Civilisations (RVC)- Mesopotamia, Indus, Egypt and Chinese. When it came to water development and management, these were reported ahead of times through advance canal irrigation systems or could be, rain water harvesting.

All ignore this positive aspect and go on gulping polluted and contaminated water, day in and day out, wash clothes and pass the residual stuff to already hard pressed flora and fauna.

Prior to going ahead, it is upsetting to note the estimated annual rise in global temperature, now, by 1.5 degrees, speeding of melting process of Icebergs of Antarctica and "authorised" killing of 1428 Dolphins on Faroe Island near Scotland as an intrinsic part of four century old tradition.

Trace From Beginning

Adam came first, to be joined by Eve. Their predestined union led to offsprings. From a family unit, it was a movement from place to place to get converted into a village, complex thereof and to associations with the passage of time. When a set of civilisation emerged, a kind of urban settlement too began being formed on fertile river banks. So settled or statics took over from nomadics from Mesopotamians on Tigris-Euphratus rivers, to Indus Valley on Indus River to Egyptians on Nile and to the Chinese on Yellow river.

Old to Present

Earlier Mesopotamia (meaning land between rivers) was thought to be oldest to have thrived during 3300 B.C. to 750 B.C. but recent archeological findings have bestowed this title on Indus Valley Civilisation, which was a force to reckon with during 2500 B.C. Even size-wise, Harappa part of it was twenty times bigger than Egypt and twelve times larger than combined area of Egypt and Meso-potamia. Its characteristic features were: standardized Weights and Measures, Seal Carving and Metallurgy with Copper, Bronze. Lead and Tin.

What Made A RVC Special ?

A RVC was supposed to be an agricultural entity or a nation located beside and drawing sustenance from a river, according to Wikipedia. Their common features were: large population, agriculture based economy, social and economic hierarchies, unique art and craft traditions and a typical system of territory administration.

Coming to faith, almost all are believed to be Polytheists or having faith in more than one God, adds the same source.

Land was found fertile and their management skills were very good with predominant canal irrigation system. Regulation of Water resources too impressed. Better utilisation of surface and ground water might have also helped.

Rivers, Dams, Waterfalls

Why only river water, as a teenager in Ranchi we were permitted to peddle to dams, such as, Kanke or Dhurwa and Waterfalls, ranging from Dasang to Jonha to Hundru to enjoy Picnic.

The stagnant but clean water would be used both for cooking and drinking, followed by a night of marvellous sleep.

Or in late Eighties, on the high altitudes of Sikkim, Himachal, Arunachal or Uttarakhand, my freshly joined Better Half would stop the old vehicle every now and then to feel crystal clear water from roadside tiny waterfalls, which would be splashed over my face without prior hint, much to her bemusement and that of late Passang, my old trusted driver hailing from Yangthang, West Sikkim. There were no mobiles, no worries, no anxieties or expectations. Life would move on without any premise, precondition or blockage.

Present Abode Activates and Ignites Mind

Living now in a modest 3 BHK apartment in the outskirts of Delhi, one notes a lot from media about high Air Quality Index (AQI) from October to February but most of them keep conveniently off from automobile noise pollution, rampant dust pollution and faster decline in the depth of ground water.

REVERSION TO MESOPOTAMIA

With this, we move on to attempt a brief case analysis of present plight of Farhat and Siruwan rivers of Mesopotamia times, passing through and supporting the livelihood in present day Turkey and Iran. One element appears common-unbelievable high degree of biotic interference, aided and abated by capital intensive projects, such as, large dams and barrages.

According to WION T.V. channel, hundreds of Iraqis had to be hospitalised some time back, upon drinking polluted water. A villager's candid view was "No fish or aquatic life was found in the dying river for a long time".

It is akin to major portions of Hindon river in NCR and may be, in some stretches of legendary Yamuna, passing through Haryana and Delhi.

Why only Iraq, parts of Syria and Turkey are also facing such challenges, albeit, in smaller degree. Its the same story pertaining to civilised people living on Siruwan river or for that matter on Great Nile river of Egypt, which appeared in September 1997, a poor reflection of its former self.

EMERGING ONSLAUGHTS

Reacting to emerging developments, while Iran is blaming construction of two huge dams by Turkey, latter has defended its position by stating that only a water divergent tunnel was under execution which may not have any adverse impact. Fact remains that both Farhat and Siruwan rivers located in the erstwhile prosperous Mesopotamia region have not only turned into lean and thin entities but are causing rapid fall in cultivation resulting into drought and famine, which is bound to lead to exodus of struggling people.

People of Iraq who have been exploited and devastated by Saddam Hussain earlier and later by the neo imperialists, continue to bear the brunt due to nothing less than onslaught on once clean, vibrant and user friendly river systems.

SITUATION SIMILAR ON HOME FRONT

Back home, on the reverse side, Ganga Mata too appears furious with her so called secular followers by crossing her banks in Prayagraj, Kanpur, Varanasi, Patna and Monghyr. Similar is the anger on the part of Brahamputra, Hoogly, Koshi, Gandak and some rivers of Andhra Pradesh, M.P., West Bengal, Rajasthan and Gujarat.

While all of us see, hear and feel, who will dare to take the plunge to indulge into a kind of unbiased thought process in this age of Global Warming and lay foundation stone for a more advanced, lasting and Sustainable River Valley Civilisation?

DO WE STILL WAIT AND WATCH ?

17

Strategy Regarding Air, Water Pollution and Landslides Requires Review[16]

November 15, 2021

In good old days, say, early Nineties we had slow but steady vehicles of all types (125 types on Delhi roads alone) and mind boggling pollution from thermal power plants. Very old diesel trucks and buses would pollute more than taking care of carriage. But things appeared somewhat "under some degree of control."

Change, coupled with strict directions and monitoring by the Supreme Court together with introduction of CNG from 1997-98 onwards could harbinger some sense, awareness, fear as also compliance of Motor vehicle rules and regulations. Further liberalised set up in respect of FDI and SUV's did go on to add to the woes, at the same time.

Linking of four to six to eight lanes of National Highways and onset of Expressways, however, raised fresh concerns from road safety point of view. Imagine, taking bold steps in a scenario infamous for road rage at the drop of hat !

Looked as if Executive had abdicated its responsibility and thereby Judiciary had no option but to enter the fray in "Public Interest".

Water Pollution closely followed up Air Pollution

Present scary number of over 75 lakh vehicles in Delhi would shake anybody's sane sense. Other three metros and Bengalore also did not lag behind.

Shall we say that rivers, rivulets, lakes, ponds were also getting polluted ? But not to the present extent. At least there was less of reporting or awareness regarding a SLOW POISON like this.

Mind Boggling Expenditure

Crores of Rupees have been sanctioned and spent under Plan & Non Plan Heads on not crossing the threshold limits in both crucial spheres.

But each year during the Peak time, we are caught "off guard", atleast in NCR due to very high density of population, rapid and unthinkable and unaesthetic constructions, fast depletion of water sources, untimely and erratic release of Yamuna water by the neighbouring Haryana Government, consistent rise in visible pollution of any water bodies and gradual lowering of ground water tables.

Are we Concerned, or Alarmed ?

Not as much alertness or advance preparation is resorted to, as it should be.

Rapid expansion of Corona virus leading to Covid-19 since February 2020 should have given us an useful lesson and opportunity on both Air and Water Prevention and control measures but we began well, went for first Lock Down for sixty eight days all of a sudden, followed again by its second version of fifty four days. However, the development of our own two vaccines and neat and clean measures pertaining to air and water pollution control measures did make some difference, Sky would appear azure blue, for a change.

Free or Discounted Diversion of Vaccines

Had we not diverted vaccines to 89 countries based on "Freebie" and differential pricing policy, we would have perhaps reached the target of vaccinating entire adult population by November 2021 and all of them by second dose also, say, by August / September, 2022.

However, while being back to crucial and focussed area of Corona prevention and control regime, we need to acknowledge fully and pat our doctors and paramedics as also ASHA and Anganwadi workers and helpers together with other identified and recognised frontliners.

While we saw many ups and downs, sometimes by applying Trial and Error methods on Covid front, by and large, water pollution and containment measures have got sidelined if not neglected, altogether. It should have been contested or fought against both in equal measures.

Doubts regarding Reporting by States

When more than 4.60 lakh Covid casualties has taken place, pan India, we are still having teething problems in some states besides a sort of attempt to undermine the real success stories in a few major states both during first and second waves. Reporting from Assam, Mizoram, West Bengal and Bihar and lately Kerala, remains a GREY AREA.

But for the advent of COWIN, data reporting,, tabulation and analysis methods would have been manipulated, further leading to faulty planning as also construction and fabrication devices.

So let us hope for a slightly bright scenario by August or September, 2022.

Pollution and Landslides

In the domain of air pollution, we had the worst scenario in the last five years, atleast concerning NCR in particular and entire North, possibly with exception of J&K, H.P. and Uttarakhand.

Last named state has seen, nevertheless, more natural calamities during the calendar year 2021 than ever in the past. Many precious lives and properties could have been saved in Uttarakhand if the state government had not signed MoU's with hundreds of hydel companies for erecting plants in fragile and precarious zones. Another major blunder by Arunachal, Uttarakhand and Sikkim were expansion of existing plants and undertaking and augmentation of water supply schemes together with large scale village connectivity works and widening of existing main roads, supposedly for religious and adventure tourism purposes under the directions of "THE TOP."

These three states have rather fragile ecology and that they have survived in general due to low population density and relatively low level of industrial activity.

Still we donot seem to be very late in these states from environment conservation perspective. Situation can be salvaged, that's my considered view.

Air pollution too is under control so far in the named hilly states as compared to the NCR or two "prosperous" states of Punjab and Haryana.

We donot wish to hint at the same time, towards the MESS on the agricultural and drugs control fronts in these two states.

Shall we not resist the temptation of pinpointing Stubble or Parrali burning therein which is a major threat to air pollution scenario in the whole of NCR, atleast in the last five to six years? The talk of PUSA "developed" mechanical device to suppress the stubble then and there and turn these residues into manure for the next round of crop continues to BE MOSTLY ON PAPER.

O Yes, unthinkable and irritating P.R. measures are always undertaken.

Clear Sky, Distant or Uncertain ?

Going by the present authentic indications, thick Smog over NCR since the Diwali day may not disappear prior to first week of February 2022.

Imagine from worst possible AQI of 990 on 4th November to a partial decline upto 400 or so by 6th November to again rise upto 536 at Anand Vihar, Delhi on 10th November, the state of hazardousness continues.

But we are still in a debating and discussing Mode.

Such a casual approach also pertaining to water pollution prevention and control measures are going TO BE NOT only unsustainable from health viewpoint but these would be detrimental equally to the needs and aspirations of future generations.

Concerted and Focussed Action Round the Year By All

Let there be concerted action plans both regarding air and water pollution side by side with adequate prevention measures against further rise in Covid and Dengue cases or any other kind of Viral fever. Systematic work without any break should be our motto.

States have to support Centre in all respects and people too have to make their viable contributions.

Celebration of Diwali should reflect simplicity, peace of mind and a fellow feeling, rather than show of wealth, shift towards reflection of road rage or aggressive behaviour. Also inhaling of toxic air for days together was never thought of or expected.

It is a matter of grave concern that no perceptible change is noticed even subsequent to special campaigns and drives.

How many of concerned and sustainable development minded citizens Refrain from having additional houses or the vehicles or Air conditioners?

To hit the current Bull or Target directly, Eco friendly and relatively cost effective harvesting machines or devices, such as, Turbo H.Feeders will have to be introduced in the farm driven states during October-November.

Compulsory compliance of orders relating to fixed periodicity of vehicles in all the metros together with re-introduction of odd and even number system may work again in general public interest. Vehicle free zones too may have to be introduced immediately.

Also there is an urgent need to stop the nefarious sell of "targetted" vehicles in other states. A pollution generator will continue to be so till finally taken off the road.

Equal emphasis has to be given for revival of fast deteriorating water bodies together with visible ban on vegetable cultivation along the polluted and vulnerable river banks.

As regards pollution of any kind, the Executive Magistrates and the area Police officers may have to be actually taken to task in case of unusual practices, rather than routine warnings or transfers.

Apart from fines, confiscation of vehicles for a limited duration can also have a deterrent effect.

18

Global Warming : Warming of Weather and Consumers[17]

August 2, 2021

One is hearing and reading about weather part of it for more than a decade. In some parts of planet it is directly being felt, in others it may generate considerable heat due to some other pressures, such as, unexpected volcanic eruptions and wild fires resulting from climate change.

Average temperature of earth is likely to get an addition of more than 1.5 degree celcius above pre- industrial levels by 2030. It has already risen by 0.5 to 1 degree celcius. In some parts, however, one also experiences overall cooling albit, for a short period.

According to latest input of Inter Govermental Panel on Climate Change, warming of surface of earth happens when Carbon Dioxide traps solar radiation in the atmosphere. In common parlance, this process is also known as Greenhouse Effect. It is caused by:

(a) Burning of Fossil fuels, such as, Coal, Oil, Wood and Natural Gas.

Alternatives already being tried are Solar power of which Germany is the leader and India too is fast catching up, and oft repeated, several New and Renewable sources of energy,

(b) High Emission levels in many sectors and countries,

(c) Alarming rate of deforestation,

(d) Growing consumption of fertilisers containing nitrogen, and

(e) Indiscriminate release of Fluorinated Gas from Refrigerators, Air Conditioners and Heat Pumps.

No doubt earth's temperature has risen 0.5 degree celcius per year but more worries may emerge in future. It is not only news or earlier prediction about melting of Himalayan Glaciers that is of concern, it is melting of Ice Shelves and Ice Bergs lately in Antarctica as well.

Recent studies and findings indicate that Ice Bergs are not only found floating but these have begun cracking and falling as well. Resultantly in some parts of Antarctica, there is addition of minus 38 degree of temperature. Undoubtedly, this could be considered very warm from existing parameters of the isolated Continent.

March Heat Felt by Indians on Weather and Consumption Fronts

Back home, Northern India and most of NCR is already experiencing an early Heat Wave, with rise in maximum temperature by five degrees in one week from 35 degree celcius to 40 degree and minimum one hovering between 18 and 20 degree celcius.

Imagine this is happening despite the region recording its wettest winter in several decades, as per the finding of Delhi-based Centre For Environment and Science. Five months period from 1st October 2021 to 22nd February 2022 was studied for this purpose.

Further, as we are aware, Delhi recorded in all 217 mm of rainfall in 2021 Winter, nearly double of 114 mm in 2020 winter, 74 mm in 2019-20 and 86 mm in 2018 -19. Surprisingly, however, Delhi also had 192 Good Air days but mostly had Air Quality Index in very poor and severe categories during just concluded tough and severe winter. If situation like this continues for a week to ten days, SEVERE HEAT WAVE ALERTS will Have To Be Issued as per the India Meteorological Department.

"Warming Up" of Indian Consumer

Less said about heat and warmth of average Indian consumer would be better.

For nearly 107 days during the Code of Conduct period of Assembly Election process in five states recently, no rise in prices of POL products, LPG, PNG or CNG was announced. Now POL prices are being increased almost on a daily basis for twelve days. As a result, medicine and edible oil prices, food inflation and unemployment have also shot up beyond unthinkable limits.

A kind of laisse faire situation was prevailing in the market, ever since election results were announced on 10th March, but formal take over of new Governments was yet to take place. So fixed income earners are on tenterhooks, due to turn and twist in the market.

Consumer's Woes Across the Borders

Crossing nation's boundaries, one is hearing of extreme heat on consumer front in Pakistan and Sri Lanka also apart from gradually being forgotten Afghanistan. While in Pakistan it may be attributable to present political uncertainty, in Sri Lanka both price rise coupled with scarcities of essential commodities are probably due to gradual exploitation and subjugation to the Chinese. Citizen led protests against ongoing economic crisis and short supply of Electricity have taken place outside the President's residence for the first time in the history of the Island nation.

While the Chinese have compelled Lankans to toe their line subsequent to their failure in fulfilling certain agreed to conditions, India's announcement of $ 1,000 Crore aid, is essentially aimed to bail out the Island nation from the current economic mess. But ethnic factor and interest inherent herein, should not be ruled out.

As petty shopkeepers are ruling the roost, prior to dictating the terms, should such a situation be allowed to continue ? We, as vigilant consumers Need To Ask Ourself.

HEAT GENERATED BY ARMS

So to say, not always in demand, Arms Bazar gets a chance to warm up mainly in war kind of situation. It is undoubtedly getting heated up owing to year long tension and build up involving Russia and Ukraine. Subsequent to sizable loss of troops in Iraq and Afghanistan, USA and NATO allies have decided to play safe by promising and actually providing latest arms to Army under stress from a " big" brother. However, when it comes to committing any manpower support, they simply back out.

Principal arms manufacturers, viz, USA(37% share), Russia (20%), Israel, Germany, France and China come in this "league".

Incidentally and ironically, these are the same countries that talk of peace, human rights and what not ? They also ask, expect and cajole others for their own advantages.

A noted T.V. channel has, therefore, rightly opined that USA, despite losing on many fronts, including recent embarrassment in Afghanistan, does not have any regrets. Rather it is a huge profit situation, as interest of their arms and aviation industry has to be kept alive.

19

World Sparrow Day[18]

March 20, 2022

By sharing some pictures of Sparrows, idea is to Remind you of the World Sparrow Day, a Day celebrated universally on 20th March to highlight reduction in numbers of the bird and thereby to raise awareness about their conservation.

In India, to my memory, initiative like this was taken a few years ago in NCT, Delhi under the leadership of Late Shiela Dixit, former Chief Minister. Subsequent to such an initiative, number of this bird is reported to be increasing a bit. They can be attracted in more numbers if nests made from items of daily use can be created and fixed in a corner at a height of minimum ten feet.

A few birds and animals, such as Dog, Cat, Parrot, Cow, Goat, Sparrow, Rabit, etc. always are found in human habitat, in all climate zones, with the exception of deserts and fully snow covered land mass.

Close link, rather relationship between them and humans, was once a foregone conclusion. Proximity would always depend on love and care, we showered on them. If elders cared, tiny tots too would imbibe good values to show affection to such useful, caring and loyal fauna. The house sparrow or Passer domesticus is a bird of the sparrow family Passeridae, once found all over world. In our infancy years, we would find them in all the orchards, courtyards and markets, wherein regular feed would be ensured.

Now that houses are no longer thatched with no courtyard, till a few years back, Sparrows would throng the balconies and terraces. But they would be more cautious if not threatened vis-à-vis life around spacious courtyards or plethora of farm land. Also there was no Mobile or T.V. tower to deter them. Each time I raise this issue and make a fervent appeal, friends, relatives and well wishers say : **"Maybe, in your area but not in mine/ours they seem to have disappeared."**

If such is the trend, such a tiny, harmless and loving bird, having an average length of 16 centimeters, with prominent colour of light brown and grey, MAY BECOME EXTINCT SOON.

There is, therefore, an immediate need to make available their preferred Feed of seeds of grains, wild grass, weeds, insects etc. A city like Delhi, Mumbai, Chennai, Kolkata or Noida (over 300 skyscrappers) is not the place for them. Friends, by taking more care and supporting conservation efforts let us strengthen our age old bond with them and also provide healthy learning opportunity to young generation, otherwise getting Glued to Cell phone, Net etc.

At the same time, there is an immediate need to reduce use of insecticides and pesticides. Compared to Pigeon these birds do not make a place dirty or are instrumental in spreading any disease.

20th March is also International Day of Happiness. So why can't we be more Happy in spreading this kind of positive message and join hands with Delhi based Rakesh Khatri, who has built 36,000 nests already and Arjun Singh of Rohtas, Sparrow Man of Bihar, who has 8000 sparrows to give company in his difficult times?

All Photographs by Author

20

World Environment Day[19]

June 8, 2022

Protection and preservation of nature should be a matter of collective responsibility for each one of us. Needless to say, threats keep emerging in the shape of global warming, sudden volcanic eruptions, drying of river basins, melting of glaciers & ice bergs, cloud bursts, untimely floods, degradation of soil etc.

The World Environment Day observed every year on 5th June is an universal platform for raising the tempo of environmental awareness and education and taking corrective action. Led by U.N. Environment Programme since 1973 it is supposed to involve millions of people across the world.

One can take up cleaning of beaches, be part of grass root movements, plant trees, organize meetings & awareness drives, take environmentally conscious decisions etc.

Ahead of main event at Sweden, I. Anderson, the Executive Director of UNEP has rightly highlighted that "Today as we look to a....future of heatwaves, droughts, floods, wildfires, pandemics, dirty air, wars and plastic ridden oceans, action is more important than ever".

Further the U. N. O. Secretary General has also aptly added "we can no longer ignore the alarm bells that ring louder every day. The only way forward is to work with nature, not against it".

THEME OF 2022 -ONLY ONE EARTH

The theme of this year's day was supposed to stress living in harmony with nature on earth in a sustainable way, as earth is only home for the entire humanity. It is significant to flag that this theme was chosen for the first conference at Stockholm in 1972 also. The humble beginning made has now spread to 150 countries.

Single use plastic products are supposed to be discarded after one time use. But in actual reality, it is not so. As a result, India alone generates around 3.5 million tonnes of such a 'difficult' waste on an annual basis. Situation has become alarming even after banning it in many states of the country. Hectic efforts have been resumed again (Sikkim did it in 1997).

Even the loud campaign of "Reduce, Reuse & Recycle" and reduction in consumption of animal products is not succeeding.

Coming to municipal solid waste, the whole world according to an estimate, generates 2. 01 Billion tonnes and 34% of that is generated alone by high income countries. Only one third of it is managed in hazardous ways. By 2050, it is expected to grow to 3. 50 Billion tonnes.

Rise In Heat Wave

Heatwaves are not only showing an upward trend this year in India despite arrival of Monsoon ahead of schedule in Andamans and Kerala but the weather continues to be humid and sticky. The emission level of Carbon Dioxide too is expected to rise. Also high demand for electricity will increase the consumption of fossil fuel against which we have committed ourselves in COP-26 summit at Glasgow in 2021.

Rampant use of air conditioners in metros and large cities further adds to the crisis.

Electric two and four wheelers & buses also are being popularised and introduced as well but incidents of fires in their batteries are also being experienced, time and again.

P. M. ADDRESS

Talking of actions taken at the central level, the Prime Minister at the event organized by Isha Foundation, in the presence of spiritual leader Sadhguru has informed that all his policies over eight years have enabled protection of environment in some way.

Be it Swachh Bharat Mission or Programme on Waste to wealth, modern sewerage treatment plants in cities, campaign to get rid of single use plastic or Ganga Cleanliness campaign. He. also later launched a Global initiative called "LiFE Movement". Its vision is to live a lifestyle that is in tune with planet and does not harm it.

In the words of P. M., "it borrows from past, operates in the present and focuses on the future."

Giving his own slogan of "ONE EARTH, MANY EFFORTS" he has declared that India was ready to lend its support to actions to make environment better and improve global wellness.

While applauding the Save Soil Movement led by Sadhguru, he termed it as huge service to humanity.

The rise in Ethanol blending in Petrol from 1.5% in 2014 to 10% now shall lead to reduction in Carbon emission by 27 lakh tonnes and saving of foreign exchange reserve to the tune of Rs. 41, 000 Crores, P.M. went on to add.

Sikkim Show

As regards Sikkim, World Environment Day state level function held at Saramsa Garden was graced as chief guest, by the Chief Minister of Sikkim. He rightly stated that protection of environment and responding to issues, such as, forest fires was a responsibility to be shared by all. Same should not end with merely planting a sampling as it was to be taken care of also. Further, in his opinion, plantation drive in uncultivated and vacant land was going to enrich the eco system.

To Sum Up, a large number of saplings are planted (including native varieties as desired by the Tamil Nadu Governor this year) on such important days. But how many of them will be actually watered, maintained and pruned at appropriate time, THAT SHOULD BE IMPORTANT PART OF THE PROCESS.

A sincere and sustainable effort by involving the common man, SHG's and Gram Punchayats is, therefore, called for.

Everyone has to realise that environment has to be protected and preserved for the benefit of future generations and pollution of any kind will be detrimental to the entire society.

21

Natural Calamities : North East & Afghanistan Scenarios[20]

July 2, 2022

A natural calamity is a major event of adverse nature resulting from natural happenings, namely, earthquakes, floods, cyclones, landslides, hurricanes, volcanic eruptions, forest fires etc which affect rural and urban areas at large and also make an area more vulnerable for a certain period.

According to International Federation of Red Cross and Red Crescent Societies, "disasters are serious disruptions to the functioning of a community that exceed its capacity to cope, using it's own resources. These can be caused by natural, man made and technological hazards, as well as various factors that influence the exposure and vulnerability of a community."

Unchecked over exploitation of earth resources, habit of people to build houses in 'Risk Zones' & sinking areas, deforestation, global warming & climate change also add to the crisis. Hence nature alone should not be considered a culprit always.

According to U.N. Disaster Monitoring System, large number of natural disasters used to occur earlier in the disaster prone pockets of Asia-Pacific region, which led to tremendous loss of human and animal life & property, loss of livelihood, communication systems and many other short and long term social and economic disruptions. These also have the potential to generate a sizable amount of waste, such as, polythene, plastic and styrofoam. Adequate care is, therefore, called for, during the rescue and relief operations while coping with air pollution, blocking of drainage, scattered dead bodies etc or else many water borne diseases and respiratory illnesses, mostly afflicting the women and children may happen.

Some of the major **Cyclones of pre-1970 era,** keeping in view high number of casualties are:

Year	*Country*	*Casualties*
1737	India	3 lakh
1876	East Pakistan	2 lakh
1881	China	3 lakh
1923	Japan	2. 5 lakh
1970	East Pakistan	3 lakh

Devastating Earthquakes of 20th Century

Year	*Place*	*Richter Scale*	*Deaths*
1905	Kangra, H. P,	8. 0	20,000
1934	N. Bihar	8. 4	11,000
1935	Quetta, Pakistan	(7. 5)	25,000
1950	Assam	(8. 6)	1,500
1988	Bihar, W.Bengal, Sikkim	(6. 7)	1,300.

Change of Focus

Natural disaster coping mechanism by providing cash & kind only to victims was never free from corruption, rather it would lead to worsening of ongoing conflicts in an affected zone. Hence, change of approach was felt necessary, which would be oriented towards disaster preparedness, duly assisted by regular sharing of data and expertise face to face as also by use of internet and mobile telephones.

Launching of International Early Warning Programme by the U.N.O. in 2000 and subsequent declaration of October 13 as

International Day For Disaster Reduction (I.D.D.R.) could be considered significant milestones internationally.

Similarly change of nodal Ministry from Agriculture & Co - operation to Home Affairs and setting up of National Disaster Management Agency (NDMA) in 2004 led to transformation of the pattern of disaster management in India. In no time State and District level agencies too came up.

These got further fillip with formation of a dedicated National Disaster Response Force (NDRF) in 2006. Now with the help of such forces at key locations as also state capitals, response is becoming swift, certain and dependable.

NDRF with 13, 000 trained professionals has been in a position to rescue over 1. 44 lakh valuable lives and has evacuated more than 8 lakh persons stranded in disaster situations.

Extreme Weather Phenomena In North East India

Extreme weather developments nowadays is leading to unexpected heat, hot, sultry & humid conditions, cold or wetness etc, posing severe risks to human life. Sometimes localised unbearable weather can also cross geographical limits, causing destruction within two to three hours.

Talking of Tropical Cyclones, these also impact marine life and coastal regions more whereas inland regions are relatively safe from strong winds due to their rapid dissipation over land.

However, widespread floods can happen even in far inland areas due to high amount of rain from Tropical cyclones.

This is what precisely has happened in the North Eastern states, especially in the second fortnight of June. According to a source, Meghalaya had recorded 203% excess rainfall, followed by Assam (170%), Tripura (151%), Arunachal Pradesh (65%), Mizoram (64%) and Manipur (20%).

When Assam and Meghalaya flood situation was grim, these were widely reported in print and electronic media. With situation improving in Meghalaya, in Manipur death of 34 persons and over 30 still missing in the biggest ever landslides(over a stretch of two kms)at a railway construction site at Marangching in Noney District on 29th June is sending shock waves. Maximum loss has been faced by the Jawans of Territorial Army, eleven of them hailing from Darjeeling and Sikkim.

Initially landslide debris had blocked Ijei river creating a reservoir. If sufficient number of excavators were not deployed, original course of the river may not have been restored which may have led to inundation of many low lying areas. Because of continuous rainfall in the area flow in the local rivers is also expected to rise.

There is a precedent of such a nature in North Sikkim in 2017 when fast flowing Kanaka river was blocked for a week by the debris of landslide and one small village was fully submerged. An artificial lake thus formed was in existence for almost two months.

As far as Assam is concerned, at one stage, 32 out of 35 Districts were submerged including many parts of Guahati. There is some respite in 25 Districts now. According to latest information released by Assam State Disaster Management Agency, the number of casualties has risen to 174 and 2. 21 million people and a total of 1,590,557 domestic animals are still bearing the brunt of unprecedented floods. Setting up of 230 relief camps in Cachar Dist and 896 camps all over the state may not be sufficient. Water level in Barak river was flowing above danger level in several areas till recently leading to immense shortage of food, drinking water, medicines and many essential commodities.

When floods and landslides happen in Assam and many other states of Eastern India every year, I suppose, local administration should make preparations in advance. All construction activities need to be halted especially along District and State roads. More damage in hilly portions of N.E. states and plains of Bihar in coming two months can not be ruled out as in many areas Monsoon has not become aggressive as yet.

Need For Restrained Public Behaviour

In such challenging situations, common man should be more vigilant and proactive rather than merely waiting for Government response.

Immediate action by the First Responders, Gram Panchayats and local N. G. O's can very well pre empt a situation and possibly turn the tide. Any action taken should be in the interest of the community at large. In this regard, the act of damage to an embankment over Barak river (less dangerous than mighty Brahamputra) by some miscreants near Silchar town was completely uncalled for.

This proves the point that NATURAL DISASTERS CAN TAKE UNEXPECTED SHAPE even when an old and organized system may be in place.

EARTHQUAKE IN AFGHANISTAN

I may be failing in my task if post earthquake pathetic situation in Afghanistan is not paid attention. The country of 38 millions has witnessed large scale devastation owing to earthquakes in the Eastern provinces of Paktika, Khost and Nangarhar. The country already undergoing acute economic crisis, following the fresh takeover by the Talibans on 15th August 2021, had to face a massive earthquake at 6.2 on Richter scale on 22nd June.

Although number of deaths reported are 1150 (including 115 children) and injuries to over 3000, in actual reality numbers may rise further due to pathetic condition of roads, rugged unattended terrain, frequent tremors, rain off and on, lack of necessary equipment and above all, a less exposed and inefficient public administration. Many people are still feared to be buried under the rubble of mud brick and other type of 10,000 houses.

Lack of painkillers and antibiotics being reported from majority of health centers is adding to the crisis.

The Indian Humanitarian Aid

Without waiting for response from the so called fair weather friends of Afghanistan, Govt. of India has despatched 27 tons of relief materials(comprising family ridge tents, sleeping bags, mats and blankets) by air. Further, 6 tons of essential medicines have been airlifted in continuation of similar assistance in the past. The decision to reopen and run Indian Embassy in Kabul and a few Consulates through the " Technical Officers" could be considered a step in the right direction.

Being unable to control the situation, the Taliban Government had appealed for international aid but response so far is far from encouraging. A few organizations, such as, WFP, WHO, UNHCR and the Norwegian Refugee Council have, however, offered some cash assistance and relief materials. An Italian NGO named Emergency is also coming forward to extend help.

As no more casualty or damage was reported, the Deputy President of Afghan Red Crescent has stated on 27th June that there is not so much of need for food or non-food items. The most critical need according to him was cash for survivors to take care of basic needs.

But the ball lies in the court of USA and some other countries to defreeze Afghan Government assets. The USA President has shown only his verbal concern and offered sympathy and prayers. USA has also promised to provide little bit of financial aid and lead the international community in responding to humanitarian issues of Afghans.

BUT WHEN AND HOW, SAME WILL MATERIALIZE, REMAINS TO BE SEEN.

(D) INTERNATIONAL AFFAIRS

Author on China Side of Nathu la Border.
Trading was resumed after 43 Years on 6 July, 2006.
Author Contributed Considerably to the Process.

22

Changing Equations in World Living and Politics[21]

September 10, 2021

Man was born free but due to his greed not need, he/she often crosses limits, boundaries, time tested customs, traditions, mores, folkways, rules and regulations. A time comes when a faith or value system may assimilate, if not integrate or unite. But varying circumstances over a period of time also lead to disagreements, dissentions and diversions resulting into suspicions and latent jealousies. A time comes when negativity begins overtaking positivity and there is no ground or scope left for morality, ethics and rationality.

Geopolitics Dominant Theme

In good old days, Geo Politics would be the determining factor when it came to societies or Zamindaris and later principalities. Somehow, individuals began feeling and believing that they needed additionalities to take care of their lust or unjustified and ineffective desires, not luxuries or necessities, per se.

We tend to have differences within, then we begin creating the same among the neighbours, followed by latent and manifest interventions. May be, Guerilla wars, occasional skirmishes, short period battles and ultimately, open and full fledged wars take place.

Post Industrial Revolution Era

In the beginning of twentieth century, "birds of same feather started flocking together". Some were having leadership qualities, others would follow either in the name of religion, ethnicity or even proximity. One block of loose nationalities began pitted against similar such groups.

Gradual developments in culture, religion and science subsequent to long years of industrial revolution and simultaneous suppression of labour, also aided and abated the feelings of dislike and hatred. Man began not only showing or expressing extra territorial interests but these would be pursued for months and years.

World War Period

World War I from 1914 to 1918 demolished notions and nations, devastated people and places and made millions hopeless and homeless. Apart from infamous Spanish Flu for two years, it led to more unlimited demands as against limited or restricted supplies.

As if this was not enough, some tensions, some simmering discontents could not possibly be resolved. These lingered on for no apparent rhyme and reason and soon, from September 1939 to September 1944, World War II came knocking.

No one can afford to forget Reign of Terror unleashed by Adolf Hitler on the one hand and dropping of Atom Bombs over meek and helpless populace of Hiroshima and Nagasaki, on the other.

Many countries, such as, India which were subservient, were compelled to side with their, the then masters and rulers. Thus, a good deal of manpower and resources had to be diverted, exploited and sacrificed.

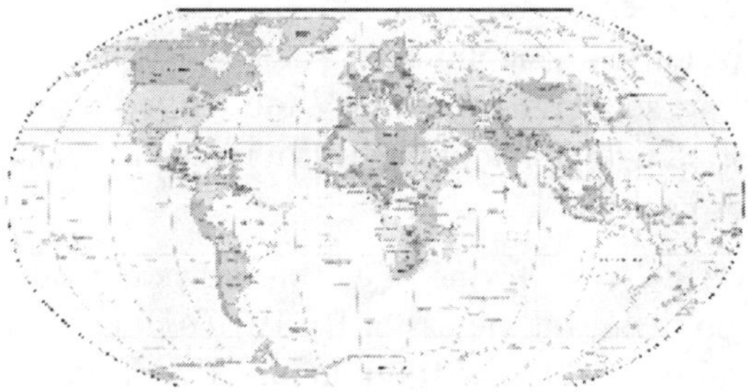

League of Nations and UNO

Though short-lived League of Nations and very soon, there after, UNO took birth but complete dominance "of a few" over the world majority got reflected in session after session. Veto power to "famous five" made all the difference. USA emerged as a leading power by outsmarting Great Britain and is reported to have made 73 direct or indirect interventions in the post-Second World War period.

Cold War and de tant

The relatively peaceful era was followed by Cold War period, when countries would differ, speak, come together for a while, to go astray again. But war in real sense appeared a distant possibility. An era of cold war between old opponents, padded by fresh alignments and realignments, therefore, became the order of the day.

With the passage of time, the world living and relationship scenario took the shape of a "de tant" or a saga, if not era of relaxation of strained relations.

Further developments in science and technology began favourably responding to change if not transition in perceptions concerning education and vocations, succeeded by fresh frontiers of neo education. An education pattern that would not only feed the mind but also the belly, as a matter of immediate necessity.

Means of Communication: Rapid Strides

A time came when need for fresh alignments without moving closer to each other, began being felt. Separatist tendencies were destined to be buried. Telephones, Radios and Transistors entered the scene but no sooner than later, T.V. too arrived, as man was not merely satisfied with listening, he was tempted to see. Perhaps to have a Better Feel.

Side by side, new forms of wireless systems, telephones, portable or cordless, hit the earth. By 1970's, Internet arrived in full force and by 1990's mobile phone network not only began expanding but these hand held tiny machines ensured more actual as also at times, unwanted volume in terms of messages and conversations. Things became loud and clear but by and large, people began taking recourse to blatant lies also. Web cameras, social media sites, as also Whatsapp kind further changed if not revolutionised the nuts and bolts of human interaction. Soon, rapid spread of Corona virus led to less physical or face to face interface and thus, reality began becoming "virtual" in a new "normal" era.

Reverting to the theme, from Geo politics, we seem to have got into a phase of Geo Economics. Already divided World was further sub-divided and began facing fresh challenges of separatism, unification and reunification, more so, in Europe. The new and decisive era of Global Village not only came but it was there to stay. I.T., Internet and multitude of several other devices spread their tentacles and mankind began feeling a justified or loose notions towards coming together of nations.

Uncalled for Interventions

Vietnam, Afghanistan, Iraq, meddling in Libya, Myanmar, Syria and Afghanistan again, showed nothing but shameless and naked dance of Neo-imperialism, as compared to erstwhile Colonial Rule by the British. What ultimately happened vis-à-vis what was planned, is now very well known to the thinking and rational human beings.

Afghan Situation

Terrorism continues to be in the forefront even after 24 days of "CHANGE" with seventeen of wanted world level terrorists figuring prominently in the thirty four member, just announced structure of soon to take over Government of "Emirate of Afghanistan". Beards and veils have returned, education to girl child is again receiving a setback and women are being forced out of offices.

Dominion Status

While Canada, Australia and non-descript entities, such as, Falklands are still ruled from Buckingham Palace, notable places like, Honkong had to be returned to "original owner", China in 1997, leading to tense situations, protests, occasional out-bursts, so on and so forth. In the post-Wuhan era, this liberated and restored piece of highly prosperous business hub, having a key location, continues to play a "leading" role.

Earlier entry and exodus of USSR into and from Afghanistan, followed by two decade long occupation by the US led Western forces, goes on to reflect that GeoEconomics too cannot succeed on its own. Same has to be given tonic from time to time in the form of Back Track and sometimes Loud and Clear Diplomacy. One may indulge in GeoEconomics but only by giving due credence to the Geopolitical constraints.

No wonder, A.B.Vajpayee, the great parliamentarian, poet and unassuming Prime Minister of India is reported to have said

"You can change your friends but not neighbours".

They exist, are destined to exist, side by side, if not necessarily bound by the feeling and spirit of togetherness.

Revival of QUAD

While fresh diplomatic moves, such as, revival of QUAD spirit by the USA seems to have got a certain nod from Japan, Australia, France and India in the name of "maritime interests" in the Indian and possibly Pacific Ocean zones, actual motive appears to check further dominance of China in the South China Sea region and in the ultimate analysis, China is not only to be "encircled", but to be kept on its tenterhooks.

Crucial Role of ISRAEL

Israel, with the background of its internecine issues with the Palestinians also appears to be changing a bit after its well established supremacy in Science and Technology, Land management, manufacture of arms and ammunitions, including the fast emerging Drones, not only traditional and known hatred against the Arab World in general and Palestine in particular is showing some positive overtones, if not an urge for a change, but she has also gone to the extent of approaching and establishing diplomatic relations with confirmed and prosperous Muslim powers, such as, Morocco and the UAE. Both initiatives were brokered by USA, their permanent mentor and guide. No wonder, recently held meeting between the Palestine President and Israeli Foreign Minister even after resumption of hostilities in West Bank and Gaza Strip assumes significance if not a departure. It happened soon after the new Israeli P.M.'s visit to the USA and requisite advice rendered, presumably, therefrom.

In the light of this, eagerness, followed by actual dialogue process between the Taliban and India at Doha should not be seen from the angle of suspicion.

OPEN OR BACK DOOR DIPLOMATIC SHOWS GO ON, THEY MUST GO ON.

Prior to leaving the "mouse," one is tempted to say:

> "Changing realities are expected to give way to changing equations in world living and politics." Mankind has to remain on Earth, unless actualisation of Moon or Mars Mission happens.

But there is no Guarantee, whatsoever, of Peace and Amity, therein also, due to omnipresent dominance of Greed over Need.

23

Afghanistan Again at Crossroads?[22]

August 7, 2021

Is this the age of Geo- Economics or Geo-Politics Revisited?

The question gains significance in view of almost certain return of Taliban to Not A God's Own Country of Afghanistan. In a sad and immensely painful situation, when not only USA and UK have given up and Russia and China may be cooking afresh, India too, having assumed the role of a Caretaker-cum-restorer for almost two decades, is also shirking its regional, if not social responsibility.

Afghanistan- a land locked, amazingly beautiful and cold country, is destined not to have semblance of peace, amity and stability, perhaps owing to its immense drugs wealth which may remind us of what Karl Marx once said-"Religion is opiate to masses."

By getting severely addicted, for decades, the neglected and self-suppressed populace has offered itself to foreign dictat every now and then.

First it was Russia through Pakistan route, the excesses of which later gave readymade alibi to the USA and allies through the Saudi Arabian route. Now in the backdrop of her certain withdrawal and "Almost Abdication" of its duty by India, stage is getting set for likely return of Putin's troops "riding Bears". Their proposed truck with China, Pakistan and some others in near future, may give additional anxiety.

Dear Afghanistan you asked for it time and again, at the heavy cost of developments in economic, educational and health fields. Think about boost in some sectors and good performance in culture and sports arena of Football and Cricket. They will be back to pavilion. Very Sad & Unfortunate.

Drugs Perpetrated Menace of Terrorism

On turning the pages of contemporary history, one may discover that the present form or shape of the menace took a solid birth with the emergence of Black September ferocious group in Palestine "Area" towards the end of sixties of the 20th Century. Not only the voice of emergence of Palestine began being heard distinctly but Israel, another entrant to the comity of nations, in a way, also got "Booster Dose" to rebuild and refurbish herself, of course with readily available US support.

No wonder, with the passage of time, not only she established herself as a world leader not only in arms and ammunition, production of latest kind of security apparatus but also in the domain of spying (Pegasus phenomenon being latest).

Good Performance Covid Wise

Side by side, Israel never ignored the vital interest of her people if very recent advent of Third Dose of Corona vaccine in their territory is any indication. This was after having claimed hundred percent vaccination coverage nearly two months ago.

The age old rivalry of once scattered two nationalities, is getting murkier and murkier with recent eleven day fierce fight or show off at the peak of Covid-19. It was at a time when the world at large and India, in particular, was adding as high as four lakh fifteen thousand cases in just 24 hours and West Europe was also grappling afresh for the second or third time.

Terrorism Anywhere is Lethal

I may clarify in all honesty and sincerity that it is not my intention to divert or evade from the main issue. Rather sole intention is to flag undoubtedly that Terrorism, per se, with all its tentacles, does not have a religion but a certain language to communicate at a virgin territory by means of soft targeting to begin with.

By nature, it is so brutal that it does not even take note of untold sufferings of Covid infected even within Palestine pockets/ conclaves of Jerusalem or horribly cold vallies of Afghanistan, wherein the Covid statistics is either knowingly suppressed or may not be taken note of.

It is not only the followers of Islam through the dreaded Taliban (literal meaning- seekers of knowledge) being signalled out in the emerging scenario or the inter or intra religion tirades, it is something which is likely to gain more momentum in Afghanistan or even parts of "dissatisfied" Pakistan.

But the plight of the neglected, poor, needy, starved and basic health-care denied to people in a situation, such as, Boko Haram, in Nigeria continues to be completely ignored.

Who will initiate, who will bell the cat or who will hold the key to vaccinate millions of poor Afghans or Africans in such a situation?

Role of WHO

So far ineffective head of WHO, given the game being played time and again from Wuhan, has warmed of more sufferings, apart from suppression of actual death figures by almost all nations, on atleast two occasions.

It has also stressed the necessity of completing the first dose first prior to proceeding for Boosters.

The so called "Human Groups" operating from centre of Europe too have given sufficient negative indications for the future.

Outlook of G-8

Further, during the recently held face to face G-8 conclave in the serene surroundings of UK, a special fund was "announced" to meet the expenses on vaccines in neglected territories of Asia and Africa.

It, however, seems to have ignored certain reports of hoarding of Covid vaccines by Canada, USA or may be, a few West European nations.

Under such perplexing and Topsy Turvy circumstances, how does one attempt to make a distinction between Visible threats (bombings, murders, suicide and drone attacks etc.) vis-à-vis non-visible ones (bio terrorism in form of SARS -II Corona Virus) in a special situation such as, Afghanistan ?

The recent decision of the virtual meeting of the CTWG of BRICS held on 28th July is bound to further amaze peace desiring individuals, when China, the alleged originator of never ending Corona virus, becomes a confidante to Counter Terrorism Action Plan of BRICS, soon to be adopted.

Are not we THUS tempted to utter the word DOUBLE STANDARD, if not DOUBLE SPEAK of Orwelian kind ?

This will be in respect of changing role and designs of both Russia and China in the region but both may be sadly compelled to avail of direct or indirect help of Pakistan in handling new Afghanistan.

The debate may remain inconclusive, perhaps.

24

Once Again.... Taliban's Afghanistan[23]

August 17, 2021

On 15th August 2021, when India was celebrating her long awaited and cherished 75th anniversary of liberation or freedom from the British rule, co-incidently and unfortunately in neighbouring Afghanistan, it was a different kind of liberation that was in the offing. Latter was sooner than expected, so much so, that the cleavage between US intelligence and the White House had become prominent.

President Ashraf Ghani lost no time in fleeing away with helicopters and four cars stuffed with cash.He seems to have taken refuse in Tajikistan or Uzbekistan. Element of hurry became apparent when a large chunk of cash was left lying on the tarmac.

While shrewd, sophisticated and westernised Abdulla Abdulla, the former Foreign Minister and outgoing CEO has declared that God will decide fate of now former President, a statement from Hamid Karjai, the predecessor of Ghani and the first President during the start of new era, is very much awaited.

Is Afghanistan in doldrums again ? What will happen to this beautifully cold, dry fruit and vast opium producing mountainous country, now that "non peaceful transfer" of power appently has become an imminent Reality, a Foregone Conclusion.

The bitter and yet again painful reality was more than assured, the day self proclaimed Supreme super duper power of the world had decided to withdraw allied forces, soon after similar act of desertion if not departure from Iraq.

Though 31st August was the 'D' date for ultimate pull out by USA, UK, France and Germany, Taliban or Talb-e-ilam (literal meaning Seekers of Knowledge) were closely watching and following the developments from their strongholds in some pockets of Afghanistan and provided bases in a handful of friendly or supportive countries.

It also looked as if support and guidance was not going to come directly only from Russia, the former ally-cum-tormenter of Afghanistan, two decades ago but also from a new interest group headed by China and a few latent if not passive forces.China, in the meanwhile has made her desire clear to have friendly ties with the new regime. Pakistan for obvious reasons, was kept subdued or she herself decided to maintain a low profile.Nobody can infer so fast.

Facade of Doha talks was created without losing time by purposely sidelining India. India's late participation in "apology to talks", at relatively low level of a Joint Secretary, goes on to prove that our Vasudhev Kutumbakam philosophy was going to receive a clear set-back. Same is happening despite her active two decades involvement in re-development forays in this "Allah Ko Pyaara" country, full of drugs, latest arms and armaments and ever ready urge or inclination to fight for the cause of Islam.

Was India's slow reaction mechanism so far, purposeful or was it due to her helplessness in given rapidly changing scenario ? India will have to be more pro-active given large presence of Afghans in India and vice versa. Only time will tell, more so, in view of silence thus far of the entire Islamic world but sudden "bold act" of recognition of the new regime by Pakistan, the longest staunch enemy of India.

Coming back to modus operandi of withdrawal by US led forces, attempts are being made by diplomatic watchers to equate this development with, or draw parallels with similar surrender process, not very long ago from Saigaon in Vietnam.

It is honestly felt that, for want of full details yet to emerge, it may not be apt to jump to any conclusion at this fluid situation stage.

One thing is certain-having announced its fresh intentions a few months ago, by seeking active assistance of Navies of both France and India to begin exercises aimed at reviving if not strengthening QUAD, USA has made it crystal clear that it is not going to forget or forgive China for the catastrophe of Corona virus and that latter's encirclement both in South China Sea region as also in Pacific region, presumably with Japan's help will be SURE & CERTAIN.

Having been so much involved in Afghan affairs over the years, India could have walked a step forward by attempting to have secret or open parleys with some of the moderates among Talibans. Reducing her present distance with Russia was also very much desirable. Now Talibans not only are changing their strategy a bit, they are also deploying English speaking spokesmen to put forward their intentions, if not evil designs coated with past gory misdeeds.

To sum up, in the new emering scenario, a big buffer state will be going out of India's hands and her surveillance over Iran and the Gulf may not be as easy as same was thought to be. Iran may react, however upon a good lapse of time, in view of recent change

of guard in Tehran. Stand of Israel in view of rapid developments in Muslim world, will be also worth watching due to her solid achievement of diplomatic ties first with UAE, followed by Morocco, both incidently brokered by none other than USA. Having become more than friendly with India despite knowing her Arab world weakness, the duo of USA and Israel may be getting ready to have ultimate decisive say over the murky waters of World affairs.

25

TALIBAN's AFGHANISTAN : Will Positive Vibes Emerge This Time ?[24]

August 25, 2021

Should we begin with a vital comment of John Gray, a London Journalist, made in 2002 in the book 'Clash of Fundamentalisms' by Tariq Ali, the then Pak Leftist leader, based in England ? He had said: "Highest Critics of fundamentalism are often Exponents of a Rival Fundamentalism".

Readers may themselves read and try to find out who is this 'Exponent' in contemporary Afghan situation ?

ADVANCE INPUTS

While the country synonymous with opium, agitated war lords and now Lithium, continues to dominate the headlines in the media, developments of last few days show some change. Violence is on, it is being perpetrated but from very beginning, to be precise, three weeks ahead of 15th August, former President Ashraf Ghani was not only made available with full intelligence assessment of situation but chances of a certain Return of Taliban were also indicated. But as it happens in such situations, his differences, may not be due to rivalry with his predecessor and Abdullah Abdullah, former CEO, may have got widened. So he was left with a narrow group of Advisors who would 'advise' according to his mood swings. Many of these disclosures were attributable to Gen. Masoud Andrabi, former Afghan Foreign Minister.

GROWING AWARENESS

While violence continued in the heart of Taliban and events preceding four days of "Fall" amplified it, people in general and young women and school going girls in particular, appeared determined to face even if unable to fight the brutal force enjoying blessing of and armed with latest U.S. arms and ammunitions, as opposed to 'AK's' of Russian era. They came out in open procession on the 102nd Independence Day of the country and some daredevil men also carried a 200 metre long Afghan national Flag through main thoroughfares of Kabul. As if this was not enough, local women T.V. anchors, doctors and H.R. activists began getting hooked up to international media in no time. In Dec. 1979, it was unthinkable. So more awareness, exposure and literacy mattered.

ASSERTION BY CRICKET TEAM

It was a change for the better, but at great personal risks. Probably, Gen. Masoud too took advantage to speak out his mind. Rashid Khan, the IPL and County Cricket Star also made an emotional appeal by risking his life, while his team mates continued to practice. Even at the extreme height of the crisis, when President Biden has hinted at possible extension of the deadline of 31/8 with understood support from UK, Germany and France, Afghan Cricket team is going ahead with its three Test series against Pakistan, though choice over a safe venue has led to short postponement. It was unthinkable in the old era of Russian domination.

Changing Colour of OIC

Another emerging pressure group of OIC is slowly asserting itself after its long silence. Subsequent to a meeting in Riyadh, Saudi Arabia on 23rd August, its General Secretary has warned Taliban and majority seem to be annoyed with their actions so far. Likes of Pakistan, Turkey and Qatar on the other hand, seem to have said, 'Yes' to their nefarious designs. Though the powerful collectivity has not made its stand clear on the issue of refugees from Afghanistan as yet, Turkey has voiced against it, having already been burdened with 1,20,000 of them. Incidently, S. Arabia, UAE, Tajikistan and Iran (a Shia super power traditionally opposed to Sunni dominated Afghanistan and Pakistan), may not oppose Taliban in the ultimate analysis but their current stand shows some signs of "positive optimism". The Islamic world being dicey and unpredictable, can not be said to have got divided over Afghanistan.

Change in Exit Route

Incidently, as opposed to earlier followed exit or rescue route from Afghanistan (through one of CIS countries) Doha route is becoming more popular and sought after by US and allies and India. Stand of Qatar on inconclusive Doha talks too may have to be watched with interest.

Afghan Refugees, A New Issue in India

Reverting to tense situation in Afghanistan, while India seems to be coming to end of its rescue mission, presumably due to presence of 6000 US troops at Kabul airport in addition to Talibans, US too has claimed to have evacuated 16,000 of its personnel. Yet thousands continue to be still trapped. In India alone, number of Afghan refugees has gone upto 21,000 (including two Sikh

Ex-Senators), necessitating a renewed debate on considering citizenship to Indians among them, under postponed CAA.

G-7 TALKS

All said and done, G-7 forthcoming virtual meeting may also throw some positive signals aimed at containing the ferocity of Taliban action. While most of US allies donot appear to be happy with their stand so far, there is going to be less likelihood of issuing of Economic Sanctions against TALIBAN, if at all they succeed in suppressing acts of assertion by Late Warlord Masoud's son in Panjshir or in some minor pockets already liberated from Taliban.

To conclude, latest disclosures made by Hashmi Ghani, younger brother of former President of Afghanistan to WION T.V. channel on 23rd August, assume some importance if they can not be considered significant enough. While he seems to in favour of Neo-Talibans, who according to him "may stabilise", he is not divulging whether the Americans or the Talibans, who marched to Kabul "ahead" of schedule, were out to assassinate his elder brother. Junior Ghani made two more important "announcements"/ disclosures:

(a) India-Afghanistan air corridor should continue, in view of rapid boost it has given to dry fruit export and

(b) both India and Pakistan should continue to have embassies in Kabul.

His concluding statement- "Afghanistan under Taliban wants to be a 'neutral' power," should be seen with a pinch of salt. Whatever it may be, it is going to be a change from the erstwhile face of Taliban, or the force now spearheaded by Badri-313, an uniformed, highly trained outfit having commandos from many countries and possessing latest US arms, gadgets and armaments.

To sum up, the new regime is expected to learn from past experiences vis a vis superpowers. A statement on behalf of their so called Cabinet signed by their supreme leader, H Akhundzada has assured the foreign diplomats, embassies, humanitarian organisations and investors in Afghanistan that Taliban was doing its best for their security and safety, so they will not face any problem.

The statement has further assured of country's commitment to all international laws, treaties and resolutions that are not "in conflict" with Islamic law and country's national values. While describing education as one of the most important requirements, the statement was largely silent on protecting the rights of women and children and preserving the gains of the past two decades.

Hence one has to wait and watch for their next move.

26

Indo-China Relations Down the Years[25]

January 29, 2022

As far as Indo-China ties are concerned, one has been hearing about Confucius, Huen -Tsang, Mao-tse-Tung, Chou-En-Lai and Deng-Xiao-ping, if not from childhood, definitely in post-Panchsheel era (29 April, 1954).

If Mao-tse-Tung, was an undisputed Chinese Communist leader from 1949 to 1976, Deng-Xiao-ping served as a revolutionary and paramount leader of China from 1978 to 1992.

Seize of Tibet

After enjoying forty eight years of freedom from Manchu dynasty, Tibet had got de facto Independence but under "Suzerainty" of China. On 17th March 1959, when Chinese forces attacked Potala Palace in Lhasa, forced exodus of Dalai Lama from Tibet became a foregone conclusion. Incognito, after a long treacherous trek with his supporters, he reached India on 31st March 1959. While he was given Political Asylum, nearly 14, 000 of Tibetans also got refugee status.

Futile Talks, War Thrust on India

Our subsequent four round of talks at PM Nehru and PM Chou-en-Lai levels, both in India and China, ultimately led sadly to India's humiliation in 1962 war. China attacked fiercely in Western and Eastern sectors on 20th October and "offered" a 3-point Cease Fire Agenda on 24th October. When China intensified their assault on 26th October, India requested USA, first for military supplies and later for air support.

USA obliged on 3rd November but before air support too was sought on 19 November, China, unilaterally announced Cease Fire and Withdrawal Declaration on 21st November, 1962.

One has no idea, however, about any passive support of Soviet Union in India's hour of crisis.

Thus, India's early initiative in extending a firm hand of friendship by establishing diplomatic ties with China as early as 1948, followed by her recognition of PRC, China on 30th December 1949, proved a waste of time and effort.

Post-1977 Period

Initially Morarji Desai led first non- Congress Government and later Rajiv Gandhi picked up threads of restoring old ties between two most populous, labour intensive and vast market nations having the I.T. acumen.

On their side, Prime Minister Li Peng of China visited New Delhi in December, 1991 and P.M. Narasimha Rao paid a return visit in 1993. President Jiang Jemin too paid a visit in November, 1996.

Undettered Vajpayee

Prime Minister A.B.Vajpayee, even after his unsuccessful bid earlier (during his visit as Foreign Minister embarassing attack over Vietnam by China took place), had the audacity and vision to extend a hand of friendship to China, when it came to resumption of negotiations and old trade routes through Shipki La in H.P. (3930 metres), Lipulekh (17, 000 feet) in Uttarakhand and Nathu

La (14, 498 feet) in Sikkim. Later in June 2014, a vehicular pilgrimage access to Mansarowar was also allowed through Sikkim route. Loss of Akshai Chin, Karakoram highway and frequent incursions in erstwhile NEFA (rechristened Arunachal in 1972) and Ladhakh were not forgotten as such but some diversion or change of stand became necessary, if not an emerging guiding principle.

Utterances

In between, one also heard loud utterance of the then Defence Minister George Fernandes that China, not Pakistan was going to emerge as enemy number one. It was nothing but reiteration of silmilar caution by Sardar Patel to Nehru in November 1950, when former termed China as a "Potential Enemy".

Indo-Pak Ties

As regards Indo-Pak ties, though China had initially supported stand of India on Kashmir and Goa, due to India's earlier support for China's membership of UNO, yet, China never supported India's permanent membership to the Security Council.

One sincerely feels that had it not been creation of Bangladesh and demolition of Babri structure in Ayodhya, aggression on the part of Pakistan could have been a subdued affair. By saying so, one is not giving a clean chit to our erstwhile 'Part' but it is a viewpoint which should not be ignored.

Tilt of Pakistan

Why Pakistan had been tilting first towards China, followed by its dependence on USA in post-1971 war scenario, was also perhaps, due to India being bound by a 20-year Treaty of Peace, Friendship and Cooperation signed on August 9, 1971 with the then Soviet Union.

Against this or with reference to it, India's extra cautious slow proximity first towards Israel and then towards France for supply of modern weapons and aircrafts assumes significance. Not only these steps may have invited wrath of Russia but initial softening of Modi Government towards China may have been also taken with a pinch of salt by her.

Why only this, setback to India's durable contribution in rebuilding Afghanistan, prior to 2021 resumption of power by Talibans, followed by her unnecessary alignment with face saving USA led initiative of QUAD, so far, has not resulted into any tangible benefits.

QUAD

As far as Joint Naval exercises of India with France and in future with Japan under QUAD arrangement are concerned, it may further annoy China. It may be also noteworthy that association of 'dormant and inactive' Australia with QUAD is not going to cut any ice. Hegemony of China over Taiwan, Hongkong and increasing its naval and air presence in South China Sea region has been always there, whether USA has agreed or disagreed.

USA, now in view of swift turn of events along Russia-Ukraine border has to decide which will be THE priority area for her. Stand of dormant NATO, also apparently, is clear. Prolonged, rather extended rounds of border related talks between India and China, also should not be undermined any longer by the USA.

Aiming for Long Term Economic Gains

Ever since USA has overtaken UK in terms of imperialism or neo-colonialsm, China has increased its presence in many diverse countries, such as, Myanmar, Sri Lanka, Maldives and Venezuela. At the same time, while exploring to silence its Islamic dissidents, China is eyeing the huge stock of Lithium mineral in Afghanistan. Needless to say, it is very vital for producing rechargeable batteries and thus sustaining portable devices, such as, automobiles with high efficiency as compared to the traditional Alkaline batteries. They are lighter, cost effective and can work well even in cold conditions.

Bravo, the strongest ever President Xi Jinping of PRC, China, The President For Life. Long Live the shrewd dictum of using an opportunity even in a distress situation !

27

With the Attack on Ukraine, is Third World War Inevitable?[26]

February 27, 2022

Will the biggest ground war begun since World War II involving Russia and Ukraine and being watched over T.V. & Internet for the second time after U.S.A.'s act of 'liberating Kuwait' in 1991, give indication for possible inhuman assaults leading to World War III ?

Entry of 150,000 Russian troops into Ukraine, which voted for Independence in 1991, from three sides is certainly an act of invasion leading to smoke, dust, screaming of helpless citizens, explosions and gunfire being heard all over. Fog of war and days of upheaval are bound to multiply worries and anxieties, more from missiles that could now be launched even from a distance of 11,000 kms. While airport of Ukraine's capital city Kyiv (3 million population) has been already shut, strategic locations in many cities, such as, Ivankiv, Lviv, Odesa, Kharkiv, Dnipro, Sumy, Chernobyl and Hostomel airport have been taken over by the Russians. With more than 200 casualties, 1100 injuries and some 100,000 displaced already in three days, one can think of scale of tragedy ahead. As it happens in such abnormal situations, apartment buildings, river bridges and schools are not being spared at all.

Emotions Will Not Work

Emotional outbursts from a former Comedian and T.V. star, President Volodymyr Zelenskiy, such as: "When bombs fall on Kyiv, it happens in Europe, not just in Ukraine", "When missiles kill our people, they kill all Europeans", "Ukrainians are demonstrating heroism" etc, may NOT cut any ice now before the tough, experienced and shrewd Vladimar Putin. Latter wants Ukraine to get rid of "drug addicts and neo-Nazis" and act neutral by abandoning its ambition of joining NATO on the path shown in 2004 by Estonia, Latvia and Lithuania (formerly part of erstwhile USSR) or face his ongoing special military operation.

Zelenskiy, in power since 2019 and already facing opposition over Covid control failure and controlling corruption in country's Judiciary may not easily surrender to threat emanating from Russian forces. It has been learnt that he was willing to discuss Ukraine's 'non-aligned' status. Russians, reportedly have offered to have talks in Belarus but only after Kyiv lays down arms. As per Russians, Ukraine had rejected their offer, suggesting a meeting in Poland, instead.

Upon annexing Crimea in 2014, latest move of Russia to officially recognize Donetsk and Luhansk areas, partly occupied by pro- Russian rebels since 2014 in the eastern Donbas region of Ukraine, could be a well thought of diplomatic move. Earlier defeat inflicted on Georgia, also should not be forgotten. Further, Nord stream 2 pipeline between Russia and Germany going underneath Ukraine is already a bone of contention between Ukraine and Russia for some time. It is significant to note that location-wise Belarus on the North of Ukraine and Poland and Slovakia on the west are not areas of concern for the Russians for the time being.

Stand of Security Council May Not Have Any Impact

Latest action by Russia has been opposed harshly by eleven permanent and non-permanent members.While India after discussing the issue extensively, has abstained alongwith China and UAE, Russia has used its Veto power. Russia had taken such a recourse on the Crimea issue in 2014 as well. China normally acts like this in such situations. According to Syed Akbaruddin, India's former Permanent Representative to the UNO, India as a non-permanent member had abstained five times when India-Pakistan question was discussed in the UNSC in 1950-51.

Plight of Stranded Indians

Total number of estimated Indians, so far reported from Maharashtra, U.P., Uttarakhand, Sikkim and some other states differs from 18,000 to 20,000, majority being medical students. Their welfare and security being very crucial, 470 students have been escorted to Romania after the Foreign Minister S.Jaishanker took up the matter telephonically with D. Kuleba, his Ukranian counter-part. The crisis, however, could have been pre-empted atleast a fortnight ago when clouds of war began hovering.We unfortunately wait till last moment and indulge into unwanted acts, such as, formal launching of a Helpline for the stranded, subsequent to closure of airspace in the devastated zone. Late reaction by the Indian Medical Association could also be considered a mere formality.

In a welcome development, Russian soldiers inside Ukraine have been instructed to allow movement of Indians towards Rumanian borders through the Purubne-Siret border crossing. Some of the Pakistani students carrying wrongly Indian Tricolour, however, were stopped. After airlifting of 242 Indians by an Air India plane from Kyiv, only two flights carrying Indian students from Bucharest had reached or departed for Mumbai and Delhi, respectively.

But are'nt these a drop in the vast ocean ?

With a view to explore alternative routes from the neighbouring countries to evacuate its citizens, Indian officials have been placed at Chop-Zahony check point on Hungary border and at Porubne-Siret check point on the frontier with Romania.

Future Nuclear Fears ?

When Ukraine is drawing international attention for right or wrong reasons, one must flash back to the 1986 nuclear Catastrophe of Chernobyl at Pryp'yat, located very close to Belarus border. Within 24 hours of 24th February, Russian forces could seize control over the shut nuclear plant, easily one of the most radio-active places on earth. It has been learnt that Ukraine has officially intimated IAEA about losing hold over its highly radioactive fuel rods, significant amount of Plutonium-239 therein possibly becoming a Nuclear bomb which could turn thousands of hectares into a lifeless desert apart from causing unthinkable health hazards for the people.

Taking cognizance, the international regulator has found that readings recorded so far may have been caused by heavy army vehicles "stirring up soil" contaminated from 1986 accident and these being low, posed no immediate danger to the human beings. According to a report, apple still grows in the vicinity but no one dares to touch it for obvious reasons.

Sanctions by USA

While USA, after literally failing at diplomatic level, has gone ahead with a series of economic sanctions against Russia, these are aimed at ensuring higher inflation and interest rates with lower investment, purchasing power and growth in Russia. According to Daleep Singh, the U.S. Deputy National Security Advisor for International Economics, these measures would give a fitting reply to physical land grab of territory, pursued by President Putin.

Late Response by Reluctant NATO Allies

Poland, Netherland, Italy, Germany, Czech Republic and

Belgium have now come out in open in favour of Ukraine and people of Israel are also extending support. Internal protests against invasion in Moscow and St. Petersberg and demonstrations in New York are also becoming noteworthy.

Whether support now from 28 NATO countries would push the humanity on the brink of Third World War, remains to be seen. Such a tragic situation in the midst of ongoing challenging fight against Covid/Omicron NEEDS TO BE AVOIDED BY ANY MEANS.

Cessession of further violence and resumption of talks is very much called for in the overall interest of humanity.

28

Tough Resistance by Ukraine to Imposed War[27]

March 06, 2022

Despite its well understood edge, Russia took nine days to enter Kyiv after securing Kharkiv, the second largest city in full measure. Other important cities too in the vicinity of Kyiv have been intruded into after encirclement of the capital city.

On the 11th day of war, issues appear clear. The Russian aggression, perhaps could be considered somewhat close to the Indian army attacking ethnic Indians during the Indian peace keeping operation in Sri Lanka between 1987 to 1990. Aim was to end a civil war between LTTE, a vocal Sri Lankan militant outfit and the Sri Lankan army. However, Difference was Crucial. Consent of the then Sri Lankan Government existed. Present war begun by Russians, is bent upon thrashing and killing the fellow Russians, more so, in Eastern Ukraine. They do not seem to be satisfied with annexation of Crimea in 2014 which is now reported to be linked to Russia by a 18 kms long bridge.

One needs to remember that Mikhail Gorbachev, the most powerful USSR President ever, himself was an Ukrainean.

Ceasefire

After days of ruthless attacks, much needed partial Ceasefire was announced on the 10th day. Though, a temporary one, it lasted less than agreed upon seven hours to facilitate purchase of food stuff and medicines in Mariupol and Volnovakha. However, banks and ATM's dissatisfied the citizens and Indian students, alike.

Alongwith the ceasing of hostilities, humanitarian corridors and Exit points too functioned for some time to give relief to the citizens in two cities, who were facing cut off electricity, food and water, apart from heating arrangements and transport in the minus temperature weather.

It reminded one of Nazi blockade of Leningrad during the World War II.

Incidentally, plenty of World War II Bunkers have been kept ready for use and those of Kyiv are reported to be in somewhat good shape.

On to violations, reports suggest that Russia, herself took the lead.

Drawing a parallel with India again, China had offered a Ceasefire after four days of attack on 24th October 1962 but went on to intensify assaults, thereafter.

Seeing no other option, when India sought US help for miltary supplies, followed by air support, China unilaterally announced a Ceasefire and Withdrawal Declaration after 31 days of invasion.

No End to Sufferings

One can not help but feel deeply concerned about the fatalities caused on both the sides together with fear and intimidation with which 1.4 million Ukraineans (UNHCR reports) have fled already, majority of them being women and children. On the contrary, more than twenty thousand Ukraineans have volunteered to return to fight for their motherland.No wonder, long ques are being seen in Kyiv to get enrolled in Army.

When food stocks and medicines are getting exhausted fast and no cash is left in banks and ATM's, yet the courage and fresh resilience shown by Ukraineans is simply remarkable.Upon trying Patrol bombs and "active resistance" against advancing Russian army vehicles, anti-tank barricades are also being fabricated by the people.

Thus, one gets an impression that the Russians even after getting isolated, as now admitted by President Putin, are fighting Ukrainean Army and the defiant and determined Ukrainian people.

Residential buildings and public utilities too are being targetted in city after city, which depicts nothing but brutal lust for " Neo-imperialism". There is no thought and care for Value of Peace.

Nuclear Dominance

While the Russians have captured the biggest nuclear plant of the world at Zaporichzhia after destabilising most of the reactors of the infamous Chernobyl plant, no thought is being spared for the injurious flow of nuclear fuel or the overall dangers to the environment from the gigantic hits and burns on a daily basis.

The International Atomic Energy Agency (IAEA) has so far issued two statements through which safe situation seems to be prevailing (?). But one should not forget that Ukrain has as many as 15 Nuclear Reactors and thus safety of civilians is threatened across both the warring nations and a few neighbouring countries of Europe.

Economic Implications and Protests

Though USA and EU sanctions continued to bite Russia to further isolate her, Russia cities are unusually calm but with price hikes in crude oil, wheat, coal, aluminium and iron ore markets. It may be significant to note that 75% of crude oil requirement of India is by means of import and Russia together with Ukraine contributes to 29% of total wheat availability in the international market. It is high time India took advantage of this situation.

DIGITAL & CREDIT CARD PAYMENT disruptions too are being faced by Russia from abroad.

While many Russian cities are witnessing daily protests against the war, Russia is showing determination to curb disinformation by declaring sentences upto 15 years against spreading information which goes against the ruling party's policies on the war.

Russia has further restricted access to foreign media websites and announced more control over Internet.

How can official media outlets refer to Russia's invasion of Ukraine as a Special Military operation, rather than a War ?

Zelensky, The Fighter

On the eve of third round of talks, V. Zelensky is showing maturity and courage.Erstwhile hero of a popular satirical show, he is no longer politically or diplomatically a Naive person, even when NATO has negated his "No Fly Zone Over Ukraine" proposal.

At the same time, how can NATO being more active than before, now say that it was not part of conflict, being a Defence Alliance. One may also ask, why are they keeping a Standby Force of Forty thousand men ?

Despite daily reports emanating from the Russian top brass that Zelensky has fled, he is reported to be in a Specially Controlled Station. After rejecting US offer of evacuation, he claims to have survived three assassination attempts. From an 'Accidental President', who knows, he may become a Legendary one ?

United Nations General Assembly Emergency Session

The session on 2nd March may not impact immediate course of action in the same way as the UNSC sessions earlier. In a historic resolution, 141 member countries deplored in strongest terms and asked Russia to withdraw troops. Only Russia, Belarus, Eritrea, N. Korea and Syria voted against, with India abstaining for the fifth time alongwith 33 members. Her stand appears to be as a result of Ukraine's recent unfriendly stands on India's requirements and changing role in World politics.

Operation Ganga

Officially MEA has confirmed to have evacuated 2900 Indian students through 63 flights so far but many are still reported to be trapped (of the revised figure of twenty thousand).Main focus is now on evacuation of 700 Indian students from Sumy.

Further, Russia has intimated the UNSC that their 130 buses are ready at crossing points to proceed to Kharkiv and Sumy to get Indian students and other foreign nationals.

In a welcome development, the National Medical Commission (NMC) has declared that the medical students who have returned to the country without completing their Internship because of "situations beyond their control", can do so in India.It has further added that Internships can be processed by state medical councils provided the candidates have cleared the Foreign Medical Graduate Examination before applying for completion of Internship in India.

TO SUM UP

MEA co-ordinated stand and that of NMC will go a long way in silencing the students who were critical of or making fun of Govt.of India's otherwise proactive role in ongoing crisis.

Shall we not say -

Three Cheers for Vande Mataram ?

29

From Kashmir to Ukraine File: Unending Seize of Mariupol[28]

March 24, 2022

One has heard and read from childhood: there cannot be smoke without fire. Both are true of seize and exodus of Kashmiri Pandits in J&K in the past and that of citizens of Mariupol and Kyiv for now almost a month.

A territory that was not only resided in but also owned by native people i.e. Kashmiri Pandits and Ukraineans repectively, has been on fire, is on fire and attack by Cruise missiles, newly developed weapons and lurking danger of a possible chemical or nuclear attack.

Strength or resistance power of Kashmiri Pandits was judged and taken care of unknowingly by the militia opposed to them gradually or suddenly in some cases. In respect of Ukraine, locals knew their "cousins" from Russia in advance. Yet they allowed women and children to take refuge elsewhere, maximum being in Poland, as on date.

But most determined men stayed back to give a fight. They were joined by thousands of ex-patriate Ukraineans.

From physically stopping attackers, to throwing patrol bombs, to erecting tank barricades, now to Guerilla warfare.

Enter Chchenya: Will it Herald a new turn ?

Available video evidence (may or may not be reliable) shows entry of Islam following mercenaries from Chechnya, on the side of Russia. Majority are reported to be under the guidance of notorious Sheikh Mansur Gang, who being inhuman and ruthless could be considered War Veterans, much ahead of earlier modus operandi of Suicide Bombing. While they appear to be hand in glove with Russian Army in surrounding Kyiv, Kherson and Mariupol, a couple of them are now surprisingly taking side of Ukraineans. Their outfit appears distinct from that of armies of two warring nations.

Seize of Leningrad

Ongoing seize of port city of Mariupol and almost encirclement of Kyiv could be compared to inhuman and atrocious 872 days of seize of Leningrad (rechristened St. Petersburg), the second largest city of Russia and always European in its planning, landscape and look.

I carry vivid personal memories of July-August, 1996 of visit to this amazing city and Vyberg, located close to Finland border.

As per inputs culled out from Google, the former capital of Russia, recorded death of one million people and Red Army defenders during 872 days of seize by the German Army. Soon all highways and railway lines were cut off. A narrow supply line through Lake Ladoga was made available. When severe winter showed minus 40 degree Fahrenheit temperature, daily ration of citizens was reduced to only 125 grams of bread and people were compelled to burn books and furniture to stay warm. Soon animals and pets began to be consumed and people had no option but to boil leather to produce edible jelly. Even grass and weeds had to be cooked at a particular stage. On top of it, hold your breath, unbelievable stories of Cannibalising the dead were heard (sic). To keep track of it or with a view to contain it, Police had to create a special division. Starvation deaths in bitter cold conditions are reported to have claimed 600,000 lives.

With the onset of Summer in 1943, some supply chain was possible through Lake Ladoga. After testing the unique endurance of city dwellers, Germans began their Retreat and ultimately seize was lifted on 27th January 1944.

Lines of comparison

Seize of Leningrad was mainly the handiwork of foot soldiers, backed by tanks and other war worthy vehicles. Air support was taken only in the beginning to set fire to a large warehouse storing food grains.

On the contrary, in the present case it is all -army, air force, latest Cruise and supersonic missiles and Submarines on the standby in regard to Mariupol. Coming to civic conditions and availability of food, water, gas and electricity, both situations appear identical. People, in a way, held captives so far, cannot perhaps have unlimited patience and perseverance akin to that of people of Leningrad.

Ironically, an Ukrainean grand mother, who managed to live through the seize of Leningrad from Sept. 1941 to 27th January 1944 by the Germans died only recently during the ongoing seize of one of Ukrainean cities by the Russians.

Putting the Clock Back ?

While the bouts of sufferings of Kashmiri Pandits are coming to the fore more from 2015 onwards, and for the first time a daring movie called Kashmir File, directed by dare devil Vivek Ranjan Agnihotri, seems to have given a fresh filip to the process, it remains to be seen whether the Kashmiri Pandits may return to reoccupy houses, now being vacated in Srinagar and parts of Jammu region.

In respect of Ukraineans, however, it may take months if not years probably to revert even if UNO succeeds or warrying nations reach a compromise soon. But shedding of crocodile tears by NATO, and a sort of lip service by the President Joe Biden of USA and P.M. Boris Johnson of UK may not stand a chance.

Tailpiece-

Just concluded Dance of Ukraine festival held at London raising £ 1,20,000 in aid of war victims of Ukraine may make little sense, in addition to some concerts or drives by many international celebrities elsewhere.

Graceful Ballet performances by dancers of Ukraine, a few European countries, Brazil, Argentina and USA is likely to soothen ruffled feathers for sometime but lost lives and devastated cities may not make a comeback. That is the unbearable impact of war.

30

Never Ending Ukraine War: Expected Conduct During Devastation and Interrogation[29]

April 8, 2022

A close look at the developments over a week or so, on the "special operation" or Ukraine war front may reveal that a sort of Retreat has begun. First, if I am not mistaken, was from Mariupol, then Kyiv, followed by Bucha and now Sumi.

Whether you call it butchery or genocide or brutality, inhuman massacre was perpetrated not for capturing but for terrorising and devastating. Human beings carried out the onslaught on the fellow human beings of once same nationality and ethnicity. Majority at the receiving end have been helpless senior citizens, women and children.

At last after taking up and failing to show a decisive and firm stand twice in a fortnight, the emergency session of UNGA has voted to Suspend Russia from the rights of its membership of the U.N. Human Rights Council (UNHRC) late on 7th April. Consequently, Russia will not be in a position to exercise its rights as a member to speak or vote. Thus, the US led Western coalition has succeeded in getting support of 93 member states with 24 voting against and 58 abstentions.

India alongwith Pakistan, Bangladesh, Sri Lanka, Maldives, Nepal, Bhutan and others, abstained even after condemning massacres in Ukraine and backing an independent probe. Russia had sought support rather than an abstention from India, thus, indicating a more difficult phase for her in international diplomacy.

Regretably, it has happened after more than ten thousand dead and 1.5 lakh persons being stuck up in acute crisis for over a month during a "special operation", for 44 days. Video and audio evidence tells all. Helpless individuals living in crammed up space, bereft of water, electricity, gas, essential food items, medicines. One can imagine their plight. Even a humanitarian corridor was mostly ruled out. One can think about pathetic condition of ventilation and sanitation also under the freezing temperature.

Future Shock Waves

More shock waves concerning war crimes and interrogations can be expected unless good sense prevails over the minds that matter. It is not that people of suffering nationality living elsewhere or those earlier dependent on trade relations with the sufferers, are unaffected. In fact, more of insanity will lead to ripples being felt everywhere. Now that indiscriminate sacrilege has "slowed" a bit and some habitations are visible, one can imagine what the scene would be when huge heap of debris finally gets cleared.

More signs of butchery, something akin to infamous Gas Chambers of World War II, are bound to surface.

U.N. Convention Against Torture (UNCAT).

The UNCAT signed by USA and 140 other countries long ago is clearly against all kinds of cruel, inhuman or degrading treatment. Though torture according to the convention is defined as the infliction of severe physical and mental suffering committed under the colour of law, under no circumstances it can be permitted. It is prohibited as such, under the customary International law. Parties to the convention are obligated to take effective legislative, administrative, judicial or other measures to prevent acts of torture, in any territory under their jurisdiction.

When one comes across torture of a Russian woman Spy (Sniper), alleged accused of having committed forty murders of Ukraineans by the people who have supposedly tortured her for extracting information or for that matter, discovery of dead bodies in Bucha, additional killing of 300 civilians or may be armymen in the same city, the US Amendment to such a Manual adopted on 6th September, 2006 may assume significance.

WHAT IS PROHIBITED?

Inter alia, it Prohibites following eight techniques in conjunction with intelligence interrogations :

(a) Compelling a detainee to be naked, perform sexual acts or pose in a sexual manner,

(b) Placing hoods or sacks over his/her head,

(c) Applying electric shocks, burns or other forms of physical pain,

(d) Water boarding,

(e) Use of Military dogs against them,

(f) Inducing Hypothermia or heat injury,

(g) Conduct of mock executions and

(h) Depriving the detainee of minimum food, water or medical care.

According to inputs culled out from Internet, USA has been "leader" in application of UNCAT towards persons captured in

Iraq and Afghanistan. (ostensively after burning their fingers, they have refrained from pushing their troops in conflict between Russia and Ukraine so far). Why only they? Neither they, nor Russia or Ukraine or Pakistan bother for standards prescribed under the 1949 Geneva Convention concerning the protection of civilians and Prisoners of Wars during an armed conflict.

While President George Bush Junior was somewhat brutal (video evidence of naked Iraqi men prisoners would be shown to tourists), the Barack Obama administration in 2009 issued an Executive order stating that all detainees held by USA during an armed conflict be treated more consistently with several domestic statutes and international agreements, including UNCAT.

Interrogation Techniques of Other Nations

Coming to Non US bodies, whether some interrogation techniques rise to the level of torture, there are serious doubts about British interrogation techniques used in Northern Ireland, as confirmed by the European Commission of Human Rights (ECHR). These relate to weight loss and adverse effects to their acute psychiatric systems during an interrogation.

In the same way, the ECHR has termed interrogation techniques of the Israelis against the Palestinian security detainees as completely unacceptable, given Israel's obligations under Articles 2 and 16 of the UNCAT. Their techniques, such as, use of loud music for prolonged periods, sleep deprivations, violent shaking, use of cold air to chill etc. are definitely more inhuman.

Signs of Change in Future ?

Even after witnessing harrowing videos of dead bodies shown by President Zelensky, whether the UN O will act more strongly against Russia, that remains to be seen. So far only country to lose its membership at the UNHRC was Libya, when long time dictator Muammar Gadhafi (1969-2011) lost power.

In all eventuality, torture and devastation by a tired Russian army may slow down but same may not end the Proxy War between the two Superpowers.

31

Praise India's Foreign Policy, Then Rake Up Kashmir[30]

April 13, 2022

Praise India's foreign policy, then rake up Kashmir issue. This is supposed to be the 'Mantra' of the outgoing and incoming Prime Ministers of democratic turbulent country of Pakistan, our 'distinguished' neighbours.

When you can not address the burning domestic issues (Inflation, Unemployment, IMF debts, language or development challenges) concerning backward areas of Sindh and Baluchistan, forget about finding a solution, this is supposed to be readily available Modus Operandi.

The new Pakistan P.M., Shehbaz Sharif has hinted at a "just," resolution of the vexed Kashmir issue, at the same time, maintaining "Good Relations" with India.

While congratulating Sharif, P.M. Modi has reminded him of India's concern about cross-border terrorism. Stopping her support to terror groups should be the pre-condition for normal ties, the P.M. Modi went on to add.

Imran Khan, the ousted P. M., by giving poor governance, leading to economic ill health of the nation, has begun ironically laying stress on "independent" approach to governance. Now he is seeking to convince the electorate that his struggle, till last ball was going to be for freedom, in view of "interference" by a foreign goverment.

As a last resort, playing a religious card, he is asking people to take (either) path of freedom or that of slavery being shown by the opposition.

If Kashmir has been a bone of contention blocking our smooth bi-lateral relations, it has been the Key or X factor for Pakistan all the time since 1947.

The new nation born out of strictly religious considerations has not been able to come out of this syndrome.

We in India, seem to be tolerating our loss of a big area of Aksai Chin, but our neighbours always rake up the "loss" of Kashmir at every conceivable forum. At UNGA, its an Annual Ritual.

And when they fail to resolve their economic ills and in a way, resort to complete surrender to fundamentalists, Kashmir Raga or Saga religiously, has to be remembered.

The tool used is that of ISI. So it may be pertinent to understand a bit of this long surviving "puzzle".

ISI, The Most Important Determinant

The Inter Services Intelligence Directorate, popularly known as ISI, is the apex intelligence agency of Pakistan. It is to Pakistan, what CIA is to USA or what KGB was to erstwhile USSR. In reality, however, it is not only an external and military intelligence organisation but in the words of Mohammed Yousaf, former Chief of ISI Afghan Bureau, it has the responsibility for all the intelligence matters at the national level. These may encompass political, military, internal and external security as also the vital area of counter-intelligence.

It is supposed to be a **Government within a Government**. It has so much of clout inside Pakistan that it is considered above law, at times. History, including events of last fortnight have shown that every government, be it civilian or army supported, has to depend obliquely on ISI for its survival. That is why Gen. Bajwa, the Army Chief and supreme commander of ISI was always in NEWS, never out of it.

Administratively, the D.G. of ISI is under the Defence ministry, but due to his direct reporting to the P.M., control of defence ministry over the agency is minimal.

The ISI has played a decisive role in compelling withdrawal of USSR from Afghanistan and was also the catalyst when USA funded and supported the "Mujaheedeen" to pursue their "Jehad". In addition, US funding, technical and training support to ISI has been substantial and continued even after two years of 'vacation' of Afghanistan by the Taliban. A part of this fund and latest weapons were later diverted to foreign mercenaries and Kashmiri militants.

The ISI was back to Afghanistan alongwith full Peshawar Division of Pak Army when Talibans recaptured power in Afghanistan in August 2021 and the difference of opinion that surfaced between Gen. Bajwa and Imran Khan over selection of new ISI Chief, Lt. Gen. Nadeem Anjum, goes on to prove the say Army continues to have in the matters, civilian as also in keeping the Kashmir issue alive for Pakistan.

As regards source of fund, the ISI, apart from annual allocation from Army, also has been getting sizable funds in form of charities from a few Middle East countries. It also has an enormous stake in the money generated from sale of drugs and small arms in the Pak-Afghan region. A major portion of their fund is spent on pursuing espionage, subversion and sabotage in J & K and many parts of India.

Rather, it can be safely stated that ISI is more strong a force to reckon with than two other Intelligence agencies of US and Russia in the sense that no Government worth its salt can survive in Pakistan, unless ISI "endorses".

The ISI has been posing serious threats to India's integrity and internal security by instigating and encouraging the disgruntled and disloyal elements, creating disaffection among the minorities, such as, Muslims and Sikhs and is also providing support to remnants of insurgents in the North East. Their nefarious designs are facilitated by factors, such as, common ethnic and cultural background of the people of India and Pakistan and existence of groups or classes who avail or surrender themselves to exploitation by it due to past affinities, common religion etc.

It has been, over the years, pursuing a module of "encirclement" of India by recruiting agents from the groups, such as, smugglers, drug traffickers, Indian nationals visiting Pakistan legally as also clandestinely, Pak nationals visiting India, Indian nationals held in custody of Pak authorities and Pak as well as the Indian nationals especially selected for espionage and subversion activities.

Special Operations for J&K

A dedicated wing called Joint Intelligence, North(JIN) used to control operations, namely, infiltration, misleading propaganda, training, supply of arms and ammunitions and regular flow of funds to the Kashmiri militants. It is presumed to be doing so even now.

Though set up by a British officer in 1948, ISI has matured as a well structured organisation. We lacked something like this in India till it was decided to set up R&AW nearly 47 years ago. But it has confined its operations only to external intelligence work.

Over the years, the salient features of ISI's India policy according to a book published in 1999, have been:

(a) To sustain Kashmir movement at a minimal cost and force its settlement on terms and conditions acceptable to Pakistan,

(b) To weaken India's potential strength and national will by hitting at its perceived "fault lines" and to pursue the policy of thousand cuts,

(c) To prevent India from emerging as a strategically dominant power in the region and

(d) To render Indian borders porous and bordering states, vulnerable.

The activities of ISI were earlier code named K-1, K-2 and K-3, all focussed and meticulously aimed at bleeding of Punjab, J&K and the North East, respectively.

In the meanwhile, ISI's links in Nepal and Bangladesh have been receiving setbacks, every now and then, to India's Advantage.

From 1988, an exclusive operation by the name of "Operation TOPAC" aimed at mass infiltration into J&K to assist the so called 'freedom struggle' has been also financed and being sustained.

To Sum Up

Kashmir issue has not only been kept alive by the overt and covert actions of Pak Rangers and ISI alone.

One should not be saying, but it is believed that vested interests among bureaucrats and politicians had kept the issue alive. Their nexus too has done a lot of harm to the country as a whole.

A fundamental intelligence input that emerges regularly on the eve of 15th August or 26th January functions is "a module with diagrams by Pak connected militants for creating disturbances".

Needless to say, that never happens.

Abrogation of Article 370 together with raids relating to misuse of development and other funds, therefore, have the potential to correct the course and to provide suitable solution to all such ills. there is no harm in trying.

32

No End to Black Outs, Shortages and Violence in Sri Lanka[31]

13th May, 2022

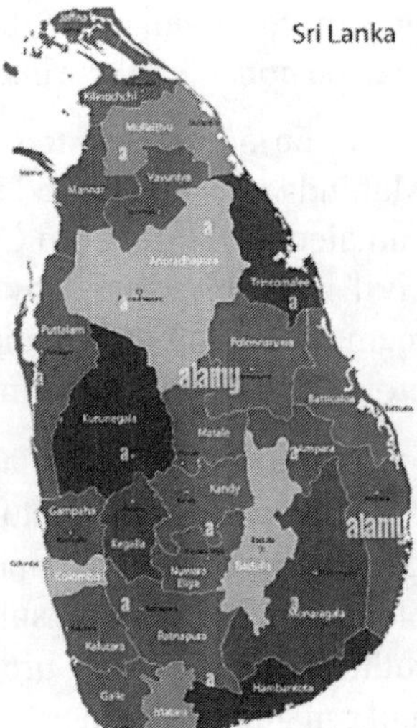

Once famous for its tea, tourism and remittance from abroad, Sri Lanka, an island nation of 22 millions is facing its worst ever economic and political crisis. Inflation is all time high, there is acute shortage of fuel, cooking gas, power, essential food items and medicines. The nation is supposed to have defaulted on a staggering $ 51 billion foreign debt. Diminishing foreign exchange reserve too is adding to the crisis. While a costly IMF package is still being negotiated, India's emergency aid of $ 3.5 billion in addition to humanitarian aid in terms of rice and P.O.L is expected to offer some relief.

Though bilateral relations were not smooth few years ago, advent of Covid-19 seems to have turned the tide in favour of India. First to be offered was our indigenous vaccine for Covid under liberal terms of trade, despite criticism at home. Why only

Sri Lanka, this assistance at the peak of second wave to Bhutan, Nepal, Bangladesh and Maldives may help in removing the 'Big Brother' tag of India. Steps could be initiated to revive SAARC summit, perhaps, under this pretext.

Pursuant to daily protests by general public, monks and now by students, leading to death of eight persons and injury to over two hundred, a State of Emergency has been declared in the country for the second time. Curfew though being defied, is likely to continue. Colombo and Kandy are no longer exotic tourist destinations.

After setting on fire to three houses of outgoing P.M. Mahinda Rajapakshe and forty one houses, shops and business units of key ruling party politicians, Army has been given sweeping powers to arrest and detain anybody for twenty four hours.

Even then blocking the main approach to Colombo airport for preventing loyalists of the ruling clan from leaving the country may be considered daring under the circumstances.

In an unprecedented development, once immensely popular Mahinda was compelled to take shelter in a Naval base in Trincomalee, 270 kms from Colombo. His crushing of thirty year old civil war perpetrated by LTTE can not be easily erased from memory of ethnic Sinhalese. Fortunately, Indians caught in the crossfire against Tamils in general earlier, have been spared so far.

Anita Pratap in her absorbing book 'Island of Blood' gives vivid description of picturesque blue lagoons, palm and cashew nut trees on the one hand and fear, horror, cruelty and anxiety factors in Jaffna peninsula on the other. One also comes across ruthless, cunning and brutal commitment of Prabhakaran, a "hit and run guerilla fighter" who got transformed into a "mastermind of conventional battles".

Ironically when Sharief brothers and a woman family member seem to have regained some lost political territory in Pakistan, in Sri Lanka, its other way round for three Rajapakse brothers and two other kins. One of them, the Finance Minister alongwith

Secretary Finance had already quit much ahead of sought after resignation of the Prime Minister.

Even appeal for help in forming an Interim Government by the President Gotabaya Rajapaksha seems to have fallen on deaf years. Opposition may not respond favourably as the current President, unless he also steps down, will continue to exercise powers to appoint and remove Ministers.

Being a former Army officer, he may manage support of Army and Police for some more time but USA, China and European Union may prefer "closely monitoring" the situation, only.

China, in view of recent setbacks to its citizens in Pakistan may be more worried to take care of its huge investments in Sri Lanka.

Michelle Bachelet, UNHR chief, in the meanwhile, has called on the authorities to prevent further unrest.

One silver lining in the rapidly deteriorating scenario seems to be proactive role of Social media. The medium has been in a position to unite the suffering populace in addition to sensitising them about day-to-day plans and developments. This medium, free from any regulation and guidance so far is doing more effective work viz-a-viz print or electronic media.

One by one, countries of Indian subcontinent are becoming disturbed. And US and China wait for a situation when in a stage of economic and political desperation, their assistance may be sought.

Ukraine right now is also not realising that they are being taken for a long ride after having all the distress, displacement and devastation, apart from quickly attending to mine clearance, rebuilding and resettlement issues.

33

Leadership Challenges in Europe, Middle East & Asia[32]

July 22, 2022

It's a strange coincidence that since February 2021 world has seen disturbances and turbulence both to leadership and state of nature in many parts of world as a result of which normal development works are receiving a certain setback.

WRATH OF NATURE

Mostly nature has been furious in terms of WILD FIRES in Australia, USA, U.K., Spain, Portugal, France, Greece, Turkey etc. It has ravaged thousands of hectares of land in addition to killing a large number of people. While 38, 000 hectares of land has been burnt in U.K., five hundred people have died in Spain and fourteen thousand people had to be evacuated in France.

In the same way, EXTREME HEAT has affected sizable parts in USA, U.K., France, Italy, Switzerland, Germany and Denmark. Maximum temperatures have been ranging from 37 degree to 40 degree celcius in many cities. Unprecedented heat of this kind, presumably due to Climate Change has not been experienced in these countries earlier.

In same way, FLOOD and LANDSLIDE have affected seven provinces of Philipines, Maluku island of Indonesia, seven provinces of Thailand, Kedah area of Malaysia and Sichuan and Gansu areas of China. Flood havoc has been also reported from Ecuador, Niger, Nigeria, Sudan and USA.

PROCESS OF POLITICAL INSTABILITY

The process of political instability began with the seize of power by Military in Myanmar, running away of elected President of Afghanistan, followed by ouster of democratically elected P. M. in Pakistan. Disturbances have been also occurring in Sri Lanka for over three months due to mismanagement of the economy and heavy dependence on foreign exchange reserves by the successive governments.

Less said about periodic change of government in the fragile democratic situation in Nepal would be better. In Myanmar, there seems to be no possibility of a democratic revival as Military rule is strengthening its hold with the support from China which has it's own sea trade plans through Myanmar.

SILVER LINING

Before we attempt analyzing a few country wise Leadership disturbances, it may be heartening to note that New Zealand, Germany, Australia and France have seen, at the same time, peaceful change of leadership together with emergence of young politicians, many of whom happen to be women. Also knocking of doors by Indian diaspora in some countries is being noted in a big way.

MYANMAR

Since its Independence in 1948, Myanmar has been under the clutches of Military rule for maximum period. A.S. Suu Kyi, Nobel Peace Prize Winner has been struggling for a long period for restoring democracy. Her National League For Democracy Party had a landslide victory in General elections held in February 2020. But military, led by Gen. Auang Hlaing seized power from her in a coup in February 2021. She had a similar setback after her notable performance in 2015 elections.

The Military government has levelled election fraud charges against her. Earlier Election Commission, however, felt otherwise.

A new Commission constituted by the Military Junta has supported the viewpoint of current Government. A conviction in the case could lead to Suu Kyi's party being dissolved and it may not be in a position to take part in the elections "promised" by the Military rulers in 2023.

The U. N. has warned of a deepening humanitarian crisis in Myanmar, with an intensification of violence and rapid rise in poverty. Also as on 30th May, 2022, there were estimated 1, 037, 800 internally displaced persons, including 6, 91, 200 newly displaced persons since 1st February 2021.

Truth does not come out from this country due to stern censorship measures and Rohingya refugees continue to flood India every now and then.

ITALY

A monarchy till 1946, Italy became a Parliamentary Republic with multi party system on 2nd June, 1946. Since it has a history of short-lived coalition governments, it was once called an example of flawed democracy. While from 1861 to 1946, there were thirty Prime Ministers heading sixty five governments in total, there have been twenty nine P. M. 's since 1946 (all men). And in last eleven years and nine months, the country has seen six prime ministers.

S. Berlusconi, former media magnate was the P.M. for altogether nine years in three spells between 1994 and 2011. Infamous for controversies, scandals and sex scandals, he proved to be a great survivor in a land that has seen variety of coalitions: from Rightists to Leftists to Liberals to Radicals to Reformists and Fascists. While for a few years, Italy had mixed coalition governments, on five occasions governments could not secure a vote of confidence. Twice the country has been ruled by Military.

In this backdrop, resignation by the last P. M., Mario Draghi, a technocrat, only after one year and five months is not surprising in a country notorious for hung Parliament, corruption, organized crime, economic disruptions, largest number of Covid deaths(at one time)etc.

Despite all this, Italy is supposed to be the third biggest economy of Europe. A highly developed country, it prominently figures in the G-7.

ISRAEL

Israel is another country which despite being ahead of many developed countries in many respects, is lacking political stability, having seen four elections in four years: April 2019, September 2019, March 2020 and March 2021. Fifth election is scheduled to be held in November 2022.

Leader of Likud Party, Benjamin Netanyahu, has served maximum as P. M. for fifteen years in different spells. Present P. M. is Y. Lapid, who took over as fourteenth P. M. on 1st July 2022 after one year 'rotation' term of earlier P. M., Naftali Bennett ended.

In a Parliament(Knesset) having only 120 seats, most of the political parties have been failing to secure even 61 seats on their own to form a Government. In the September 2017 elections Benjamin Netanyahu's Likud party failed to secure a majority but he managed to run the show. Decisions of the Knesset to dissolve itself have not been free from controversies.

Elections in this multi party country like Italy have seen malpractices and controversies many times. Despite all this, Israel continues to be a force to reckon with. It ranked 19th out of 189 countries on the 2019 U.N. Human Development Index. Considered to be a high ranking country by the World Bank, it has also secured 17th rank in Global Innovation Index. Its recent initiative to establish diplomatic relations with Morocco, Bahrain and UAE may go a long way in ensuring more peace in the Middle East.

LEADERSHIP CRISIS IN U. K.

Of all the countries, it is the dramatic developments in U.K. which is baffling everyone at present. In 2019 parliamentary elections Boris Johnson (BoJo) led the Conservative party to the largest ever election victory in three decades. A message of political stability was given when they won 358 seats out of a total of 650 seats. The main opposition, Labour Party had to be satisfied with only 200 M.P.'s.

The flamboyant former Mayor of London and former Foreign Secretary in Teresa May's government sporting an unusual hair style, defeated Jeremy Hunt in the leadership run off. Hunt was offered a Cabinet position but he turned it down. A great deal was expected from this young Tory leader but he went on getting involved in one controversy after another since November 2021 even after managing an honourable Exit for U. K. from the European Union and raising the level of confidence of Ukraine vis a vis Russia during the ongoing war.

Following mass exodus of his cabinet, BoJo decided to quit as P.M. on 7th July after three years in office against the backdrop of many scandals, including a party at 10 Downing Street which violated Covid-19 protocol, no confidence vote and a matter of sexual misconduct against a senior Tory M.P.

With his resignation, race to replace him has picked up momentum. Taking due note of high inflation and rising cost of living in the country, most of the initial eleven contenders, had pledged to lower taxes and begin with a clean start.

Ms. Priti Patel, former Home Secretary was the only one out of race as her priorities were reported to be country's unity and security.

After rounds and rounds of internal voting, Rishi Sunak, 42 year old former Chancellor of Exchequor having Indian origin is being seen as a credible contender even though he is facing a tough competition from Ms, Truss at the time of Parliament going into Summer Recess. Although he has taken a pledge to restore trust, rebuild the economy and reunite the country, his foreign origin and rather late entry into House of Commons as compared to Truss may not appear convincing to a large number of Conservative party members who are yet to open their cards.

Hence in all probability it may be Truss who may become eligible to succeed Boris Johnson on September 5. Only factor which goes against her, is her initial disagreement on Brexit.

Since new P.M. is unlikely to take over before first week of September, for the next two months, BoJo will have to act as a Caretaker P.M., which has been opposed by John Major, a former P.M.

Incidently, such a phase in U.K. Parliament system could be compared to Code of Conduct period ahead of Assembly and General elections in India when no major policy decision can be taken for about two months. In Italy also, now similar situation may prevail. In Sri Lanka, however, with swearing in of new President followed by appointment of a new P.M. and eighteen Ministers, things may become somewhat normal as the present incumbents may have full powers unlike caretaker heads of governments in U.K. and Italy.

PATHETIC CONDITION IN SRI LANKA

Having discussed the ongoing political developments in the country of erstwhile Colonial rulers, let us shift our focus to Sri Lanka, one of the former colonies of erstwhile British empire.

Apparently, due to the misdeeds of Rajapakshe "dynasty", the island nation has become bankrupt in the words of former Cartaker P.M. Ranil Wickeramsinghe, now elected as President by the country's Parliament. Incidently, this was the second time in nation's history when Parliament of the country had to exercise its power to break the leadership deadlock. Excercising his powers, Wickramsinghe has appointed Dinesh Gunawardana, a former Education & Foreign Affairs Minister in Gotabaya's government as the country's new P.M. together with eighteen Ministers.

Widespread disturbances due to power, food, fuel and fertilizer shortages have become every day affair for now over 105 days. Twice the Government had to declare a state of Emergency and imposed Curfew to suppress the agitation by the common man and Buddhist Monks, a decisive group in influencing public opinion in Sri Lanka. Agitators have been refusing to give up despite having only one meal a day.

Responding to humanitarian issues, India while standing with people of Sri Lanka has so far given a loan assistance of $ 3.5 Billions to pay for vital supplies. In addition, supply of rice and P.O.L. continues to pour in from India in a regular way.

While people were dying of hunger and fuel issues, the former President Gotabaya Rajapakshe was adamant not to resign before 13th July. After fleeing to Maldives, he sent his resignation by e-mail from Singapore, only after securing a safe place for himself.

For Sri Lanka, very much under the debt trap diplomacy of China like Maldives, Nepal and a few African countries, crisis period is not yet over. In view of the fact that Parliamentarians themselves are a divided lot, prospect of an all party government appears dim. Rather, it may continue to face an uncertain political future.

The European Union and USA governments have urged Sri Lanka government to co-operate, focus and work quickly to achieve a peaceful and orderly transition.

While talks are being held with IMF for over two months for a rescue package (presumably on the lines of Pakistan), fact remains that present government will have to take some strict fiscal measures to cut down expenditure and explore ways and means to raise resources. The Government now headed by President Wickeramsinghe continues to face the wrath of protestors. Regaining their confidence may not be easy.

Its high time from a humanitarian angle, some members of G-7 come forward to bail out Sri Lanka. But no one can possibly extend a helping hand in settling their huge debt issue with China.

(E) IN PUBLIC DOMAIN

Pakyong Airport, Gangtok, Inaugurated on 24 September 2018, Most Notable Achievement Of Author

34

Bureaucracy and Corruption[33]

Corruption means deviation or distortion from an established, expected or a desirable path. The Oxford Dictionary describes a corrupt person as dishonest, especially, the one using bribery. It has been rightly considered an immoral activity. Meaning thereby, what ought to be, becomes infructuous vis-a-vis what it is. This is why it becomes difficult, if not an impossible proposition to detect and pinpoint such an unfair means.

Corruption, *per se,* may not only refer to the practice of giving and accepting money for a normal, day to day work. It also has a dangerous combination of cash as well as kind. In addition, there are individuals who neither take cash nor allow any perceptible flow of goods into their household but they may resort to a corrupt means of an invisible nature. Still, there are people who are different from the lot described. Such persons, by their "honest" looking deeds, may guarantee inputs in cash or kind to others, thus ensuring for themselves a position or a rank not normally possible to get through fair means. Besides, they also succeed to build a good, enduring and usable image.

However, there is another group of individuals who may not be habitually corrupt but they definitely fall in the category of occasionally corrupt. By all these parameters, it is impossible to locate an extremely fair and honest person. While one is ready to express concern against such an unworthy practice, it would be safe to state that, both in developing and developed economies, corruption exists in some form or the other and that it would be difficult, if not impossible to uproot such a perpetual malady. One can, however, always hope to minimise its impact.

Kautilya's *Saptanga* theory or the theory of seven elements of state threw sufficient light on the conduct of the *Amatyas* (encompassing the Ministers and the Officials). They were required to be *Dharmopashuddha* (morally and ethically pure), *Arthopashuddha* (honest in financial matters) and *Charitropashuddha* (of good and pure character). Some other virtues, according to Kautilya, necessary for a person to serve as a state official were - a person of infallible memory, friendly nature, wisdom, patience and endurance.

On the other hand, Ziauddin Barani, a notable historian and political thinker of the Tughluq dynasty opined that the Sultan (king) must rely on the learned, experienced and well-wishing *Wazirs* (Ministers) and Counsellors. He prescribed 24 *Nasihats* (advices) for an ideal Sultan. One of the *Nasihats* as given in his scholarly work, *Fatwa-i-Jahandari,* pertains to appointing just, honest, truthful, reliable and intelligent officers. He considered that the king should appoint officers who do not accept bribes or presents or accede to recommendations and that the revenue collectors will always refrain from misappropriation of revenue.

Generally, it is observed that corrupt people are by and large competent and the mere fact that they outnumber the honest, they are not only in a position to survive but they also thrive beyond imagination. When we make a premise of this nature, we do not mean to say that honest persons are incompetent. But it is also a fact that those having an unusual mix of integrity and competence, by and large, are troubled and harassed in the most inconceivable ways.

Apart from the mental and semi-physical torture, these "marginals" are, many a time, denied access to the normal facilities, which may appear privileges or perks in the eyes of the "mainliners". This is why, it is often said, good is bad in government or public domain, and that rating such as very good and outstanding are more often than not managed by unfair means.

It may not be out of place to mention the timely observations of the Supreme Court in Dev Dutt vs. Union of India & Others (AIR 2008 SC 2513). The court ruled that, "...higher posts which are in a pyramidical structure, where often the principle of elimination is followed in selection for promotion, and even a single entry can destroy the career of an officer which has otherwise been outstanding throughout. This often results in grave injustice and heart-burning, and may shatter the morale of many good officers who are superseded due to this arbitrariness, while officers of inferior merit may be promoted".

In bureaucracy, one also comes across a situation, such as, "you show me the person, I will show you the rule." As a result, rules and regulations are twisted and partially amended or sometimes changed altogether to suit a vested interest. When these things do not appear helpful, one indulges in corrupt means by following the "safe" path of interpretation or drawing inference. Also, the oft-repeated *modus operandi* is to suggest "to read between the lines". Generally, "I help you, you help me, kind of 'brotherly' phenomenon" comes in the way of delivery of fair and impartial stands, decisions and judgements. And the actually honest, fair, quiet and non-assertive types continue to suffer at the hands of the self-proclaimed honest and competent superiors.

Corruption is found in some form or. the other in every sphere, in every country and social system. In a developing economy, it takes a manifested shape or face in the economies of polar opposite scenario; it may be more prevalent but perhaps with a latent face. While the former may see the use of unfair means at every step, in case of the latter, a certain degree of sophistication may act as a cover, though the stakes may be much higher, involving risks of the bigger magnitude.

No wonder, a country like Bangladesh which is at the lowest rung of development, figures right on top when it comes to the menace of corruption. This is despite the stupendous success of the micro-credit phenomenon, triggered and guided by the Nobel Laureate, Md. Yunus. India does not lag behind either. The Transparency International in its latest release has considered the world's largest and the most vibrant democracy as the 85th most corrupt country in the world. This is unfortunately in the backdrop of the unprecedented positive impact of the Right to Information Act and more vigilant consumerism.

While the country has a sizeable chunk of black money and soaring Hawala transactions, $ 1.5 trillion worfh of deposit (seven times the size of the Union budget) has been reported to be in the safe custody of the banks of Switzerland and other countries since the year 1947. A disclosure to this effect was made by Professor R.Vaidyanathan of IIM, Bangalore, while delivering the Nani Palkhiwala Memorial Lecture on "Tax Havens and the Illegal Wealth of India" at Chennai on 29/8/09 (The Hindu, New Delhi, dated 30th August, 2009).

Apart from the money that living tax evaders may have kept therein, a large amount cannot be retrieved because those who managed to open such "safe" accounts (presumably by taking undue advantage of our lax tax collection machinery) have died without informing their family or heirs of all relevant details. Needless to say, with the passage of time, the bank in question freezes or swallows such deposit. Further, our populous country has allegedly lost more than $ 20 billion during 2002-06 alone. There is also an apprehension that these tax havens are used as a source of funding spying, terrorist, insurgency and other undesirable activities.

The prevailing practice of subsidised food grains, seeds, fertilisers, kerosene oil and other essential items not reaching the intended beneficiaries also causes overwhelming concern, apart from adversely impacting economic growth and giving a setback to the efforts to build a just, fair and equitable society. Also the pitiable and rampant habit of late submission of the progress and utilisation certificates, diversion of funds for non-targeted spheres, plea for revised estimates, subsequent to time overrun etc., go on to consume a large chunk of our scarce resources which could be better utilised in many other priority sectors.

Enough institutional mechanism is available in the country to prevent and check corruption, right from the Vigilance Cells and Anti-Corruption Bureau at the State level to the Chief Vigilance Officers and the CBI at the Central level. In order to plug the loop hole, the central government has recently decided to set up 71 CBI Courts. Expected to function as model courts, these are to hold day to day proceedings and avoid unnecessary adjournments. After so much of hue and cry, the institution of *Lokayukta* has seen the light of the day only in a handful of states and not all of them are in a position to show their teeth. Either they are helpless, or rendered useless by the non-cooperative attitude of the government of the day. The preliminary requirement of giving permission to prosecute a public servant takes months and sometimes, years. The institution of *Lokpal,* supposed to cover the Prime Minister, is yet to become a reality, despite the frequent confabulations about it right from the date of lifting of the Emergency in 1977. **In such a dismal scenario, the honest and dedicated officials toil and suffer, while the corrupt and the inefficient continue to have a field day. Resultantly, the habit of corruption continues to pose a bigger threat to the country than external aggression or internal disturbances of the kind of Left-wing extremism.**

Corruption is something that captures the imagination of everyone but very little has been done to "catch the big fish". Addressing the 17th Biennial Conference of the CBI, Anti-Corruption Bureaux and the Vigilance agencies recently, Prime Minister Manmohan Singh called upon them to accord priority to rapid, fair and accurate investigation of corruption in high places. They were expected to act firmly, swiftly and without fear or favour in view of the constitutional and legal protection available to them. He also called upon them to look at themselves critically and introspect deeply to fine-tune the functioning of their organisations. He has also gone to the extent of admitting that the fear of harassment and damage to reputation makes the officials unduly timid and slow, thus rendering the whole government machinery ineffectual. Also, expeditious conduct of trials is as important as hastening the pace of the investigations. While on the one hand, one can see a glimmer of hope, on the other, clear sign of desperation is visible at a time when the Second Administrative Reforms Commission has submitted its wide-ranging recommendations so that the poor are not disproportionately hurt because of corruption and carelessness.

In addition, the Minister of State for Personnel, Administrative Reforms & PMO, while inaugurating a conference of secretaries of administrative reforms departments of states has also admitted that the Indian bureaucracy is inefficient and corrupt. He seems to have favoured a focused approach to implement the recommendations of the Second Administrative Reforms Commission within a realistic time-frame and also an amendment in the RTI Act with a view to ensure more transparency in public administration. Is it not ironical that the same "inefficient and corrupt" lot is expected to examine the recommendations for improving the efficacy of the system, reduce corruption and ensure transparency?

Similar conduct is expected from the judiciary, if we are to follow the candid and meaningful write-up of Justice V.R. Krishna Iyer in the Hindu (31st Aug. 2009) on the stalemate over the issue of declaration of assets. According to him, "The best judge has nothing to hide and everything to discover without fear or favour and do justice to everyone, be he high or humble, without affection or ill-will". He goes on to add that "the real cause of the pathological arrear syndrome is the absence of accountability and transparency and that creation of more courts would result in more arrears and more lazy judges". To him, "a capable judge with sound social philosophy is a better instrument of justice than a dozen mediocre, indolent, ignoramuses who will merely add to the adipose of the system."

The mere fact that the reluctant judges at last gave in to the public pressure pertaining to declarations concerning disclosure of assets and the ruling of the Delhi High Court (The Hindustan Times, New Delhi dated 3rd September 2009) that the judicial power is accountable to the Constitution of India, proves the logic and necessity of transparency in public life. The judgment in question is unprecedented as this is the first time that a High Court has decided on a matter involving the Supreme Court judges. Thus, it has been maintained beyond doubt that the office of the Chief Justice of India did not fall outside the purview of the RTI Act.

The enormous power available to the judiciary, revenue collectors, police, municipal bodies etc., has not succeeded in reducing the might of the lower level officials, bent upon behaving like extortionists rather than protectors and regulators. The people in general, and the captains of industry in particular, contribute immensely to the mess by showing their ever-willingness to pay at every step, while resorting to short cuts and thus undermining the compliance of the rule of law.

The officers in general not only suck systematically and consistently our welfare state during their long and eventful service career; they also do not refrain from locating and finding a lucrative position in some commission or the "public service" body, subsequent to their superannuation. In this way, the phenomena of dismal performance combined with non-accountability perpetuates at the cost of the paramount interest of the poor, ignorant and toiling masses.

It goes without saying that barely 5 per cent bureaucrats are honest as on date and that together with 10 per cent of their corrupt, yet efficient brethren, they ensure functioning of the system. Isn't the time ripe to downsize the bureaucracy and to recognise and motivate the non-descript looking honest, hard-working and upright bureaucrats with a view to weed out corruption and complacency?

One cannot ensure total purity in people's behaviour in the public domain, but one can always make an attempt to reduce or minimise the use of unfair means. Or shall we believe an experienced, qualified and non-vocal urban housewife when she says, "Corruption will end only when the universe will come to an end".

35

Election Tourism in India[34]

February 17, 2022

As unseasonal floods and volcano fires abate and new equations build up in the Middle East with the visit of Israeli PM to UAE and Bahrain and virtually no chance of de-escalation of tension along Russia-Ukraine border even after frantic efforts of French President E. Macron and German Chancellor Olaf Scolz, India is in thick of yet another mini General Elections for 625 Assembly seats in five states: Goa, Manipur, Uttarakhand, Punjab and U.P. (Immediate previous such Mini Event for 824 seats was in March - April, 2021).

Corona or Covid or Omicron, its Business As Usual. Public sentiments are not only appealed at, depending upon mood and 'setting', these are also taken for granted.

Topsy Turvy Phase

Its a span of nine to ten weeks from announcement to the conclusion of process of elections.

Looks, festival of Holi with all it's fun and frolic, may be preponed for a few. Everything appears moving except further slowing down of work in Government offices or common man targetted projects and schemes.

So to say, another adventure has been set in motion by the vigilant and hard tasking Election Commission of India (ECI), upon test of first endurance amidst Covid syndrome in Bihar, West Bengal and four other states, subsequently.

Real Issues Take a Back Seat

It is not that indispositions and casualties donot happen and religion and secularism do not assume fresh 'Avatars', but the fact remains that vital figures are under reported, if not suppressed altogether.

Fresh but futile debates on Secularism and resultant Rights and Duties begin even when one needs to be "vocal about local", as such, mainly local issues matter during an Assembly poll. No need to think and touch even the vexed topic of a population policy or minimizing corruption (as it can't be Eradicated) OR Need to get rid of Black Money which, otherwise are responsible for most of the ills and challenges in our country.

One has no hesitation in expressing that regular studies of children and their examinations have to wait or postponed for no valid rhyme or reason but elections (even if term of some legislatures may not have expired) have to be held in the name of Jumhuriat (democracy). One is also supposed to IGNORE large number of casualties during the U.P. Panchayat polls.

Advent of Election Tourism

One gets an impression therefore, that elections may not be a necessity always, rather these are taking the shape of an 'Exercise in Tourism'.

What is not there to be witnessed which a normal, relaxed tourist does not desire or aspire. To be realistic, a tourist looks for the Best Season. Likewise, is the election time for a politician.

Generally one finds perceptible change in Civic Sense as well. For a change, politeness and humility replaces curt and rash behaviour on the part of vote seeker, while those exercising franchise display some what orderly and disciplined conduct.

Some booths having Web casting are well decorated to attract for the specially arranged 'Festival'.

Thrill, adventure, rural-urban exposure, interface with regional lyrics, idioms, songs, music, dances, cuisine, artificial or superficial contact and temporary sympathy with the masses, all can be experienced. With a view to dramatise if not to divert always.

The exercise so made available or imposed, provides seasonal engagement as also employment, apart from rise to fresh caste and class alignments.

ON THE POSITIVE SIDE

Unemployment is ENSURED to Baddies & Ruffians due to tightening and efficient measures through the Booth level functionaries.

Actually needy at the bottom of the ladder too receive food and cash, when an aspirant wishes to secure his/her future for five years.

On the contrary, a tourist too spends, but out of his hard earned savings.

From health point of view, Elections serve as a Litmus Test for Covid related measures. Stalled and neglected infrastructure projects, too are promised to receive a kick.

One also gets to know the short-lived proximity between primordial loyalties and status patterns springing from upstarts on the one hand and gradually picking up Start Up phenomenon.

Lofty Promises

Promises are made without proper assessment and appraisal of individual or community resources. Element of violence and muscle power may look subsided. Truth invariably takes a back seat. But liquor gets a new lease of life.

Free flow of allegations and counter allegations have a field day. Even fissures within a dominant family surface to suit personal interests. Upon victory or loss, they get re-united, like last scene of a popular Hindi film.

Groping in dark or promising castles in the air does not cost anything. Mere play or shuffling of words would do. You have to have a knack for it.

For print and electronic media and those aiming to make a fast buck, elections provide a ready made opportunity. It's also the ideal time to try fresh networks, harbour relationships or get acquainted with psedo think tanks, out of action journalists or actual intellectuals.

Who knows, a situation of win or loss in political spectrum may open other flood gates ?

Assumption of role of fixers, mediators, critics, analysts and upcoming election guides-cum-managers, based on past trends and projections is also very much possible. This is how the Science of Psephology and opinion polls get sustained.

This never ending show will go on. Has to go on. One has to live with it, unless an alternative emerges.

To Conclude, in the words of Dr. M.S. Gill, a former CEC "Election is a Festival of Democracy. We should let it prosper, rather than throttle the process".

36

2022 Mini General Elections: Modus Operandi, Trends and Patterns[35]

February 24, 2022

Every representative body has a fixed term. Election is supposed to be conducted as per a guiding legislation, well honoured and to be followed by everyone in black and white. Model Code of Conduct becomes a cardinal principle. Any deviation may raise genuine eye brows depending upon conduct of involved players or performers. Extreme or exemplary punishment, however, hardly follows.

Significance of Voters

While seeking a mandate, every eligible voter looks important. No sooner than later, he/she loses primacy. Those remembered fondly once, become redundant with change in circumstances.

Many a time, change of constituency may lead to shift in loyalty or following. In the event of repetition, electorate have to weigh rightly gains or losses or cleavage found between expectation and actual fulfillment. Bond between voters and voted is supposed to fructify if requirements pertaining to basic or minimum needs are appreciated and achievement process is within the purview of managed resources. Dissatisfaction or resentment begin developing if representative's personal acquisitions begin getting precedence over that of collectivity.

Caste and class equations, in Indian situation disappear faster than expected. A certain resolve to pursue self-interest becomes prominent.Family members friends and other relatives, instead of fine tuning, mostly darken the interface.

Trends and Patterns: Dismal If Not Pathetic

A close look at last Mini General Election involving West Bangal, Assam, Tamil Nadu, Kerala and Puducherry and the current one having Uttar Pradesh, Uttrakhand, Punjab, Manipur and Goa in the fray, reveal the following:

- "Local" is crucial but it has the propensity to get transformed into "Regional". A drift from "National" may not be advisable. As such, we lack National Character,
- Show of strength gets confined to a series of allegations and counter allegations, sometimes over petty issues,
- Owing to Covid, whether a rally is virtual or physical, no oratory skill or articulation may be needed.Quality of speeches or utterances mostly reflect warnings and threats. Politeness or humility is either absent or sidelined or gone,
- Parivar Vaad or Family rule has to be mentioned even by those having a Bachelor or Spinster status. Their number is growing incidentally. One may ask which outfit does not promote kith and kin, election after election, either in a latent or in a manifest way ?
- Ironically, a voice is also heard off and on: Good, honest, qualified and experienced should enter the political arena,
- Chief Ministers have begun playing a more robust and leading role and that so called Star Speakers do not matter any longer or simply have outlived their utility.

- Talking about ending freebies, subsidies, eradicating black money, proper upkeep of health, education, water and sanitation assets at the cutting edge and spelling out a Population policy do not get the attention that they deserve.
- In a span of nine to ten weeks from announcement to the end of process of elections, further slowing down of work in Government offices and public oriented works and schemes is seen. It happens against the backdrop of a long wait for examinations for degree or employment oriented courses.
- Corona or Covid, Long Covid or Delta or Omicron, elections have to be held in the name of Prajatantra (Democracy).
- In sum and substance, a ground for a sort of Election Tourism emerges with least risks involved.

Whether such trends will also affect or impact the next General Elections in 2024, only time will tell. Any sooth saying will be futile.

Events Akin to Tourism Scenario

In the present spectrum what is not there to be seen or experienced that a normal, relaxed tourist does not aspire ? Thrill, adventure, entertainment, suspense, songs, music, dances or superficial contact and sympathy with the masses ? Tensions get heightened. Nature and functioning of political parties too undergoes a temporary change.

Seasonal employment or engagement opportunities also emerge away from the grip of primordial loyalties.

No harm comes upon making promises bereft of assesment or appraisal of individual or community resources or capacity. Element of violence or importance of muscle power may look subsided with tightening of control but truth still takes a back seat. Groping in dark or promising castles in the air does not cost anything. Mere mincing or shuffling of words should suffice. Rumour mongering and something "becoming viral" over social media also has a certain impact over the psyche of voters.

For people employed in printing, putting up banners, video film making, stage and event management, transportation or those aiming to make a quick buck, such occasions provide a readymade opportunity.

It is also the ideal time to try hand at fresh networks, harbour relationships or get acquainted with actual and serious intellectuals, forgotten commentators or pseudo "Think Tanks".

One may never know, victory or defeat in an election may pave way for other avenues.

37

U.N. Population Projection: Concerns For India[36]

July 21, 2022

An United Nations report brought out on 11th July 2022 shows that population is growing at a slower pace, the world over, whereas in India, it is other way round. As per report, population of India will reach a figure of whopping 1.428 billions as on 1st July, 2023. It will be marginally higher than 1.426 billion figure of China at that time. At present, India's population is only 8.7 millions less than that of China. Both are labour intensive economies from economic growth point of view as compared to countries of Western Europe and U.S.A.

India, unfortunately may hit the top position in terms of population ranking with 1403 millions by 2025 and 1,697 billions by 2064. One, therefore, gets an impression that national population policy of China has proved effective if their statistics is to be believed but only after proper verification. From earlier One Child norm, they are advising couples to have atleast two children. As such, China's population has begun showing a decreasing trend from 2021 onwards. It is felt that more strict Covid instructions issued for the last four months also may have a bearing.

The U.N. report, released every two years, contains population figures of past in addition to projection of population upto 2100.

Rise in global population is reported to be in line with the increase in Life Expectancy (L.E.) at birth till 2050. This figure of 71.7 years in 2022 may rise by almost five years to 77.2 years by 2050.

When it comes to India, L.E. of 68 years for males and 71 for females in 2010 will rise to 72 and 76 years respectively by 2025.

In the same way, Indian Sex Ratio of 932 in 2000 may rise to 950 per thousand males by 2025. The Demographic Bonus may also result in an increase in Working Age population (15 to 64 years) from 603. 98 millions in 2000 to 942.54 millions by 2025.

Demographic Dividend (D.D.)

Scenario as above is normally expected to ensure better opportunities for economic growth of the country or favourable demographic dividend as eloquently highlighted by the Prime Minister from time to time in his speeches.

Since it will also lead to boost the rate of urbanisation and industrialization, more investment in physical and human infrastructure would be possible. However, D.D. can also turn into a liability if India does not produce enough job opportunities and required skilled workforce.

According to Confederation of Indian industries (C.I.I.), India's working population is not sufficient for it to sustain the needed economic growth. In view thereof, enhanced level of education and skill development aligned to needs of industry is very much required. India thus can become a global production hub, at the same time, more consumption of goods and services will take place.

C.I.I. further cautions that in view of the fact that majority of the children did not have the benefit of face to face education for two years due to Covid pandemic, it may add to Learning Gaps. As such, only 3% of labour force of India is formally skilled as compared to 80% in Japan, 68% in U. K., 52% in USA and 24% in China. So Multi Skill training institutes in MSME clusters are very much needed in our country. With more close collaboration and partnership between the Government and the industry our number of formally skilled labourers is bound to rise.

Most Populous Countries

According to the U.N. report in question, five most populous countries as in 2022 were: China (1426 millions), India (1412 millions), USA (337 millions), Indonesia (275 millions) and Pakistan (234 millions).

These were closely followed by Nigeria, Brazil, Bangladesh, Russia and Mexico. By 2050, India is expected to be topper with 1668 millions, followed by China (1317 million) and USA (375 millions).

While China and USA would have controlled their population by 2050, Nigeria, on the other hand would increase it to 375 millions as against 216 millions in 2022 and Pakistan too will have a rise to 366 millions as against 234 millions in 2022.

Need For Fresh National Population Policy (N.P.P.) In India

For a long time we are not having a National Population Policy. The last such policy was given shape by the then Planning Commission in 2000. Whenever such demand is raised, including in Parliament, Central Government sources say that so far Fertility Rate is satisfactory in India. If that is the case, how the latest U.N. Report speaks otherwise ?

Incidently, U.P. is the only State which is thinking positively to have such a policy. But as per some observers, the proposed policy may target a particular community as their fertility rate is much higher.

The U.P. Population(Control, Stabilisation and Welfare) Bill, 2021, introduced on 7th July 2021, aims to control the population of the state. Its goal is to reduce state Fertility Rate (F.R.) to 2.1 per thousand population by 2026 and 1.9 by 2030. Current F.R. of the state is 2.7 per thousand population. It aims to help in improving the overall welfare of the people.

The Bill is said to divide the population into two groups:

(a) First encouraging individuals alongwith their spouses to go for voluntary sterilization after having two children,

(b) Secondly, debarring individuals with more than two children from applying for Government jobs, promotions & subsidies.

Earlier two child policy initiatives of Assam, M.P. Haryana, Rajasthan and Odisha have led to sex-selective and unsafe abortions. Abandoning of girl child or even husband deserting his wife alongwith girl child may be possible, or same may be happening already.

Apart from further improving the financial condition of a family, improving literacy can certainly help. Delaying marriages is bound to be one of the best measures. At the same time, male participation in the sterilization processes can also help in improving their health.

N.P.P., 2000 had identified 13 Social and Demographic objectives, the target year for which was 2010. However, no follow up report has come in public domain.

IMPACT INDICATORS

These were:

- Total Fertility Rate was to be brought to Replacement Level,
- IMR was to be below 30 per 1000 Live Births,
- MMR was to be reduced to below 100, per one lakh births,
- Girls were not to be married before 18 years,
- Given targets for contraceptives, health infrastructure and personnel were to be achieved,
- Universal Immunisation was to become a success,

- 80 % Institutional deliveries were to be achieved,
- State governments were to ensure cent percent Registration of Births, Deaths, Marriage and Pregnancy.

In addition, the NPP also stressed on PROGRAMME INDICATORS, such as:

- Free education upto 14 years of age,
- Drop Out rates were to be reduced,
- Universal information and Counseling,
- Wide choice for Contraceptives was to be offered,
- Incidence of AIDS was to be contained seriously,
- More control over Communicable Diseases was to be exercised,
- Convergence with social Sector programmes so that Family Planning could become a public Centre activity. Further F.P. must be adaptive to changing needs.

Scenario For Period 2001 to 2026

It was noted that eight States of country will have only 15% population as Replacement Fertility Rate would be already achieved. These would be, Kerala, Tamil Nadu, A.P., Karnataka, Punjab, H.P., Goa and SIKKIM.

However, ten states of Arunachal, Bihar, Jharkhand, M.P., U.P., Manipur, Mizoram, Meghalaya, Nagaland and Rajasthan would still contribute to 48% of India's population as these states will have relatively higher fertility rates.

TO SUM UP

In view of above facts and statistics, one can sense and expect an alarming scenario on population front. It is still the root cause of most of our social ills leading not only to rise in crime but emergence of crimes linked to day to day technological advancements.

In good faith, therefore, following measures Need To Be adopted in India if objective of Population Stabilisation was to be achieved:

Immediate Reduction of IMR & MMR,

Vasectomy To Be Given More Impetus,

More rise in Female Literacy, Awareness & Further Empowerment of Women,

Improvement in the domain of Infant Nutrition (Anganwari Workers and ASHA's have to be more alert)

Institutional Deliveries will have to be insisted upon to ensure better health of women.

Raising of Age of Marriage to 20 & 23 years, respectively,

Increase of Gap Between Two Births,

Together with Reduction in Fertility, Efficient Health Care Management Will Be Needed,

Improve Administrative Capacity & Organisational Efficiency, and

Controlled Urbanisation and Migration Strategies to be stressed upon. N.C.R. may have to be specially taken care of.

38

75 Years In Retrospect[37]

August 15, 2021

As is well known, this year's 15th August will be a special and memorable one. While owing to supreme sacrifice of our simple freedom fighters, FREEDOM was won, some builders of modern India have also contributed immensely to its further development, growth and sustenance. Whereas being a young country, we seem to have done well, there have been setbacks, not failures, per se, in some sectors. If Credit for former should go to people with tact, control and acumen, Discredit part for the latter will be attributable to road blockers among us.

Most significant causes perhaps, are, our utter failure on DEMOGRAPHIC FRONT and being a party to perpetuating corruption and inefficiency.

Moral standards are going haywire, may be beyond redemption. We are still away from self respect situation.

What to think even of building a National Character?

One can go on and on. However, in order to come out with a perspective in retrospect, it would be desirable to analyse some of

the key sectors in the midst of Covid crisis and apparent flavour or boost provided by the encouraging performance of our youth in Tokyo Olympics.

Before we proceed ahead, if we do not mention about rapid fall in our moral standards and the way we make a mockery of rules and regulations both indoors (be it offices or Legislative institutions) or out in full public view, we may be committing a blunder at the very outset.

To mark the sombre occasion, monumental Tricolours, more than a hundred in number are going to be put up in several spots. Maybe, we see felicitations to a chosen few apart from Olympic participants and a couple of special people, as also new welfare programmes and schemes are very much expected.

A very pertinent and apt question could be posed, however – Can't Rs Fifty Crores to be spent in Delhi alone on Tricolours go for meeting the basic requirements of still struggling families or thousands of shattered children who have been deprived of their parents in the course of dreaded Covid-2019 ? This will be in addition to hundreds of children who go missing every day through the train on to the 'Dhaba' or 'Kotha' route.

Secondly, during the uncertain Covid times when we are socially distanced but mentally connected by Net and Cell, we may be also tempted to ask -Independence for Whom, From What?

FREEDOM NEEDED FROM VISIBLE CHALLENGES

Spirit of FREEDOM needs to be sought in the given scenario of pressure and anxiety by the common man, who may dare to break the shackles of mind boggling corruption, cracks in social fabric, unpredictable weather, instances of low wages and labour law violations and also trying to withstand waves and mutations & Delta offspring of "Corona Auntie".

It is the time, when instead of uniting to fight the never ending pandemic, we have been compelled to become more "practical" and self focused.

Setback Among Students and Office Goers

We seem to have come to a situation when students have been forced to be away from educational institutions since March 2020 and when Govt. Offices as also legislatures, look to be paralyzed. But daily expenditure on them never stops. As if this was not enough, ahead of time infrastructures are being built by getting rid of durable and aesthetic super structures and trees. Name changing is also on in full speed, thus drawing unwanted attention. and expenditure. Do we do everything in one go or take a break in between the targets, keeping in view other priorities?

When we are supposed to look after the health, well being and minimum needs of our own countrymen, we are expressing a lot of concern about such challenges in the so called friendly countries. It takes ample time and networking to realise that they are basically **fair weather friends.**

When we were down with creeping economy, rising inflation, imposed unemployment and rapid fall in morality and ethics, the encouraging victory in Tokyo Olympics has come as a breath of fresh air. While being in high spirits we donot ask ourselves: How come such a hardworking and talented youth make such a feeble contribution? Listeners and watchers not only become crazy by ignoring their normal duties but unwanted traffic jams too happen.

UNREALISTIC NOTIONS

On such happy occasions, we not only have short term elation, we also have the false notion to be part of a nation. This, despite NOT having a National Character.

If something binds and unites us even in a superficial way, I suppose same is welcome to heart and mind in a country having 20% of its people suffering from anxiety and depression. The restlessness or lack of self-confidence among the youth, comprising 45% of our population needs to be taken up on top priority, if true feel of INDEPENDENCE is to be ensured.

Experiments With Untruth

When we are still unable to guarantee adequate health, job and social security to so called 'outsider' citizens, the tall talk of food security may appear out of context. While responding to rush and crush situations, we seem to be drifting away from age old values and falling prey to the shrewd dictat of Net and Cell. Mentally we have the wrong notion of being connected but physically our standards are having a rapid fall. Such technologies are capable of taking us to a stage when Untruth and Sycophancy seem to have become emerging harbingers of TRUTH.

Secular Credentials Revisited

It may not be out of way to state that half hearted attempts to redefine our secular credentials by sidelining a sizable social collectivity through the majority route may bring in more animosity in the long run. One may not forget that the spirit of freedom, we take pride in on such occasions has a firm cultural genesis or a binding, in Indian situation. Afterall, we have been birth place to four religions of the world and that our ethos and ethnicity have been discovered even in far flung countries. Thus, we should have renewed faith in the essence of Mutual Co-existence.

Changing Diplomatic Scene

Our neo Geo-Economics or neighbour tilted diplomacy, in view of our short period chairmanship of Security Council should be also guided by our historicity and being leader of the Non Aligned countries, once upon a time.

We may have to determine quickly whether West is best or is it other way round, or we prefer or pretend to be flexible to adapt to any situation such as fast deteriorating situation in Afghanistan. But element of INDECISIVENESS should not be our hallmark.

Friends and Neighbours

Mostly our friends and neighbours tend to play safe with us in times of need (such as Covid) but succumb to pressures of tall and mighty, in no time. They surrender rather meekly to non-visible threats or ensure, obliquely, a division in their own country through pressure groups and business interventions in the name of Foreign Direct Investment (FDI). Periodic or long term loans in a developing country too perpetuate a situation. Since they aid and abate DEPENDENCE, How would one rejoice INDEPENDENCE?

Internal Threats and External Constraints

While internal security threats continue to engage our attention, there is hardly any respite from perceived or sudden external hicups.

Earlier crude oil was a strong weapon, now its place could be soon taken over by Covid vaccine. Few superpowers have ensured procurement more than their actual requirement. So the DEPENDENCE factor is bound to be more clumsy and tiresome.

Weather Crisis

To add to the crisis, weather Gods seem to be playing against the will of humanity at regular intervals. Young formation of Himalyas is cracking under hydel power projects, road constructions and climate crisis. Never before we had such extended spells of warming, "wetting" and cooling phases.

Number of cyclones, flash floods, forest fires, landslides etc are multiplying. After Chamoli episode in Uttarakhand and two terrifying Cyclones, it is the turn of these. It has been further observed by the scientists that perpetual freak weather conditions may continue, may be, due to our adoption of unfair and unsustainable means and partly due to overall Global Warming phenomenon which is adding to earth's temperature @ of 0.5 degrees every year. In Brazil, this threshold has been crossed by 5 degree celcius, already.

ENVIRONMENT ISSUES NOT TO BE NEGLECTED

We play at the cost of flora and fauna too with series of Governmental as also private developmental actions. Even though they pose threats to conservation of Bio-diversity, yet we take pride in their heritage quotient. Coming to the need for existence, spirit of mutual co-existence between animals and human beings should normally prevail. Thus, Food chain may also remain unaffected apart from saving the fauna from regular attacks.

STEPS FOR BOLSTERING INDIA

From a positive perspective, It may appear unfair if not out of place, if we fail to flag unprecedented, long term reforms in health, education, rural development and many key areas in social domain.

Also, it has been a long cherished and welcome development to get rid of hundreds of useless and meaningless acts, rules and procedures, inconveniencing one and all.

Given the limitations, it would not be possible to throw light on all aspects of public life. Some of the Path Breaking Initiatives that could be discussed are:

MISSION INDRA DHANUSH: launched for comprehensive immunisation in 2014 has made a distinct mark to enable tiny tots to get FREEDOM from many diseases. However, despite its success in two phases, more than three hundred children have been recently found Covid positive in a major state (similar to USA). PMSSY, another notable scheme aimed at improving and fine tuning tertiary healthcare, has seen setting up of a few regional AIIMS hospitals and that twenty six such speciality hospitals are going to come up almost in all states, apart from 'KAYAKALP' of C.H.C's/ District hospitals and approval given for 189 new medical colleges (of 558,269 will be private run) Needy citizens should take adequate advantage instead of rushing to old, yet far off major hospitals.

Yet it is unfortunate to note that 34% of kids below five years still suffer from malnutrition.

Ayushmam Bharat, world's biggest health project is already having the desired positive impact, in continuation of the earlier mega project of NRHM. Both have identified and filled up crucial gaps in infrastructure, manpower and transport areas. Requisite confidence too needs to be developed on the part of people.

FRESH STEPS FOR PEOPLE LITERACY AND EDUCATION

These can not be easy exercises in a diverse, vast and highly populated country of 140 millions especially when all encompassing corruption and multitude of road blocks come up at delivery of services level, coupled with ever depressing scenario of drop outs.

Once an individual is secured from health and education angles, he should comprehend the responsibility towards the country to feel Liberated on the eve of 75th year of Independence.

However, it is also a fact that as opposed to physical medium of instruction, plagued by two waves of Covid, On Line Education came up as a temporary measure. Nevertheless, doubts will remain regarding it's worth and effectiveness in the days to come. The affordability of Smart Phone and availability of network during the required hours continue to be grey areas. Also one would be incomplete in analysis if we donot highlight the fast emerging hypertension phenomenon on the part of caring, yet anxious mothers.

Further, recent decision of the CBSE to declare all students of Classes Xth and XIIth "Pass" shall have adverse repercussion on future development of youth. Besides, it is likely to disturb the mental state of present students of these classes. Won't things go Haywire if there is no consciousness about an Examination? Such Freedom or Independence in the crucial year of 75 years of Independence was not at all desirable.

TRANSFORMING RURAL SCENARIO AND NRLM

The National Rural Livelihood Mission, presumably on the lines of Rural Livelihood projects of World Bank and other Multilateral organisations already concluded in a dozen states (four in North East) apparently looks impressive, forget about it's being hugely capital intensive.

It should have been appropriate to draw only significant lessons from the experience of the past decade to pinpoint and exclusively focus on region specific livelihood activity. Also correct time after due consultation with the Gram Panchayat members for 'Village Immersion' should be chosen besides adding an essential Sun Set clause, or else it will be a never ending mission. Stereotypes prevalent in the old era should never be repeated.

Ultimate Freedom from the syndrome related to credit/ loan from World Bank etc has also to be ensured in view of rather convenient availability of adequate internal finance. It is also high time, we clearly comprehended the difference between anti-poverty programmes as opposed to asset generation ones.

SHG's, ANGANWADIS AND ASHA's

The massive success of Self Help Groups, Anganwadis and ASHA's even during two Covid waves may need special mention as these bold people have ensured substantial if not full Freedom from constraints of micro finance, saving habit, potable water, minimum nutrition, immunisation, taking care of teenaged girls and breast feeding mothers and what not ?

First step towards voluntary healthcare and initial vital lessons at primary socialisation level have been notable success stories of such interventions. These can have future sustenance factor also unless target groups stop referring to past for their own standard motivation. Collective satisfaction would be possible only if each one of us has a focused desire and skill to climb up the economic and social ladder.

ODF, SANITATION & FREEDOM FROM SMOKE

Advent of Open Defecation Free villages in a record time (Sikkim being the first state) in all nooks and corners has been truly the most revolutionary step of past few years, side by side with success of other sanitary steps and cleanliness (Swatchhata) drives with active participation of rural folk. It has brought fresh vigour and vitality especially among the women folk.

Freedom from Smoke for mothers, sisters and spouses has been also a resounding success Saga. It is helping also in rapidly improving the health status of minor children. Beneficiaries too need to meet the cost of cylinders themselves rather than expecting a permanent free supply. Criticisms over T.V. channels and social media are not desirable. One should not expect spoon feeding from the Government.

To Sum Up

Self Help and Awareness will have to be The Mantra which may raise hopes both for minimising corruption and lightening the burden of the Government.

It has been attempted to throw light on fundamental aspects, changes in which were necessary. Further, yeomen service has been rendered in Communications and IT sectors, accelerating pace of road constructions, provision of free as also charged electricity and potable water. While role of major players remains to be in or out of domain of discussions, achievements, such as, unique Code based D. B. T. facility could be considered a revolutionary step. In addition to ensuring a monetary benefit to a deserving beneficiary, steps also, such as, Bank Sakhis, Bank Mitras etc. are likely to go a long way.

Present level of support system to the individual at last mile, may have to be scaled down gradually. Chinese logic or philosophy of teaching Fishing, rather than giving free fish is VERY MUCH CALLED FOR.

Being prisoner of one's thought process is Not Desirable. One has to think and Go Beyond. Game changing, not merely playing, should be the Need of the Hour.

Real key to Happiness and Freedom should be to expect less from the Government as in many countries which were successful in crossing the barriers of poverty and relative deprivation.

LET US NOT SURRENDER. LET US CONTINUE OUR SINCERE EFFORTS

(F) EMINENT PERSONS

39

Relevance of Gandhi in Present Context[38]

October 21, 2021

It goes without saying that Mohan Das Karamchand Gandhi or Baapu, the Patron Saint of Porbander, was the most formidable public figure in the country's Freedom Struggle. His almost "non-violent tirade" was not only exceptional, he also tried his basic tenets of peace, truth, non-violence, passive resistance, self purification, Swatchchata etc, exceedingly well. Impact of such time tested "mantras" is discernible even now.

His economic thinking and diplomatic nuances inferred possibly from his writings and speeches, should not be discussed here as these did not have relevance to his focussed domain of liberty from the British.

More and more indulgence in the rude actions, perpetrated by our lust for neo colonialism, amid actions guided by the emerging developments in Science & Technology also aided by Narco Terrorism, not only force us to review and re-work our strategies, continued loss of manpower and property also has adverse effect on the imagination and initiatives for multi- pronged development. No doubt, at the face value, they may attract, yet, these may not be sustaining, keeping in view the needs of Future Generations.

It has been widely felt that the Sustainable Development strategy should be the leading light in a plethora of human endeavours. To a great extent, the spike in the cases of Covid-19 especially in the second wave, should have put us on alert immensely, if not adequately compensated for the Needy. But what we feel and experience is generally an opposite phenomenon with shaky foundations.

No longer apparent patronage and "support" of UNO or much subdued WHO, continues to be a silent spectator to spate in mass killings, volcano eruptions, forest fires, landslides, cyclones, chemical & Bio warfare etc.

Also in what manner can we justify irrational acts and unsustainable designs that are made to appear as acts of accidents?

At the drop of hat, normal physical or the arms power is considered synonymous to combat opposition. Recently one has seen atrocious mayhem in Afghanistan. Voices in the lowest rung of society and of women folk in general, something Gandhi jee always advocated for, are being systematically suppressed. Those who led from front, are now lying low. Many of the perpetrators also not only appear helpless but they may modify if not endorse the "new" modus operandi altogether.

Basic aim and endeavour of Marxism perhaps has been to capture the throne with Gun Power. And all the Naxal hit Left Wing Terrorism states are witnessing use of hatred and fire power against the State, per se, first hitting the local Police, before often marginalizing the Central Police forces. How can Truth and non-violence work in such trying circumstances ?

Communal Twist

While the supremacy of the State & its unquestioned authority, has been correctly asserted time and again, yet there are foreign elements who tend to exploit the economic condition and relative educational level of a vast population, mainly from religious viewpoint.

Mostly Indoctrination begins at a young age by exploiting the loopholes of out-dated rules and regulations of the British era. Commendably, more than a hundred of these have been declared null and void, yet we have miles to go.

Most of the time, the State may and should appear as Protector & Saviour but they may appear helpless if not infructuous, if people in general provide adequate and regular support.

Constructive Feedback

Feedback, not necessarily criticism, should be forthcoming from both the beneficiaries and to the identified human targets.

Sustainable Planning for the masses is possible in a peaceful setting, Not amid almost a year of blocking of important national highways, first at Shaheen Bagh and later at three points at the Delhi 'Border', by a large section of the so-called Kisan agitators.

Is the Redressal of Grievances An Ongoing Process?

When most of the key grievances are being listened to and ventilated even after applying non Gandhian methods, road and rail blockades, and two national level "Bharat Bandhs", there has to be a reciprocity, if not an apology to a dialogue process.

Maligning the Father of Nation ?

It has been observed that we tend to also take the fair name of RASTRAPITA to begin a struggle or a strike or a bandh but very soon, we show a tendency to become outright Violent.

We should not forget that soon after burning of a Police station at Chauri Chaura, Gandhiji had called off the Non Cooperation movement.

Drawing a lesson, the Kisaan Agitation should have been CALLED OFF on 26th January 2021, when the Red Fort was desecrated.

It has been observed that not only the activists are self sustaining, rather, a tacit support, including money from powerful countries keep emerging and seen prominently, time and again.

One may carry out amendments, ensure checks and balances but the extent of fire within us is difficult to measure if not impossible to gauge.

Gandhiji may have met his nemesis on 30th January 1950 but his spirit must Light our young nation having centuries- old sustainable and tenable traditions and scientific brains that developed, ahead of times. They had the required inclination and propensity.

All anger may be foolish. Acts of violence nowadays are bereft of reason and rationality. The state can and must be the Watchdog but the populace too have to understand their basic, minimum responsibility for the process of nation building.

Rights without commensurate duties may appear unreasonable & unsustainable and one may perish because of this in the long run.

When weapons of Satyagraha and Strike augmented things to the detriment of British, they began resorting to 'Divide & Rule'.

While Chauri Chaura incident led to withdrawal of Non Co-operation Movement in1919-20, the Kissan Agitation sponsors too Need to read the "Writing On The Wall".

Similar perilous trends are noticeable in other areas too. Not only the expression "Harijan", coined by the Mahatma, has been misused by vested interests, but reservation meant only for ten years, has NEVER been Halted. Its very purpose is being defeated, apart from addition of the EWS to the domain of the highly misused "Protective Discrimination" strategy.

Vested members of media not only get sarcastic pleasure in their unique modus operandi, occasional or professional activists are also projected as Heroes, thus ignoring the very cause of sufferings of the common man. And the expression "tool" too gets converted into that of "Tool Kit".

'Aam Aadmi 'under any regime has to be dependent upon' Khaas Aadmi', when even the Leftists appear themselves clad in the attire of capitalism.

Last Line Connectivity (LLC), actual redressal of issues relating to Delivery of Resources (DoR) is becoming increasingly a farce.

Caste base or factor takes the Access to essential Class Base according to the whims & fancies of the Power Elite, who, as per Wilfredo Pareto have a tendency to "Circulate".

In Gandhi's India, we seem to be extra critical without contributing to a Solution Mechanism.

No wonder the Supreme Court has wondered – "How can Kisaan Agitation go on indefinitely when bills in Question HAVE BEEN PUT ON HOLD ?"

40

Gandhi Smiriti :
SAB JAN HITAAY, SAB JAN SUKHAY[39]

October 16, 2021

By design or accident we seem to be living in a crazy and mobile dependent, materialistic, fairly educated, yet confused world. Nuances thereof, bring in an element of grief and depression. One should not say but carelessness relating to the wavering life styles impacts our anatomy, every now and then. A simple variation of bodily temperature takes the shape of a viral cum long gestation fever, which becomes more viral, thanks to our casual approach, if not on account of application of specialised knowledge through medical science in a larger entity called Global Village.

TALE OF CASUALTIES

Losing 4 lakh 51 thousand Covid patients in India may not reflect only statistically but more than six times of it is the actual reality, as per the WHO, therefore, it is high time we did a fair, impartial and unbiased statistical introspection. But ironically, we do not mind more than 30 lakhs dying every year, due to TB and heart diseases.

Learning by Remembering

On the day of Mahatma Gandhi's 152nd birth anniversary, we should have drawn some lessons from the idea behind confession or the need to express Regret for commiting a Sin. One may try to surmise and introspect on a particular day, followed by a systematic confession, the following day.

Sin and Good Deed

Paap (sin) or Punya (good deed) could be two sides of a coin. Unless we commit mistakes, there can not be a scope or ground for correction or repentance or improvement. Failure, if we follow the instance of "Spider Entangled In a web", must not discourage or deter us. These are supposed to be stepping stones to partial, medium or complete success situations, as emphasised under the basic tenets of Gandhism.

Other Anologies and Influences

In addition, if we are also to draw a parallel from Maslow's 5 stages of growth, from the stage of Take Off to the climax of Self Actualisation in real life, it may seem to be a misnomer, if not out of context, altogether.

ROLE PLAY AS PER STATUS

We should not forget that human beings are the products of the same social system, yet we are "allotted" myriad roles as per our heredity, education and background, and achievable quality or sustenance factor. We may not succeed, yet there should be no harm in climbing up the ladder. Sky may not be the limit, yet one should have the conviction and courage to create a hole in the round but revolving Earth, without bothering much for an "orange" or Black Hole or changing perceptions about statics and dynamics, Physics or hot theme of Global Warming.

As we would know, Black Hole suspense was further supplemented to by Stephen Hawking (a Divyang scientist) having unimaginable power to influence or convince ablest of all.

Gandhi's Relevance

Against such a backdrop, we may pose a pertinent question-" Gandhi Kaun, Kaisa Gandhi or Kind of Gandhi (Who is Gandhi?, What kind of Gandhi? and Whose Gandhi ?)

I may not say so but remembering Bapu appears to have become an annual ritual, equally participated by White Clad Politicians and Gala Band bureaucrats. No "national" speech is complete without him. We tend or pretend to know Gandhi also on the eve of launching a Rastriya Yojana or a "plethora" of these, in the rapidly changing virtual or physical era.

However, forgetting the Mahatma, too has become a kind of fad, if not a fashionable device. Why should we do it or why should we undermine, if not denigrate, the equally remarkable roles played by the likes of Bhagat Singh, Bal Pal Lal, J.L. Nehru, Rajendra Prasad, BR Ambedkar or Kriplanis of the bygone era and Ram Manohar Lohia and J. P., unquestioned doyens of the contemporary period.

Re-ignite the Fire

Rightly, it is the correct time to re-ignite the fire within us in respect of Sardar Patel, another stalwart, if not superior to, but definitely of the same level and stature as Nehru. Needless to say, historical evidence shows and oral traditions support that Nehru became the first choice of the Mahatma for the coveted position of the P. M. of Aazad Hindustan at the stroke of Midnight.

Even if his nocturnal experiments with young female relatives or Noakhali happened at the brink of disaster, leading to unbearable partition of the country, and widely reported economic philosophy and diplomatic inputs of Gandhi did not see the light of the day, over all contribution of "Porbander Ka Sant" in liberating us from the clutches of foreign rule must never be doubted. It is something akin to a Gospel's Truth. Having a debate, none of us can prevent.

In the post-independence period, the Iron man of Indian Politics was relegated to the background of playing the second fiddle as new Home Minister. His onerous task was to win over some Muslim ruled Princely States, a responsibility that became synonymous with unification of the Country. The greatest Barrister cum first recognised peasant leader of Bharat Varsha rightly lived upto the promise of unifying and maintaining the spirit of just passed by 'Gulaam Bharat' within the available, if not assumed limits of perseverance and tolerance.

Drawing Parallel ?

At the same time, it is honestly felt that Sardar's stature should not be equated through the tallest statue vis-a-vis Virgin Mary. That may perhaps give sleepless nights to numerous international level freedom fighters inside their graves.

A man or woman begins by taking birth from a divine mother, to grow slowly by sucking the pious milk (collastum) from her, so ananology of present kind concerning Sardar Patel vs Virgin Mary may not have guts to justify those recording history or the political undercurrents.

To slightly disgress, one thing is becoming somewhat clear that one should not impose nationalistic feelings in a situation when the very basis of a national character is conspicuous by its absence. Needless to say, young and devastated nations such as, Germany, Japan, Singapore, or Israel could instill the required sense of nationalist feelings fairly early and this must have ensured their rapid economic growth.

Do we still at this stage, try to inculcate an urge for national character among the countrymen ? It may benefit or not but it will certainly NOT result into loss. The post first and second wave Covid stage is the right time to think, introspect and act for a true nation in the 75th Year. It may perhaps be the true tribute to the ideals and teachings of the Mahatma.

To proceed closer to end, barely after 75 years one can not and must not try to reach Moon or Mars, all of a sudden. Making a concerted endeavour should not be construed as a specimen of utopian way of thinking. We shall have to move much ahead of talking about Aryabhatt, Charak, Chanakya, Ramanujam or Patanjali, and take pride in our recent achievements amid suspicion or doubts pertaining to our civilisation, as per Western financial "Experts" or neo-Philosophers.

After all, with umpteen limitations and mainly demographic constraints, we are not only developing but growing faster than many so called developed nations and that temporary threats, such as, Covid or unforeseen natural calamities, leading to anxiety sort of situation may not and should not deter our firm convictions.

Whether at this late stage, we become Hindu Rastra like Nepal or Islamic like Saudi Arabia or Indonesia or Pakistan, that should not be a priority item. We have lived and thrived under the time tasted garb of a Socialist, Democratic and Secular Republic. It should see us through the almost bipolar and murky waters of World politics. Gandhism not Gandhian Socialism as mis-interpreted, may give us the needed strength to swim further without aligning with any powerful block or a block gradually disintegrating under it's own lofty ideals, once applicable during the post World War era.

Prior to lifting the mouse, Gandhi jee, subsequent to advocating the cause of Truth, Non-violence, Passive Resistance and Self Sudhikaran, made clear the distinction between the Means and the Ends. It is the means that justify the ends. It can not be other way round.

While re-iterating it, let us also continue to have a demarcation between Need and the Greed, especially during Navratas and other festivities, when tons of food items will simply go down the drains. Suppressing the fear and intimidation factor and reign of terror, the World over through Gandhian methods also may have to be attempted to. Of course, the complicated modus operandi of the times has to be taken into account. Common man, by regaining confidence and stamina should try for a deadline for actual reforms. Our thinking, assessing and acting patterns must also undergo a change, at the same time. Then only the call of SAB JAN HITAAY, SAB JAN SUKHAY can become a reality.

Apostles of Saint of Porbander, are you listening or you may prefer to wind up this universe by further stressing upon the application of unsustainable means of development?

41

Nelson Mandela

Mahatma Gandhi was nominated more than once for the coveted Nobel Peace Prize. But he was never conferred with this honour. Some of his followers or apostles, nevertheless received the same. Rolihlahla Dalibhunga or Nelson Mandela, who languished and underwent humiliation in a white controlled jail for twenty seven years was one such public figure.

Although he could achieve his objective of getting his country freed from the clutches of an outright pro-apartheid regime during his life time, he could not enjoy political power for the reasons of age. A reign of more than five years, perhaps could have legitimately assisted him in actualizing many of his unfulfilled pro-people dreams and aspirations.

On the contrary, for no fault of his, he had to suffer immensely on personal front. All the tragedies were tolerated with such a dignity that they hardly impacted his largely transparent public life. On being reminded of his sacrifices, he would retort" I am not the only one to do so. Others too have done that". Mandela, therefore, deserves to be admired and respected for his vision, tolerance, intellect and integrity.

Several heads of states, public figures, activists, artists and sportspersons would come out with words of praise in his honour now that he has breathed his last on 5th December, 2013 but how many of them actually comprehended the basic tenets of passive resistance he championed, will be anybody's guess. Our mystical yet materialistic world has always moved like this. It may continue to progress in this manner in future also.

With the advent of Drone, upgraded cell phones, automobiles, communication devices and automatic weapons, EXPERIMENTS WITH UNTRUTH are flourishing in a mathematical progression. No one even on tasting setbacks appears interested in drawing a line between the need and greed. Commodification of the human-kind, vociforously opposed to by Gandhi, Karl Marx and Mandela, goes on unabated in one form or the other.

Fondly called Madiba by his countrymen, the 95 year old statesman who began his career as a security guard, effectively anchored a non -violent tirade without having met Mahatma Gandhi even once. In his autobiography "Long walk to Freedom", he, however, acknowledged as to how the Passive Resistance Movement led by two Gandhian followers against the Asiatic Land Tenure Act in South Africa had influenced him. In addition, choice for India for his first ever foreign visit on being released from the prison had it's own weightage and significance. All said and done, South Africa may continue to be relevant for India even in the post- Mandela era.

India on it's part had always given a loud message to the world by voicing its unequivocal opposition to the racial regime in South Africa, such as, UNO, NAM and CHOGM. Same was logically followed by conferring the Bharat Ratna on Mandela. Incidently, this was only the second time that the highest Indian Civilian Honour was being bestowed on a foreign dignitary. Earlier another Gandhian, Khan Abdul Gaffar Khan was chosen for his non - violent initiatives in the North West Frontier Province of Pakistan.

Though his credentials as a non-violent crusader can not and should not be doubted, it is also a fact that after African National Congress was banned in 1960, Mandela became impatient and desperate to the extent that he had to resort to an armed struggle against the state. This would not have found favours in the Gandhian era. The cancellation of Non - cooperation movement by Mahatma Gandhi in 1919 in the wake of Chauri Chaura violence is an effective case in point. Another digression, perhaps was Mandela's consent to share the 1993 Nobel Peace Prize with the last South African President of the notorious apartheid era. How could a reward in recognition of a mass mobilization of the sufferers be shared with the very perpetrators of crime ?

His deteriorating physical health, presumably owing to bouts of sorrow and solitude in a tiny cell of 5 x 6 feet at the Robben Island, impelled him to enter the wedlock thrice: 1944, 1958 and in 1998. In between two divorces took place. Having lost three children and a great grand daughter, he was survived by three daughters, seventeen grand children and fourteen great grand-children at the time of death.

While we mourn his irreparable loss, shall we hope and pray that his close associates and followers will continue to sustain the struggle for justice, human rights and a society free from racial discrimination ?

May South Africa progress at a rapid pace with or without the aegis of BRICS as it has to catch up fast the lost opportunities and decades.

42

Lata Mangeshkar : Nightingale of the World[40]

February 6, 2022

Sur Kokila with an unthinkable patriotic spirit, She is Gone Forever Mortally, but perhaps Not from Our Heart and Mind.

Those of us who not only Feel but Believe That– Music Has the Aura, Strength and Mesmerìsing Ability to bind, Give Us a Solid, unbreakable company at all the situations, All the twists and turns, All the Joys and Sorrows, One would get Solace always in Her Memories.

A person of her stature, she cannot be adjudged as a legend after getting immersed with five elements of nature in the evening of 6th February, 2022. She was already an undisputed legend, a giant personality with unimaginable humility, passion and professionalism even when she would walk and gently speak and sing in her life time.

Beginning from a tender age of 12 years, she took up little bit of acting in non-descript roles in Marathi films, to graduate into leaving an indelible mark as a Singer of Repute, earlier than one would have expected.

It took place upon losing her affectionate, caring and music oriented father. She had the responsibility to look after widow mother, four sisters, a brother and a Mausi (mother's sister).

What one gathers, she took her role so seriously that she became a singer par excellence, no doubt but side by side, also took adequate care for singing career of her three sisters and later music director brother.

It was perhaps an onerous or honourable responsibility, not everyone is capable of shouldering. And then deciding not to enter the wedlock at all.

That was the mettle and make of Lata Didi or Lata Jee.

More than 30 thousand songs in 36 languages, all delivered with command, acumen and wide following, universally.

On losing such a rarest of rare Ratna, one is generally tempted to say routinely- "Void left by her Cannot be Filled". She deserves to be showered with all conceivable adjectives ....

But in case of Lata Jee, in view of her range and impact for 80 long years, one may have to struggle, finding a suitable or befitting expression. Recording a song at the ripe old age of 90 years is not easy. Only she could do it.

Show by such great show person has to go on and on but who will actually fit in that role, will be difficult to pinpoint in present struggling, Covid ridden circumstances. Incidentally, she herself became a victim of same.

It is not only her rare talent that needs to be mentioned. Her devotion and stamina was apparent from the fact that she stood for eight hours at a stretch to record the song "Luka Chuppi" for the director, Rakeysh Omprakash Mehra.

Probably the best tribute was paid by singer Kavita Krishnamurti :

"From the time I have known what music is, she has been an angel in my life".

Further another budding singer, Shreya Ghoshal had following to express :

"Yesterday was Saraswati Puja, Today Ma took her blessed one with her. Even the birds, trees and wind are silent today".

Lata Jee and her Evergreen Charisma Rest in Peace.

43

Dilip Kumar, an Uncrowned Legend of 20th Century[41]

July 7, 2021

Md. Yusuf Khan or Dilip Kumar who breathed his last at the age of 98 years in the early hours of a sultry 7th July 2021, could be unquestionably considered as the first super star who dominated, rather ruled the Mayanagri of Bombay for 54 long years. No other actor, not even Rajesh Khanna would come close to him.

An unassuming actor, par excellence, his contribution to Indian cinema was extraordinary. Which role did not he play with an elan-tragedy, romantic hero, comedy or historical icons?

Known popularly as the first Khan or Yusuf Saheb, he was born on 11th December 1922 in Peshawar. He was blessed in the prised company of eleven siblings.

His father, being an orchard owner both at Peshawar and Nashik, preferred keeping him in Barnes school, Nashik. Subsequently, he tried his hand at selling sandwich.

His foray in filmdom began with his introduction in 1943 to Devika Rani, reigning star and owner of Bombay Talkies. He also came in touch with Ashok Kumar, another star on the horizon.

His impressive Urdu and English made him a script writer.Prior to making his debut in Jwar Bhata in 1944, he did not forget to change his name to Dilip Kumar, presumably under the influence of Devika.

Becoming popular with Jugnu in 1947, he gave two popular films- Saheed and Mela. But Andaz in 1949 proved a true turning point when he acted with confidence with Raj Kapoor and Nargis, other famous stars.Two films in 1955-Insaniyat with Dev Anand and Devdas with Suchitra Sen made him a household name.

The 1957, film Naya Daur, followed by 1958 block busters- Yahudi and Madhumati not only added new feathers to his glittering cap but he climbed to the Dizzy heights.

Sooner than later, he established his solid image as a tragedy king and became the first actor to be conferred with the first Film-fare award for Daag. He went on to win this award 7 times more.

In 1950, he became the first actor to charge Rs. One lakh for a film (US $120, 000 in 2019). Sensing his fading status, he rightly took a break for five years in 1976 to re-emerge again as a force to reckon with as a Character artist in mega films such as, Kranti, Vidhata, Shakti, Karma and Saudagar.

All good things come to an end and Dilip saheb could not remain in galaxy of stars forever. Having compromised with loss of glamour, his last appearance was in Qila, a non-descript movie. His last two films are yet to see light of the day.

Last couple of years he ran into inclement weather to face property related issues with neighbours etc. concerning his 2400 sq.metre area bungalow (currently priced Rs 350 Crores) located at extra posh Pali Hill area of Bandra in Mumbai.

His second marriage with Asma Rahman in 1981 was a sad and short lived affair. His first and present surviving spouse Saira Bano could not cope with it.

I began watching Hindi films in 1967 and the first one in this order was hugely successful film Ram Aur Shyam in which Dilip Kumar had a memorable double role. The number one villain of this era Pran gave remarkable performance too, so much so that if he was sighted outside the Ratan Talkies of Ranchi, he would have been thrashed by my feeble hands.

His friendship with S.N. Ganguli, owner of three cinema halls in Ranchi resulted into another hit in form of Sagina Mahto, a bi-lingual film. It was preceded by Ganga Jamuna and followed by Gopi.

His restrained portrayal of Prince Salim together with fine performances by Prithviraj Kapoor and Madhubala in K.Asif's magnum opus "Mughl-e-Azam" made the movie the highest earning one for eleven years. Originally a black & white venture, it was turned into a coloured film in 2004 and was re-released as well.

Talking of much subdued heroines of the era, Dilip Saheb gave seven hits in the company of accomplished Vyjayanthi Mala during his hey days. All the then top heroines, namely, Madhubala, Nargis, Waheeda Rahman, Mala Sinha and Saira Bano shared screen space with him. Drawing a comparison with the tough time faced by Rajesh Khanna, another super star at the last phase of their career may appear relevant.

Khan Saheb, apparently never used to divulge his miseries in being child less or suffering from Bronchial Pneumonia, advanced Prostrate Cancer & kidney ailments but he was suffering always from within. On the contrary, Rajesh Khanna after departure of Dimple would find company in drinks and women, so much so that he was viewed married only for namesake. Dilip saheb, on the contrary, despite acting in sixty five films and facing competition from many talented artists of his era, kept his morale, image and standards high. A world without the thespian may appear isolated and barren. It may be difficult, if not impossible to fill the void.

44

Rajesh Khanna : End Of An Era[42]

Marriages are made in heaven but performed on Earth. Very few, however, understand it and certainly the most prominent Superstar of Hindi movies Rajesh Khanna (R.K.) did not fall in this category.

Failed marital bliss with an equally talented person's pains and instant saturation, soon gave birth to heavy alcoholism and gradually led to his unfortunate death on 18 July 2012.

R.K. also lovingly called Kaka, was an icon, a craze, an enigma and a phenomenon, not only for a large number of women(many would splatter windscreen of his swanky cars with lipstick), but he was also a tremendous source of inspiration and style for youth in the seventies and eighties.

Who can forget or undermine his unique hair style, distinct buttons, dog collars, large shades and of course the Khadi Kurta which would simply sweep the nation in epidemic proportions?

UNBROKEN RECORD

The first and only Superstar of Hindi cinema had delivered twenty consecutive hits between 1971 and 1985 as a solo hero, a record unbeaten till date. Jatin Khanna, the adopted son of well heeled Chunnilal Khanna, was famous for visiting studios in expensive cars in search of a role.

Though he began his innings in 1966 from the film 'Aakhiri Khat' directed by talented Chetan Anand, followed by 'Raj', directed by G.P. Sippy, IT WAS ONLY WITH 'Khamoshi' (Director Asit Sen), 'Safar' and 'Anand' (Director Hrishikesh Mukherjee) that he was recognized, talked about and ultimately made an indelible mark.

He catapulted into instant stardom with 'Aradhana', opposite a senior and more accomplished Sharmila Tagore.

A star was thus born, not to fade or set but to live on for posterity. Once a clear winner out of ten thousand Filmfare contestants, R. K. was determined to establish his credentials in a sure and certain manner.

STELLAR PERFORMANCES

His hit songs 'Roop Tera Mastana', 'Yey Jo Mohabbat Hai', 'Yey Sham Mastani', 'Zindagi Ek Safar Hai Suhana' and 'Jai Jai Shiv Shanker' were, perhaps, most powerful and memorable picturisations ever. Histrionics of R.K. and Sharmila in sensual scenes carried out superbly through their eyes and a sensitive rendering of emotions, did not call for the overtly sensual scenes exhibited in modern day hits, such as, 'Munni Badnaam Hui', 'Shiela Ki Jawani' 'Chikni Chameli' or 'Fevicol Sey'.

There are many tales surrounding the life and times of R.K. but the most significant fact is that in the fierce competitive world of celluloid, he could grab the bull by horns and attained success after success. Soon he became the archetypal hero, popular, flamboyant, charming and magical.

A time came when he became larger than life, often outliving the script and the prescribed frame. Romance was the popular leitmotive that ran through Hindi cinema and R.K. was personification of same. It lingered on in the era of multi-starrers but ultimately had to take a backseat when anger and aggression became the hallmarks of popular cinema as depicted in 'Namak Haram', 'Zanjeer' 'Deewar' and 'Sholay'.

R.K. was partnered perfectly in romantic scenes with the likes of Sharmila Tagore, Asha Parekh, Tanuja, Hema Malini and Mumtaz. Out of these he shared excellant screen chemistry with the last named heroine. Although there were few innovative and excellant directors and script writers, who were in some measure, responsible for his success, it was the contribution of ONE & ONLY Kishore Kumar that led to the epic success of Kaka. Indeed if Kaka was the body then undoubtedly Kishore Kumar could be called the soul. In his movies he played out many death scenes to perfection, like the one in Anand, until actual death overcame him in his home 'Ashirvaad', now rechristened 'Dimple'.

Not only did R. K. embody the innocence and struggles of the common man, he had tremendous ability to connect closely with the audience. But at the end of the day, he was a lonely man. He gained in name and fame tremendously but was vanquished on the conjugal front. Like highly pampered prince of 'Premnagar' he would search for his 'Mahbooba', ostensively with the help of 'Lal Rang', evening after Evening. He would resort to contemplation in isolation with no company from his erstwhile fans, foes, friends or political aides.

LEGENDARY FIGURE

R. K. had an unusual and powerful image. The trademark movement of his right hand, twist of the neck and gestures conveyed thorough his eyes made him a legendary figure. Surprisingly, though he acted in over one hundred and fifty films and was a gigantic source of revenue for lakhs of people, he could receive only three Filmfare awards as the Best Actor.

ON A STICKY WICKET

In 1992 he delved into the uncertain world of politics from the prestigious New Delhi constituency with former wife Dimple and two charming daughters in tow. The 'connection' and 'dis-connection' with this teenage sensation of 1973 continued to be part of his life until he actually called it a day.

LIFETIME ACHIEVEMENT AWARD

Like any yesteryear actor or artist, he was conferred with a Lifetime Achievement Award of Filmfare in 2005 by none other than Amitabh Bachchan, his "Babu Moshai" or 'foe' of yore. He made an unsuccessful comeback in a T.V. serial and a B-grade movie, as also a non-descript advertisement for a ceiling fan.

Big B appropriately has said "Rajesh Khanna entered into heart and mind of every Indian".

However, Raj Kapoor's words perhaps define life's reality more tellingly:

"The show must go on, because it has to go on".

An illustrious career has come to a standstill. One can bid adieu to the once brightest star with an epitaph that he would greatly approve of-

"Zindagi Kaisi Hai Paheli, Kabhi To Hasaye, Kabhi To Rulay".

45

An Afternoon With Khushwant *Singh*[43]

It was a somewhat pleasant and relaxed day in November 2001. I had the mandate if not the instruction to seek the concerted views of some eminent people from various walks of life on two unprecedented documents brought out with *care,* caution and hope by my State Government. The idea was to learn from wide experience of such people and to take fruitful and sustainable initiatives for further improvement. The task in question enabled me to meet some distinguished citizens. *One* of them, Khushwant Singh, I can not easily and possibly forget. Each time I read about him or for that matter, get a chance to read his latest works, I am privileged to be reminded of my close 'encounter' with him.

It is a known fact that this magnificent genius does not hang a name plate over his main door, rather one historical and legendary board welcomes the visitors in the following way : *"Please don't ring the bell unless you are expected"*. I ventured into his habitat, obviously upon getting *an* appointment. I was under the wrong impression that one of his personal staff would lift the telephone number 24620159. I proved *incorrect* when after repeated yet patient attempts, I tasted *success.* A grave, blunt voice greeted me. It was the celebrated, prolific and the controversial man himself.

I was measured in my words while conversing. My more than adequate explanation convinced him. Thereafter, I was granted *one* of the rare opportunities of my life to meet a reputed intellectual, who was my consistent and favorite idol since the college days.

True to what I had heard and anticipated, despite all the wealth, Khushwant Singh appeared very simple, down to earth and straight forward. His drawing room, undoubtedly reflected his stature and personality. Ahead of taking a seat, I was rather distressed to see *an* ailing but beautiful old lady, attended to by two domestic helps. I gathered later that it was his life partner who had virtually become a vegetable due to some incurable disease. I was immediately reminded of what Khushwant had written about her in his controversial, informative but widely read autobiography "the day she departs I will stop writing". The celebrated old man, however, has refrained from fulfilling his resolve. After her death, he has churned out more than four books. This speaks volumes about his depth, aptitude and a remarkable urge to share his feelings, emotions and wisdom *as long as* he *can*.

The moment I explained the purpose of the meeting, he retorted "Be reasonable, how can I go through these voluminous documents at this ripe old age of 86? Nevertheless, do convey my thank/to your CM for remembering me". When he asked for my name, I disclosed. His immediate reaction was, "So you are a Kayashtha. We have a Kayashtha Damad, married to my grand daughter". Before I could venture to introduce my small and beautiful State, he recalled fondly his only visit to the then Himalayan Kingdom in May 1975 prior to its joining the main stream of the Nation. He was very nostalgic about Mrs. Dorjee, wife of late Kazi Lendup Dorji, the first CM of Sikkim. It transpired that this famous historical lady belonging to Belgium was a school teacher in Delhi and that she had successfully taught one or two foreign languages to his kith and kin.

He remembered the narrow, serpentine but clean *roads* leading to Gangtok, the Ridge Park adjacent to the Royal Palace, simple people, bright flowers, exotic handicrafts and a very very soothing view of the Mount Khanchendzonga. He did recall his interaction with Palden Thondup Namgyal, the XIIth and the last *Chogyal.* Subsequent to patient hearing of his anecdotes ably supported by his elephantine memory, I ventured down the memory lane and was aptly reminded of the brilliant cover story penned by him *as* the editor of now defunct, The Illustrated Weekly of India in June 1975. I did recall my mother showing me the copy in question in November 1984 when I was allotted the cadre of Sikkim. Needless to say, it turned out to be my first introduction to the State, wherein I was to spend my lifetime. Hats-off to my mother, the issue of the 'Weekly' was preserved neatly in her tin cash box, presented to her by my late father in the early sixties.

Contrary to initial impressions, the element of hesitation gradually paved the way for a very enlightening face-to-face communication. The World famous Sardarji sporting a casual and unimpressive 'Patka', no wonder heads a flourishing writing 'industry' with a wide readership in not less than seventeen languages. Though only half of his works are considered scholarly, he evokes indelible mark on the mindset of the readers by what he calls - 'provoking, amusing and informing'.

His insistence on punctuality prevented me from getting more insight into the mysteries of his writing world. After half *an* hour or so, it was the time to leave the famous address of Delhi- 49 E, Sujan Singh Park. Even though my hunger to acquire more knowledge from my idol could not be fully satiated, I was victorious in ways, more than one. I said goodbye to him by gently folding my hands. He did not show any change in his posture but his eyes and facial expression conveyed what I had aspired for. While getting into my car, I remembered his famous words uttered at the time of launch of one of his numerous books: "even if I write trash, not only I get published but I also get undue publicity". His another famous statement speaks high of his candid and fearless mind: "no power on earth can ever invent a condom aimed to impede the flow of my pen".

46

Sachin Tendulkar, Epitome of Simplicity

Once Indian Men's Cricket team had taken a commanding three hundred and thirteen run lead over the West Indies and had also claimed their three wickets in the second innings of the Wankhede stadium Test, it looked certain that Sachin Tendulkar was not going to get a chance to play Test Cricket again. In view thereof, I thought it prudent to scribble the following lines in his honour.

To begin with, I am in a dilemma. For, I am not qualified enough to write about a man who is so unique and incredible, who often makes difficult tasks so simple. He has no aura, no airs. He is unassuming to the core. Will perhaps never make you bore, with his antics, smile, camaraderie and performance. He does not hurt. He has rarely entered into or created controversies during the momentous twenty four years, he had the honour to play for the country.

Sachin had his ups and downs, climaxes and low points, wins and defeats, setbacks, a few embarassing moments, yet he could carry himself with grace and dignity, without hurting teammates or spectators. His extempore speech at Mumbai on the day of naming of a sports complex after him will be permanently etched in one's memory. He spoke from heart, to say the least.

15th November 2013, a cool Friday will be the most memorable day for the living legend. On this day, twenty four Springs back he donned the country's colours in Pakistan as a tense sixteen year old teenager when the Test cricket, per se, was dominated mostly by the middle aged men. The Australian and Pakistani fiery speedsters were knocking out every budding, conceivable and emerging talents. AND money power too was yet to show its glamour, attraction and tentacles. But Sachin Ramesh Tendulkar was not only determined to make a statement, he was also there to stay.

He did not score a ton on debut but with his grit, hard work and overall balanced conduct, both on and off the field, he gave enough hints for a long, consistent and sustained stay in two forms of Cricket. The latest one, i.e. Twenty Twenty, turned out to be too much in view of his advancing age as also emergence of many fit and young brethren, at least in non-IPL tournaments.

Over ten days, the whole of country led by crazy Kolkata and now Mumbai is singing praises (including Chalisas), discussing, confabulating, displaying and reminiscesing about the Master Blaster and rightly so. One can learn a great deal from the career of this genius, for, name and fame never really got into his head. He was never perturbed or shaken by the debacles in Australia, a decade ago or in England in not too distant a past or for that matter, the biting tongue of a handful of Australian Cricketers.

His forty six test wickets, sixty eight half centuries, one hundred centuries(51+49), fifteen thousand nine hundred and twenty one Test runs, eighteen thousand four hundred twenty six One Day runs are by any standards no mean achievements. It may be futile to say that such a record may not be equaled or broken. For, that will go against the very spirit of the game, of any competition. Once upon a time Sunil Gavaskar from same Mumbai was on top of the world, that too without helmet, for more than a decade.

Thereafter, another Little Master - Tendulkar sprung up and rose further to make a mark.

While paying rich tributes to him, one should not, however, forget that he had become a spent force, if not a liability, on many occasions in recent past, yet his past accomplishments and selfless service to the nation carried him to dizzy heights. He was, in the ultimate analysis, rightly given chance after chance till his own conscience convincingly conveyed-" I hereby hang my gloves for the sake of other deserving lots".

Sachin deserves to be remembered and followed like an Idol or Role model in every field of human endeavour. Let us not belittle him by discussing whether he should be conferred with the Bharat Ratna or whether he is greater than the game itself.

Dissemination of his vast knowledge, technique and style through setting up a politics free Cricket Academy would be more appropriate and sound proposition. The game of Cricket will continue to be played with more gusto, action and enthusiasm but in the words of the "Nightingale" Lata Mangeshkar, " pinch will be noticeable in days to come".

47

Fantasy Soccer With Bhaichung Bhutia

It was the solemn occasion of Pang Lhabsol. Being a holiday, people of Namchi, South Sikkim appeared in festive after a Puja at Alley Monastery. Weather looked congenial despite light showers experienced previous Evening. Soon after Breakfast, all the paths & steps led to the picturesque Dist. ground. It was decked up to host a friendly 'nine a side' football match between District Officers (D.O) and the local gentries (LG).

When sufficient spectators assembled, a request was made to area M.L.A. and Minister to grace the event as the Chief Guest. Having arrived in advance, he was busy interacting with his constituents in P.W.D. Guest House.

Usual pomp and show was visible at the jam packed ground. The Minister was accorded a traditional welcome. After a 'Teeka' was applied on his forehead, he made the waiting girls, representing three communities, richer by Rs 300/- each. Thereafter, a band of local boys played a soothing tune in the middle of ground.

To start the process, the Minister got introduced to the rival captains and team mates. Next, it was the turn of Minister to kick the ball. The way he did it, spectators got an inkling of his sporting past.

The match began with a fair degree of action, fun and enthusiasm. Spectators took time to notice the presence of Bhaichung Bhutia, local celebrity and the India Skipper, playing for the D.O.

Bhaichung and a few former players displayed their skill and tricks right after kick off. Resultantly the L. G. looked concerned if not perturbed. Since the weather was fine, natural play was very much possible. Nevertheless, as per usual experience in such a game, a few felt breathless, to begin with. The spectators dressed up in their traditional attires looked engrossed. But children forming the largest group, made their presence felt by shouting, yelling and supporting the players in attack mode.

Despite fast movement of ball, coupled with good footwork, the first twenty five minutes were devoid of any result. By this time, however, a kind of manifest division was seen among the jubilant spectators. While the stand on the side of Youth hostel was cheering the D.O. team, those occupying West and North stands were seen shouting in favour of L.G. team. Just before the whistle for the breather, Bhaichung, aided by a superb pass from Chhetri the upcoming star, could reach the goal area of the opponents. He got past the athletic goalkeeper and scored a remarkable field goal. Apart from the visual retreat and thunderous applause, same was confirmed by the Referee in his typical dancing style. Spectators now had a lot to cheer and relish.

In addition to giving an upper edge to D.O., it restored interest in the game, which, so to say, was waning, thanks to goalless first twenty four minutes.

As unusual warmth and bonhomie was witnessed during the 'half time'. Both the teams were offered Glucose, water, Squash and juice in addition to unusual items: steamed Momos and appetising Chicken legs. Discussions took place in both the camps on the strategy to be followed in the second half. The idea was not only to score goals but also to provide adequate humour and entertainment to the Festive crowd, watching the game with rapt attention. Unlike in regular matches, the Referee volunteered to play the second fiddle in the second half. The Younger but experienced Lineman, therefore walked into his exalted shoes with a beaming face. The play, nonetheless, could, resume only after the new Referee took a “Bathroom Break”, something he could have easily availed of during the breather. Since plenty of time was available, he was allowed this unforeseen liberty.

With the passage of time, the stamina of players began getting exhausted. Certain sections of crowd, however, could discover peculiar ways to boost the morale of their respective teams. The L.G. displayed a picture of renewed confidence with fresh young blood entering their ranks. Their team work and occasional picking of speed bore fruits in the last ten minutes. Though they could not score a field goal, Garjaman Gurung, their oldest player, backed brilliantly by a Jorethang ‘Sardar’ (contractor), managed to convert a Penalty Corner to perfection. With this goal, things became more interesting.

At the time of Free Kick, the strategy of D.O. team was discussed by Bhaichung Bhutia in a professional fashion even when they exceeded the time limit. The field placements too underwent change with more active players occupying the Forward positions and the hefty and tired one’s relegated as Defenders. D.O’s effective Goalkeeper too had to be replaced to enable him to attend to an emergency at his village home in Nandugaon. Many of them had to be politely requested, in addition, not to divulge in any chit chat with the spectators.

At last, the second goal for the D.O. was scored by me as Captain, as a result of a fine pass by the combined initiatives of Chettri and Bhaichung. Even after getting confirmation of same and self being hugged and patted by the fellow players, I would not release the ball. Afterall, it was a defining moment for our team. The Referee, however, showed his reluctance to pronounce the desperately needed verdict in our favour. He ruled that the Captain was 'Off Side'. Same was later confirmed by the Linesman.

****

Sudden bout of pleasure, however, vanished in thin air.

I could feel being awakened by Tom, our pet, who was a cute, quiet cat. To my shock, I discovered that I was not in Namchi, rather, I was sleeping to glory in New Delhi. May be, I actually had a sound sleep, which was instrumental in producing this nice dream. Even if it was momentary, not only I smiled but felt fully elated. The dream, per se, brought back sweet memories of the District days.

I made no mistake in ringing up Bhaichung Bhutia, a dear friend. I eloquently shared the experience of the match that never took place. Fresh from his Asia Cup triumph, Bhaichung burst into laughter and reciprocated his feelings, in his usual cool way.

(G) MISCELLANY

48

Sikkim Expedition to Mount Everest[44]

Named after legendary mountaineer and first Everester from Sikkim, the Sonam Gyatso Mountaineering Institute (SGMI) was set up at Gangtok. From its modest beginning as an adventure club in 1961, it grew into a full fledged mountaineering institute by 1963. With its breathtaking beauty and many peaks above the height of 22,000 feet or 6700 metres-Mount Khangchendzonga, Mt. Kabru, Mt. Talung, Mt. Siniolchu, Mt. Simvo, Mt. Pandim, Mt. Rathong, and Mt. Paunhari, Sikkim was considered the right choice for training and pursuing the sport of mountaineering and adventure activities. Much ahead of this significant step, the H.M.I. at Darjeeling had started giving basic and advanced training to the budding mountaineers by using Yuksom area of West Sikkim as its base.

Though Sonam Gyatso, Phu Dorjee and Nadre Sherpa (all from Sikkim) had achieved the difficult and challenging feat of climbing Mt. Everest, a need was felt to form a fresh group comprising of both mountaineers from Sikkim and from other states and undertake an expedition to "Sagarmatha".

As a result of hard and sincere work, commitment and painstaking planning for several weeks, a twenty member team was finally selected under the leadership of Sri G.D. Bhutia, the former Principal of SGMI. Dr. D.S. Burfal, an experienced mountaineer was chosen as the Deputy Leader and the expedition doctor. Of the twenty members, two were women, who hailed from Sikkim. One of them, Phulmaya Tamang had already figured in the H.M.I. expedition to the world's highest peak in 2003 but unfortunately could not reach the summit.

Upon filling the basic requirements and completion of necessary formalities, the team members had to undergo various sessions to determine their grit, stamina and determination. Objective was to put a sizable numbers of mountaineers on top of Everest. The team finally left Gangtok for New Delhi on March 16, 2008. After some briefings, interactions and sensitizations for nearly a fortnight, the team members landed at Kathmandu.

Subsequent to arranging essential climbing and camping instruments, food items and medicines, the work relating to logistics was tied up with an experienced and reputed company of Kathmandu. It took them another six days before they reached Lukla. The weather was great. Days were cool and sunny, while the nights were not very chilly. Team members were in good health and high spirits. The only setback the team faced was near Namche Bazar (altitude 11, 000 feet) when Sri Bishnu, one of the fellow members suddenly became ill. He had to be evacuated to Kathmandu for further treatment.

Following a trek of another ten days over forty odd kilometers (25 miles) and acclimatization at high altitudes, the team set up its first base camp at an altitude of 5334 metres (17,500 feet) on April 15. Many of the members had the experience of earlier expeditions. Their inputs proved invaluable. As it was the main climbing season, there was a lot of activity on the surrounding rugged terrain. Team members did not forget to take part in a comprehensive puja for their well being and the overall success of the expedition.

The team's next destination was the Khambu glacier. The climb was steep, therefore, tough. The steep and hard ice walls on the way tested the technical skills of the climbers. They had to negotiate an ice maze using ladders, fixed ropes and ice axes.

After two days of hard work in the beautiful surroundings, the team organized its first Acclimitization camp. Some of the members, tested here by the Deputy leader for their endurance skills, had to withdraw on health grounds. With the passage of two more days, the team climbed to a height of 6, 000 meters, followed by another climb of 400 meters in the next five days. Camp II was pitched at an altitude of 6,400 meters on April 26. Fourteen of the original twenty members had made it to this point. The intense cold, strong winds and avalanches necessitated adequate precaution, especially afternoon onwards.

The fourth Acclimitizarion camp was set up by April 30 and soon after the team members received the news that the Govt. of China had imposed restrictions on the more difficult and treacherous Northern Ridge approach to the peak. This was to ensure unhindered movement of the Olympic Torch. The expedition members, therefore, were left with no option but to modify their approach route and suspend further activities. They were, thus confined to Camp II until May 10, without any notable activity. However, they kept themselves in good humour and upward movement began once the Olympic Torch rally got over.

Camp III was set up on May 13 after tremendous hard work and braving inclement weather at an altitude of 7,200 meters. The team was now ready to plan the final summit ascent on Mt. Everest. A tedious climb over the next seven days took them closer to the Lhotse Face. The view of Mt. Nuptse, standing tall at 7,879 metres(25, 850 feet) was simply awesome.

On May 21, the climb began rather early for the South Col (7986 metres). Late in the afternoon, the team approached the site of Camp IV at an altitude of 8, 000 meters. The sight of Mt. Lhotse (27,890 feet) from here was simply overwhelming. Since the weather was relatively congenial, it was decided to make the summit attempt on Mt. Everest, the same evening.

D.D. Bhutia of Kalimpong was the first to leave for the summit at 19. 30 hours, followed closely by Kunzang Gyatso Bhutia of

Sikkim. Eight trying hours later, Bhutia stood on the summit at 29,035 feet at 5.30 a.m. on May 22. Though very tired, he was elated. It was a dream come true. It was enthralling and mesmerising for him to be on top of the world. Peaks in the neighbourhood were also visible clearly.

Before Kunzang Gyatso Bhutia could make it to the summit at 5.40 a.m., the famous mountaineer, Apa Sherpa of Nepal reached the peak for a record eighteenth time. K.G. Bhutia was immediately followed by Ram Singh of J&K. He proudly displayed the Indian Tri colour and flag of J&K Police also at 5.40 a.m. The summit was full of colorful prayer flags and many other things left behind by other mountaineers.

The two women climbers from Sikkim, Phulmaya Tamang and Yangdi Sherpa followed next. They set foot on the highest point of earth at 6.30 a.m. By doing so they became the first two women from the North Eastern Region to accomplish the feat. Recalling their experience and feelings, later they said "It was unbelievable. We felt as if we were in the Sky. Everything else was down below. We closed our eyes on reaching the top. We thanked God and offered prayers (Mt. Everest is considered Chomolongma or the Mother Goddess of the Earth by the Sherpas). Given a choice, we are ready to climb again."

Another five members, Ashish K. Singh of Uttarakhand, Nima Wangchuk Sherpa of Sikkim, N. Suraj Singh of Manipur, Yaduram Sharma of Siliguri, Atul Karval (I.P.S) of Gujarat, reached the summit between 6.30 and 8.30 a.m. Relentless hard work enabled Karwal to become the first All India Services officer to achieve the distinction. Nima Wangchuk at age of fifty nine years and seven months became the oldest Indian ever to accomplish the feat. According to him, it was the greatest achievement of his life. He was working very hard for it for forty long years.

May 22 was a very busy and lucky day a top the Everest. Twenty seven mountaineers from different countries, including ten from SGMI made it to the summit. Overall, it was a show of camaraderie and high performance by the Sikkim expedition. Putting ten climbers on top in one attempt without any accident or casualty was an incredible feat.

On May 23, the team returned to Camp II at 6,400 meters and the following day reached the base camp. While Dr. D.S. Bursal, P.W. Sherpa and S. Pokhriyal stayed back at the base camp for May 29 Everest Marathon organized by an Expedition company of Nepal, the rest of team members left for Kathmandu on May 27. The Everest Marathon, incidently is supposed to be the highest Marathon venue in the world.

With a sense of immense pride, the team returned to Kathmandu on May 31. Some departed for N. Delhi, while those belonging to Sikkim and nearby states returned to a rousing welcome and reception by the Sikkim Tourism Department at Rangpo on June 5. People from all walks of life in Sikkim appeared overjoyed. It was a resounding success after a gap of 43 years (Late Sonam Gyatso had climbed the Everest in 1965). Sri Pawan Chamling, the Chief Minister of Sikkim, expressing his extreme happiness, congratulated all the expedition members.

The expedition had some more satisfying moments to their credit, apart from putting ten members on top of the Mount Everest.

- Nepal Army was assisted in building a helipad at the Everest Base Camp for emergency evacuations. Same was used a couple of times in their presence.
- In a rare humanitarian gesture, Ashish K. Singh gave his Oxygen Cylinder to a Vietnamese climber when the latter had exhausted his own. Thus a precious life was saved during the return journey between the summit and the Camp IV.
- The medical team of the expedition saved the life of Ms Kalpana Das, a single woman climber from Orissa. On May 21, after scaling the peak she had developed severe dehydration and abdominal pain. She was kept on

observation at the Base camp for more than twenty eight hours and was given all possible care. Ultimately she recovered upon being evacuated by a helicopter to Kathmandu.

- Thirty nine expeditions from different parts of world were also given free medical aid.

One hopes that more youth from Sikkim and N.E. region will be inspired by the marvellous achievement of this expedition. They, may perhaps be encouraged to take up mountaineering more seriously and diligently than before.

49

Tokyo Olympics: Best Ever Performance by Bharat Desh[45]

August 8, 2021

When twenty three year old, tall and handsome Neeraj Chopra of Panipat, Haryana, the Asian Games and Commonwealth Javelin Gold medalist was inching confi-dently towards victory, at 5.09 pm on 7th August 2021, hearts of Indians rightly stopped beating for a few minutes.

Not having seen but on the basis of "hearing" I was too tempted to utter "its going to be Neeraj, Neeraj And Neeraj all the way".

After first two or three rounds, his fellow competitors began trailing badly which improved our hope quotient.

One further felt in mind "If he manages GOLD, it will be after 13 years. In 2008 Olympics Abhinav Bindra had won it in shooting."

Praiseworthy and Deserving

Now extremely capable and once badly injured but ultimately well deserving young Indian has done all of us immensely proud.

A few words would not suffice. It is to be felt deep within, during present tough Covid times.

It was best ever performance by India in Olympics Last Best was win of six Medals at 2012 London Olympics, by Sushil Kumar-Silver (Wrestling), Vijay Kumar- Silver (Shooting), Gagan Narang - Bronze (Shooting), Saina Nehwal - Bronze (Badminton), Yogeshwar Dutt-Bronze (Wrestling) and Mary Kom-Bronze (Boxing).

Unfortunate Indians

By whiskers, Mary Kom, Indian Women's Hockey Team, Golfer Aditi and Archers Deepika & Tarun Rai narrowly missed grabbing medals, or else, overall tally would have been atleast ten.

Swift Jump in Medals Tally

Neeraj's win gave India a remarkable jump from 66th position to 45th.

In 121 years old history of games, India could never manage to win even a Bronze in athletics.

When account was finally opened, it was with a solid bang which may have shocked and silenced many critics for a moment.

YES IT WAS A GOLDEN "Start"

Thus, far, best performances by Indian athletes were : Great

Flying Sikh, Late Milkha Singh, 4th place, P.T. Usha-again, 4th place, while international High Jump record holder Anju Bobby George had slipped to 5th place, unfortunately.

Is it not an unbelievable rather incedible performance to date by Indian sports persons ?

Could Performance Have Been Better ?

However, despite improved and many a time, record breaking performances in the recent past, expensive foreign training opportunities, relative calm and quiet atmosphere of two Covid waves and additional one year preparation time by postponement of current Games, overall Indian tally of medals could have been still better.

One is hearing from childhood that smaller and relatively less developed countries, such as, Serbia, Jamaica, Kenya, Netherland, Italy etc manage to get more medals than us. It would need deep study.

Considerate and Understanding P.M. at Last

In retrospect, extra filip was definitely given by Sri Narendra Modi, the extra dynamic PM who wished, inspired and motivated sportspersons both in victory as also when they lost. One has no hesitation in admitting that such a sporting and encouraging P.M. we never had.

Such a positive and determined boost goes a long way. Shall we hope to increase our medals tally at most of International events in Future?

Viewpoint of Viewers/Watchers

From the viewer's perspective, there is no harm in concluding that by nature we become too emotional on such occasions.

We also tend to misbehave with losers.

A balanced and rational behaviour should be always displayed by feeling "Indian ness" within us.

When are we going to have a National Character ?

Lower Middle Class, Clearly Scored

Last but not the least, the majority, may be with the exception of Neeraj, shooters and the lone woman Golfer belonged to lower or lower middle classes who have to mostly struggle for good balanced and nutritious diet, potable water, coaching facility at the "cutting edge", amiable peer group company etc.

Besides many had to walk a few kms prior to getting lift from truckers or crowded buses or taxis. Chanu, Dahia, Punia, a few Archers and Hockey players belong to such a category.

It is not only "Taking" which should find mention.

Chanu did not forget the gratitude of sand truckers of Mizoram. She not only hosted 150 of them but also felicitated them with her meagre resources at her ordinary house in presence of her tea seller mother. But these can happen only in the North East with due regards to other fellow Indians.

Hats off to Chanu and Loveina, similarly inclined sports persons, our country MAY see STILL brighter days in Future.

****

Seven medal winners and also other members who tried their best, deserve to be felicitated by the PM at Red Fort on 15th August, 2021

Long Live India !

50

Civil Services Day : Frankly Speaking[46]

April 21, 2022

Civil Services Day is being celebrated on 21st April every year since 2006, to commemorate the contribution of Civil Services to the society. This year it is 15th such day.

Ever since the Britishers left India, such days were a regular feature by the Defence, Police and many such services in a befitting manner. But the Civil Servants who are the "Steel Frame" of the country according to late Sardar Patel, never thought of celebrating one for themselves till the former P.M. Sri Manmohan Singh was approached for the purpose. Compared to any uniformed service, it is a sombre and low key affair even when the Prime Minister holds the centre stage.

Awards for extraordinary innovative work by the District Administrators have become the annual feature nowadays. It is an opportunity, we in service in our hey days or formative years were never given. On the contrary, our Police Service colleagues are regularly conferred Presidents Medal for Distinguished service at the fag end of one's service career, merely by virtue of seniority apart from one for gallantry or bravery.

It is never too late, one should say. But why to restrict Civil Service Awards to the level of District Administrators? Why can't we confer it to a SDO level officer in the second year of service with a view to encourage him to build more confidence for future and also to Senior Secretary level officer as a matter of recognition for his / her outstanding service so as to inspire others to replicate or go beyond a Success Story?

One expects thought provoking if not substantial pat or guidance from the Prime Minister at such annual functions and that routine talk may not carry weight. Not finding a mention about need to have a New Population Policy, Reduction in Corruption and extraordinary punishment to non-performing human assets, etc. belied expectations even this year. Nor was there any talk of hijacking of Executive functions by the Judiciary or a review of Disinvestment of the profit making "Ratnas" of public sector, or downsizing the strength of bureaucracy or adoption of ways and means to save useless expenditure. A thought needs to be also given to utilise the Retired members of service, who have had a remarkable reputation and public image, yet they may have been victims of unfair system of empanelment.

Among the five priority areas in which 16 awards are to be conferred during the next year, only promoting Excellance in Sports and Wellness makes sense. Rest are routine, usual or repetitive, which generally get neglected when one is at the helm of affairs.

As regards delivery of services, it should not be our endeavour only to provide encouragement by a system of awards but also by a system of punishment or dismissal, if need be, from service. It has to be built in the event of poor or under performance. That way one can identify "Black Sheep" easily and swiftly. Calibre, vision, knowledge and character should have an edge.

New energy, new enthusiasm, new order were all stressed at the end of "Straight From Heart" speech of a performing P.M. and he rightly deserved the standing ovation from the talented and trained audience. But how and in what manner programmes and schemes will be tailored and executed, that remains to be seen.

Politicians who speak on such occasions are tolerable. The serving and retired brethren on the contrary, expect you to follow some thing which they may not have followed themselves in their "illustrious" days. Most of them, being opportunists, expect juniors to be fair and independent in taking decisions.

One should not be saying but it is a cardinal truth that merely 5 percent of the Civil Servants happen to be honest and upright. Rest toe along the dotted line. Some of them continue to be H.M.V.'s even after superannuation. Do we have courage and conviction ?

NO.

51

The Umbrella[47]

During the initial years of service, I came across many interesting individuals and experiences. Whenever I recall and am tempted to narrate, my joys know no bounds. One such incident happenend in the thick of Monsoon at Mangan in North Sikkim in 1991. Having disposed off first half work, I took a lunch break, something not permitted officially those days. Before I could complete the process, I was pleasantly surprised by sudden entry of an old and graceful Lepcha couple. They hesitated to utter a word upon discovering that I had not finished eating. Omkith, the woman understood my predicament faster than Passang, the man accompanying her. While she turned towards the door and signalled her companion to follow her, I felt for them. Afterall, it was raining cats and dog outside. They appeared very pleased upon getting a seat on the sofa. I promised to speak to them soon.

First I listened to Passang. Theteafter, I gave a patient hearing to Omkith. It was revealed that the couple hailing from the picturesque Hee-Gyathang Panchayat had got 'separated' upon getting an 'order' from my predecessor's Court about four years ago. A certain amount of money was fixed as 'maintenance allowance' for Omkith. With the passage of time both of them had got remarried according to local customs to some other persons. To my utter surprise the Maintenance allowance was neither reviewed nor stopped on ascertaining the sound economic status of the second husband of Omkith, residing in adjacent village of

Lingdong. Since they had added to their number of children even after remarriage, Passang was dragged to Court in the hope of a possible enhancement.

A perusal of the 'Act' revealed that my predecessor had no authority to decide a Maintenance allowance. Thanks to the innocence of the people of the area, matters beyond one's jurisdiction were not only heard but expeditious disposal was also ensured. When I explained my compulsions under the circumstances, the couple tried to follow but they won't leave. They preferred a 'review' of the earlier order by me rather than going all the way to the next nearest Court at Gangtok.

I had a look at the law book again and I also broused through some of the old case records. Upon not getting any precedent, I took a break of few minutes to relish a hot cup of Temi tea. The trick not only energized me but also gave me a clue to resolve the issue. I called the couple after some thinking to my Court room. I made it clear that I was not going to write anything on the case record, however, I would be willing to consider a sort of "Milap Patra" to be jointly signed by them, provided it was counter signed by the area Panchayat members. This formula had worked earlier, hence I was somewhat optimistic about the success of same in this 'marital dispute'.

To my relief and satisfaction they gave their consent and returned within half an hour. They had all the required signatures on a white crumbled sheet. When I expressed my surprise over the signatures of Panchayat members, apt came reply "they were already in the Court building in connection with some other case". After some arguments, an amicable amount was agreed to. This paved the way for a solution to be confirmed verbally by me. I was led to believe the famous saying "all is well that ends well". I gave them a five minute breather before making up their mind, more so in view of the fact that Omkith had mentioned about her regular attendance at the time of Wedding of her former children, otherwise staying with Passang. Perhaps he was destined to pay more also in view of his sound economic condition in comparison to the second husband of Omkith. Though they were hardly on talking terms, participation of Omkith during the marriage of her former children reflected a very strange relationship. Here was persistence of emotional bond even in a situation of physical separation.

When everything got over and the couple had left quietly, my clock showed 3.30 p.m., meaning thereby, I had to continue in office for half an hour more without any visitor or engagement. As expected, my P.A. and C.A. had left for the day when I was engrossed in hearing the Lepcha couple. Upon turning towards window I discovered that rainfall was not in a' mood' to relent. Sharp at ten past four, I gently walked towards the portico. To my utter surprise, my old peon Tashi had taken his 'fill' for the day and appeared determined to lock the office. I waited for five minutes for the driver but he was not to be spotted anywhere. I was left with no option but to enter the Gypsy vehicle through an open door. Fortunately, key was very much there. Therefore, there was no point in waiting.

I was driving towards my bungalow carefully not because I was a learner but the heavy downpour had resulted into overflow of nearby drains. The road was completely isolated in the stretch of the first kilo metre, nevertheless the vegetation and rocks were dazzling with freshness. Suddenly at a sharp turn, I was compelled to slow down. I noticed two people walking hand in hand under the cover of a torn umbrella. Before I picked up momentum again, I was curious to know who were they braving the intermittent rain. To my utter but pleasant surprise, I discovered that they were none other than Passang and Omkith. Perhaps the adversity of Mother nature had brought them together even though it was a momentary affair. I was simply stunned. No word would come out. By the time I decided to reignite the engine of the vehicle, I heard a very feeble, yet audible "Khamri (Namastey in Lepcha language)". I was deeply impressed by the collective and forceful voice and togetherness of the estranged individuals. I was tempted to give them a polite reply by nodding my head. Before hitting the pillow, I was still thinking about them huddled together under a torn umbrella but facing the wrath of nature in unison.

52

Demise of A Promising Teenager[48]

Many a time, Winter nights can bring bone chilling cold, despite all comforts, one can afford. To break the monotony of Secretariat life, I decided to undertake a tour of two districts, braving inclement weather. Generally leaving of bed is early on hills but lying down with eyes wide open has its own charm.

Tour was to commence at six a.m., but I took time in getting ready after hurried bath and cut short Puja. To save time carrying packed break fast appeared better option. Though we were behind schedule, yet the vehicle would not pick up speed due to dense fog. Thanks to experienced hand of Basant, cutting across meandering road, we arrived at Ranipool, the upcoming township. Looking at the isolation one gathered that my past and present office colleagues may be thinking to take a stroll or deciding to postpone it due to chill in the air.

Drive along Rani khola upto Singtam (29 kms) was a little faster owing to loss of altitude. It was irritating to see concrete constructions, bereft of architectural touch, on both sides of highway. Lost time made up on the way enabled arrival at Food Godown, Singtam on time. Prior to routine inspection, it was relieving to munch local corn flakes and milk less Temi tea.

For drive of another thirty three kms upto Namthang, one had to climb from Mamring. Crossing Teesta bridge was a thrilling experience. There were a few landslide and sinking points when vehicle regained height. Due to many engagements in afternoon, only half an hour each was spared for Namthang and Namchi Godowns. Most of these godowns presented a depressing picture. One at Namchi elicited some promise mainly on account of better skills of the Manager. O yes, view of Namchi and Samdruptse looked awesome.

Halt at steep portion of Zoom via Jorethang for late lunch or early dinner was correct decision. Having covered over one hundred kms by now, vehicles too deserved rest. Upon finishing meal, I did not forget to jot down some notes in my diary. When asked, Namgyal Bhutia, the D.D. West Dist. informed about night halt at a village home, ahead of Soreng. Though there was no appetite, warmth of food and unassuming behaviour of our host impressed immensely. Prior to hitting the pillow, I did not forget to try neck rolls, shoulder rotations and spinal stretches.

Next morning, one left bed at 6.45 a.m. Unlike scenario of previous morning at Gangtok, it was bright and sunny. Sun, having risen already was spreading brightness and beaming faces all over. While birds and animals were already up and kicking, our hostess was having tough time to prepare children for school. Subsequent to a good walk in the serene and pollution free surroundings, I felt energized. Fragrance of soil could not be explained, it had to be felt. After ethnic Break fast and hot glass of cow milk, one felt further fresh. Prior to our departure the lady of the house insisted on presenting some ‘Basti’ Ghee and honey. As per custom, I slipped commensurate money into the pocket of eldest son of the family studying at S.S.S, Soreng.

One could not notice much change in Soreng town, though it was upgraded as Sub - divisional H.Q. in 1985.

Road from Soreng to Sombaria was clean but deserted. Hectic construction activities (foot paths, school buildings, culverts and bridges) was noticeable in an area that had thick vegetation, once. Whenever wheat and vegetable fields would be visible, one would stop to 'shoot'. A few non descript water falls also came on the way. But having heard about mammoth Geetang waterfall, I was very eager to witness it.

What a sight it was ? It turned out to be very high and ferocious. Water was clean, cold and tasty. Steps leading to top were in need of repairs and protection. Though it was much more scenic than waterfalls around Gangtok, tourists would hardly have a footfall. I decided to take up the matter with the concerned Secretary.

Around 11 a.m. we reached Food Godown, Sombaria, close to Darjeeling Dist. boundary. Building was not old but was completely under utilised. Meeting with employees and F.P. shopkeepers did not reveal much. Neither they had any issue nor they could express any desire. Contented lots, I told myself.

When I ran through Attendance Register, most of the employees were found absent. It was gathered that same was due to a tragedy at Watchman's house. Immediately I decided to visit the bereaved family, the approach to which was through two hundred steps. Typical Lepcha house made of wood without using nails had two storeys. Ground floor had space for cattle, poultry and firewood. A dog was found barking.

Though tragic death of a daughter of Karma, the watchman, had happened and relatives and visitors had begun thronging, the whole family looked busy in serving tea, milk and fermented Bear in Bamboo containers. Upon being seated, I too was offered something but had to politely deny, as it was time to offer condolence. Meeting Karma was sentimental but in order to tide over his tragic loss, he appeared to have got drunk. Like his family members, he would not shed tears but his expression was loud and clear. I also had a brief interaction with his two wives (Jethi & Kanchhi), two daughters and three sons.

It was learnt that Nim Doma, the deceased girl had complained of light fever and headache upon returning from Govt. School, Sombaria, of which she was a bright and disciplined student. Normal milk, food and fruit offered to her were flatly refused.

She was taken to the local PHSC, wherein a Nurse examined her in a routine way. They were advised to approach Soreng P.H.C., which was better equipped. By pooling money, a Mahindra Taxi was reserved. The doctor at Soreng too examined her in a casual way. As fever was not subsiding, he referred her to Dist. Hospital at Namchi. Since the Sombaria Taxi driver had not returned, seeing the deteriorating condition of the patient, he agreed to drive up to Namchi. Though the hospital was fairly large, having all the facilities, in view of loss of valuable time in commuting, efforts of doctors in normalising Nim Doma proved futile. By late night, she breathed her last. She bid farewell to this mystic world, far ahead of schedule.

Gathering strength, I entered the tiny room where the dead body was kept. There was a pin drop silence. In the corner I had first and last glance of a fair and charming teenager. As per custom, one bent down to offer "Khada" (scarf) and an envelope containing whatever cash, I had. Her eyes were closed permanently but face was beaming. She had worked hard for studies on her own, bereft of any support from her father who would often get drunk. As some young men brought a Tea box for putting the dead body, I shifted to common area. While packing the dead body took time, I was determined to be with the family slightly longer. Among the visitors, a few recognized me as the erstwhile D.D.O. of West Dist. Fondly, I was reminded of some help given.

Upon conclusion of the chant by the Lamas, final journey began. I stood up, bowed and quietly left for Food Godown. While climbing, I felt that without knowing Nim Doma personally, I seem to have developed a strange bond. I could not have even a fleeting glance at Sombaria Bazar to see the changes, therein.

Drive down to Daramdin, "Rice Bowl Of Sikkim", reminded me of an Inspection of R.D.D. office I had undertaken in August 1988 as D.D.O. Verghese, the then host was very proactive.

Leaving behind memories, when we reached Tharpu, I saw some smoke rising above Sombaria sky. Perhaps the pyre of the dead was lit. A promising teenager was leaving the world forever.

Without confirming the origin of smoke, movement ahead began. While journey from Gangtok had begun on a bright note, it was sadness all along, on return. All have to die one day but if a known or dear person departs, we begin discussing if not questioning death.

Grief comes and goes but a few deaths leave an impact. Nim Doma's was one such demise.

53

Torepkiu of Wapher[49]

In the remote village of Wapher under Samator Block of Tuensang District of Nagaland, 75 plus Torephkiu, Head Gaon Bura, was basking in the eco-friendly compound of his house. 2nd of August, 2010 was a warm day in this high altitude village. It had rained the whole of previous night leaving a severe impact on electric supply. After a long interval, a senior Civil Servant was visiting his forgotten and neglected village. He had extended his helping hand to the Village Council Chairman, Shuhven, an ex-serviceman as also a Pastor in making hectic preparations for the visit. The slushy foot path leading to a meeting hall constructed under BADP had been cleaned, pot-holes were filled up and a fixed sum was ear marked for tea, refreshments and lunch.

Though news had been spread a few days in advance to call the working SHG members of the village, half of them had not understood the purpose behind the meeting. This much was sure that some announcement was going to be made in respect of a new scheme or two.

Torepkiu, proud owner of six Mithuns was leading a contented life with lukewarm backup of his second wife, 20 years junior to him in age. While most of his five children from the deceased first wife had settled in life, three of the off springs from his latest bride were attending a dilapidated Government Junior High

School,closeby. While giving coins to them liberally as an incentive to concentrate on studies, he would not hesitate to extend this facility to all the neighborhood tiny tots on almost regular basis. Some of them would also get financial assistance for buying school uniforms and paying monthly fees. They would avail of a self declared holiday whenever the footpath leading to school would get submerged/become slippery as a result of heavy downpour. They would be also 'eligible' for a holiday, each time the teachers decided to have a gala time in Tuensang or Mokokchung.

When the entourage led by a senior officer of Union of India arrived at the village gate, Torepkiu's joy knew no bounds. Though the Council Chairman, and the Pastor took lead in welcoming him, Torepkiu did not want to lag behind. A nagging pain in his left calf muscles did not deter his spirits. Rather, wearing a half-sleeved orange coloured vest and non-ironed black shorts, he attempted to walk fast with the help of a stick.

After exchange of pleasantries, the convoy slowly moved through the flat grassy land. Some of the women and children witnessed the whole development with interest. Otherwise also, the day had turned bright and sunny after almost a week. The brightness ensured quick drying up of wet and smelly warm cloths apart from organizing a sort of 'sunning and airing ceremony' for the household items of daily use.

Subsequent to a round of the village, including youth dormitory, the formal meeting was called to order in the modest, wooden meeting hall. The guest was welcomed with a traditional woolen shawl bearing the symbol/logo of the dominant tribe of Wapher. The speakers included the Council Chairman, the Pastor and Shuhven.The last named became an Interpreter due to his command over Hindi language. In the normal course, Torepkiu's turn would not have come. When the guest evinced keen interest in his background and experience, he not only became vocal, he also threw sufficient light on the constraints and development prospects of the remote village. Like a seasoned leader, he would crack jokes in between while making submissions. Despite the dismal record of poverty alleviation schemes, he expressed a ray of hope for the toiling masses, without following a bit about the emerging group oriented approach of the Government.

Useful notes were exchanged, experiences shared and vital information was gathered, both in respect of functional and defunct SHGs during the course of interaction. Also on being asked, a fervent desire was expressed for coming under the umbrella of new SHGs depending upon the promotion prospects of a particular trade or activity.

It appeared that the villagers in general were miles away from the ambit of modern markets, what to talk of transporting the surplus products or adding value to them. The thrift habit was yet to pick up, though there was an urge for same, more so, among women in a society otherwise fully dominated by hefty and tall men. Credit link with the banks was also ruled out, as the nearest branch was located at a distance of 35 kms, requiring an irritating journey time of minimum six to seven hours.

As per prevailing tradition, the women were kept out of the meeting. Their role was limited to serving ethnic snacks, cold drink and tea. They could, nevertheless, be contacted near the gate when the GOI functionary expressed a desire to meet them. In his opinion, they were going to be main beneficiaries of the scheme, he had come to explain and advocate. This interaction made possible with the help of Torepkiu and the village Pastor could invite useful insights into the overall potential of the community. Within no time, the present villagers could regroup themselves into five to six new self help groups. They appeared more interested if not motivated.

The delayed lunch at Chairman's traditional villa turned out to be a more relaxed affair. Varieties of ethnic non-vegetarian dishes were served with care and smile by four daughters of Chairman. Fortunately, three of them were studying and one of them had a plan to go to Kohima for higher studies. Torepkiu, despite being requested, refused to eat, for, in his scheme of things, meals were to be taken only twice- 9:30 AM and 5.30 PM.

Sharp at 5pm, it began getting dark. It was time for the guest from Guwahati to leave. Accompanied by the District and Block officials, he summed up the nuts and bolts of the project to the eager villagers. Getting into his fur jacket, he did not forget to thank one and all, apart from showing them some semblance of optimism. He got an opportunity to shake hands with everyone except Torepkiu.

When the convoy of four Jeeps passed by the high and impressive traditional gate of the village, the uniformed Village Guard gave a smart salute. A few children ran from behind to bid good bye. Away from the gate, near an unused bus stop, a man hiding under an old thick blanket was also seen waving at the Jeeps. He uttered to himself-"whether they do something for the village or not, I have done my duty, to the best of my ability". Can you guess, who was he?

The emerging, crystal clear rainbow from the nearby Myanmar border at dusk attempted to narrate a story with a tinge of hope and optimism. Without noticing this rare spectacle, the Govt. Jeeps picked up momentum to reach Tuensang.

Within a few months, the Civil Servant in question was transferred, leading to a situation when no dent could be made in the fragile socio-economic structure of the village, despite dedicated efforts.

POEMS

54

Rabdentse Scenario

Sky Is Dustless, Blue and Clear
Distant Objects Look So Near
Seen Are Bermiok And Rinchenpong
Invisible Are Namchi And Kalimpong

Down Below Is Bazar of Gyalsing
Its Beauty One Can not Help Appreciating
Tree In Front Abounds In Peaches
Ground Below Has Insects And Leaches

Flowers In Their Full Bloom
Appear Tempting From Room
One Comes Out For Close Look
Leaving Aside An Absorbing Book

Near Lamp Solar Photo Voltaic
Orchids Look Lovely & Exotic
They Last For Many Days
Unaffected By Rain & Sunrays

Lawn In Front Is Lush Green
Cold Wind Goes Down One's Spleen
Yet One Is Immensely Keen
To Admire The Beauty Rarely Seen

Who Says Rabdentse Life Is Boring ?
That All The Time One Feels Like Snoring
Innumerable Are Beauties Of Nature
All Types, Large, Small And Miniature

One Needs Imagination To Catch
And Right Mood To Match
Go For A Drink Or Admiration
Or Resort To- Contemplation In Isolation

55

Syndrome of Economics

Producers Organise To Produce
Investors Plan To Manipulate
Retailers Dominate To Sell
Labourers Toil, Consumers Need To Reduce.....

Demand Can Not Command
Supply May Play Hide & Seek
Strange Are Forces Of Market
Money Has To Come From Tight Casket

When You Venture To Spend
Have To Plan And Comprehend
Struggle, Please And Appease
Perhaps Indefensible To Defend

When We Decide To Borrow
Should Not Be Affraid Of Sorrow
Loans Have To Be Repaid
While Floating In Profit
Or When Fortune Is Unmade

If We Can Not Pay Tax
We May Not Relax
Invite Worry And Machinations
Implications May Lead To Complications

Assets Are Also Liabilities
These Have To Be Maintained
And Greed To Have More
Has To Be Contained

Private May Look Active & Attractive
At Times It May Deviate
Public May Appear Outdated & Dormant
Being Safe, It Is Certain To Alleviate

56

Life in Fast Lane

With rise in income
Come myriad false notions
You soar in the sky
Unaware of the reality,
Resort to lies of variety.

You think of yourself as wise
And cajole the fellow beings
To give up 'outdated' notions,
Honesty, simplicity and traditions
Slowly, the rising income strikes

To pay you back in your own coin
Having forgotten that you came naked
Will depart in company of cloth of loin

Your decorated pyre will be lit
You leave behind
All your notoriety or fame
Are confined soon in a garlanded frame.
Your erstwhile drawing room
Instead of drawing,
Will lead to withdrawal
Of relatives and friends

The world is a gigantic stage
Human beings are mere players
The moment a call comes from above
We fly back to wide open sky
Like a sparrow, parrot or a dove.

56- A

कविता

मैं कविता लिखता नहीं,
कविता मुझे लिखने लगी है।
वे कहने लगे-सामने है आलोक,
पर कोई रोशनी दिखी नहीं।।

मोतियाबिंद चाहे हो श्वेत,
या हो इसका रंग श्याम।
जब डाक्टर भरता जेब सरेआम,
जूझता रहता है आवाम।।

चोरी और सीना जोरी

मैं चोर हूँ, पर ईमान बेचता हूँ,
यही दुनिया का रुतबा है।
ईमानदार को मूर्ख और सुस्त,
और बेईमान को मानते दुरुस्त।।

उनकी ही सदा चलती,
वे निरंतर करते हुड़दंग।
मौका मिले तो क्यों ना करें,
हम अपनी आवाज बुलंद।।

बदलाव

मंडप के नीचे,
घूंघट के पीछे,
चपल चंचल चंदा।
लग रही थी–
चंद्रमुखी सी।।

समय के अंतराल पर,
ख्यालों और बंधनों के जाल में,
तारों से नाता टूटने लगा।
सूर्य की रोशनी चुभने लगी,
दिखने लगीं *सूर्यमुखी सी।।*

जीवन की चिंता कहें,
या मानें समय का प्रेशर।
संसार के प्रति मन उचटने लगा,
ज्वालाएँ बढ़ने लगी,
प्रतीत होने लगीं, *ज्वालामुखी सी।।*

सितारा

जीवन में एक सितारा था
शांत, सुशील और प्यारा था
एक दिन वो टूट गया
दुनिया से नाता छूट गया।

वृक्ष की ओर देखें हम
पत्ते सूख और डालियाँ गिर जाती हैं
पर ऊपर बढ़ने की अभिलाषा
फिर हरियाली ले आती है।

पीना और जीना

मैं पीता नहीं,
पीने का नाटक करता हूँ।
वे पीते हैं, पर पीकर,
जीने का नाटक करते हैं।

भविष्य

बुझ जायेंगे चराग
खत्म हो जायेगा नजारा
बुलंद रहेगा सदा
अखंण्ड भारत का सितारा

(H) ANKOOR'S SECTION

Star In The Making

Being only 13 has not hampered Ankoor Srivastava from trading the path of some serious creative writing. Though a lot more is to come both in quantity and quality

by Prakriti

HE scribbles about the scenario in Gujarat, muses on the paradoxes of life, writes and short-stories that distinctly have the 'Saki' flavour to it. "Yes, I read the story 'The Dusk' by saki and got the idea to write," Ankoor Srivastava is quick to admit. Pleasantly strange. Though not surprising because it comes from this 13-year-old budding writer, who has been recently enticed by dual charms of the poems 'n' prose.

■ Master Ankoor Srivastava

A self-satisfied loner, Ankoor was encouraged to pen down his reactions and thoughts by one of his grand-uncles. Being a *Star News* and *Discovery Channel* bill only facilitated the "penchant to express," as he admits.

A class eight student of Sanskriti School, he's all praises for it, though confesses not having shown any of his creations to his teachers. Why? "Just like that," he responds shyly. A typical trait of being the only progeny of an IAS dad and a home-maker mom. That by no means indicate that he's a *bookish-keeda*. "I like to play football, table-tennis and cricket," he quickly adds before you can make up your mind on the stereotype. Talking of the *kitaabs*, he fondly reads Enid Blytons, Hardy Boys and loves to linger on detective novels. At the moment, Harry Potter occupies this roly-poly teenager's fancy.

Talking of the other side of adulation, of whether he has a critic, Ankoor replies with maturity far beyond his age. "No, I don't. But even if I would, I'd welcome it, as it would only help me get better." As for future plans, he has set his eyes on being a doctor, biology being the subject of his taste. "But I want to continue writing, even if I get very busy."

> A self-satisfied loner, Ankoor was encouraged to pen down his reactions and thoughts by one of his granduncles.

Not a bulk of creation to his share at the moments, but Ankoor Srivastava has definitely boarded a train to the fascinating journey of creative writing. So bon voyage!

Excerpts from his poems:

Violence, Tolerance and Innocence

They killed people
They killed the peace
Which killed the emotions, feelings, and sentiments of people
Secularism fell prey to the evil forces of fanaticism
Gujrat was shaken
When it was taken away by the rioter

Excerpts from his poem:

Bed of flowers and thorax

This world consists of a heaven and a hell
This world consists of dense forests and deserts
This world is like a coin consisting of two sides: head and tail. ♦

analysis January 2003

57

Violence, Tolerance and Innocence

Gujrat was shaken
When it was taken away by the rioters

They killed people
They killed peace
Which killed the emotions, feelings
and sentiments of the people

They burnt the train like petrol
They burnt the people like wood
They burnt the houses like undesirable grass
Secularism fell prey to the evil forces of fanaticism

Gujrat was shaken
When it was taken away by the rioters

They spoil the lives of many
They boiled up the blood of many
They violated the rules
People tolerated their wounds
Wounds were terrible
Life of people has become miserable

Ahimsa and truth has been hampered,
Hammered and trampled
Gujrat was shaken
When it was taken away by the rioters

This mutiny by the devils and evils has
Broken the unity of the communities
Land of peace has been broken into pieces

The imperialism of innocence by violence has
Sown the seeds of communalism
This feeling of communalism has separated
The people on the basis of religion
The riots were regional
But effect was national

Gujrat was shaken
When it was taken-away by the rioters

The riots have brought the homeless on streets
Who cannot give themselves a treat?

Children have no books
Without which you cannot prove yourself
They have no clothes
Without which you cannot go on roads
They have lost their beloved parents
Who were very relevant to them

Gujrat was shaken
When it was taken-away by the rioters

The political parties have a lust for power
Although they are just

This has awaken them
They have taken steps to fight communalism
Have tried to bring about secularism
This secularism has been derived from
the writing of the great people

Gujrat was shaken
When it was taken-away by the rioters

God is one but people lack oneness
All religions teach us same things
So we should live in harmony
Seven colours of rainbow
Together form the ray of sun

We should replace the narrow beliefs
By broad beliefs
Communalism by secularism
Violence by unity
Above all, we should be united

Put an end to this violence
Before it becomes endless

58

Nature-A Human

If this planet is a human,
Then the trees and plants are its lungs,
Nourishing every organ with air.

The ocean is its heart;
The rivers are its arteries and veins;
The canals and the streams are the capillaries,
Carrying water which is its blood and life.

The animals who maintain the ecological balance
Are its organs that float in water.

Natural calamities we face is its immune system,
Protecting it from the..........

The humans are the parasites
Causing damages for their greed, not for need.

These are the diseases that Nature suffers from,
But unlike humans, it only gives, does not take.

Swinging from Present to Future

Forget the vast past
Never regret about it
Remember your present
Enjoy it

Remember faithful God Always.
Have a tint of the future
Present is the foundation stone
Laid by you
And the future is supported
On this stone.

59

Dramatic World

This world is a stage
You are the actor
God writes dramas
You are given a role in each drama

You have to perform
You act well
You are awarded
You fail to act
You are punished

You get a better role if you act well
It becomes easier for you to get freedom
From this weird, dreadful, regretful,
Revengeful, world
And get entry into
Beautiful, delightful, graceful,

Lovely world-**heaven.**
You get an adverse role
If you fail to act in the drama
It will be difficult for you
To get freedom.
You will be a colonist of the
Most dreadful, regretful,
And revengeful world-Hell.

60

Bed of Flowers or Thorns ?

World consists of Ups and Downs
Of Victories and Defeats
World consists of Good and Bad Times
Of Happiness and Sorrow

World consists of Love and Hatred
Of Rich and Poor
World consists of Champions and Losers
Of Mistakes and Corrections

World consists of Merits and Demerits
Of Pleasures and Difficulties
World consists of Comforts and Hardships
Of Desires and Contentment

World consists of Truth and Lies
Of Violence and Non-violence
World consists of Rights and Duties
Of Communalism and Secularism

World consists of Beauty and Beasts
Of Pride and Jealousy
World consists of Strong and Weak
Of Advantages and Disadvantages

World consists of Whites and Blacks
Of Praise and Criticism
World consists of Friends and Foes
Of Saints and Terrorists

World consists of Dense Forests and Deserts
It Also consists of Heaven and Hell

World is a Coin Having Two Sides: Head and Tail

Head Depicts A Bed of Flowers
On Which It Is Easy To Walk
Tail Depicts A Bed of Thorns
On Which It Is Difficult To Walk

****

World Also Consists of A God and A Devil
Who Reside In Our Heart

Follow The God
To Reach The Top
Follow The Devil
To Land In Miseries

World Consists of A Faithful,
Loving, Kind and Great God
Who Gives Good and Bad Times

In Bad Times We Always Whine
In Good Times We Have No Time To Thank Him

We Remember Him In Distress Times
But Forget In Our Best Times

STORIES

61

A Tale Of Two Families

Alirampur was a small village in the North West Frontier of Hindustan. A large number of Hindus and Muslims lived here. The village was famous for its Hindu-Muslim unity. The name itself talks about this unity. Ali is a Muslim name while Ram is the name of a Hindu God. The people were helpful, compassionate and generous. They did not see the religion of a person. All were given equal importance.

Even secularism prevailed in this small village as the Hindus did not find any harm to visit mosques. Muslims also visited temples. All the families lived in peace, harmony and happiness. Such two families were the families of Ram Babu and Muhammad Ali Khan.

Ram Babu and Muhammad Ali Khan were Good friends. Their wives shared their techniques of cooking with each other. Two families had often dinners together. The Hindus considered cow to be a sacred animal while Muslims would not eat pigs. Both the families were well informed about this and did not, therefore, offer these two meals to each other. They celebrated festivals of each other together. The Muslim family lit lamps on Diwali nights. The Hindus greeted the Muslims on the eve of Idd. The children studied together. They helped each other during times of difficulty.

This unity between the two families continued for a long time. Many years passed by. Ram Babu and Khan became Grandfathers.

Twenty two years had passed. It was the magical year of 1947 for most of the Hindustanis, but not for the two families. Can we guess why ?

The two families had gathered in Khan's house and were having nice talk, full of gurgling laughter when they were joined in by Laxman's family. He was another jovial villager. He had a serious face that day, though he was very cheerful.

Looking at his face Khan asked him why are you looking so "sad"? Said Laxman very loudly "I am very sad. Have you read newspaper today ? continued Laxman in his loud voice "It talks of policy of separating this great country into two parts, namely, Hindustan and Pakistan. But I have good news as well. Due to efforts of great people and freedom fighters the British are thinking of leaving India.

"Oh what a good news ?" said Ram Babu happily.

The others also expressed their happiness by shouting cheerfully.

"We are free from the clutches of the British" said all with joy and happiness.

"Yes we are free" agreed Laxman. "But those British are dividing our country into two parts. They have formed Muslim League against India which is demanding a separate nation for Muslims- Pakistan. Pak means pure while tan means land. This is because of the British. They have shown the seeds of hatred and communalism in the mind of people and are dividing the Hindustanis on the basis of religion".

On hearing this everyone showed concern and were tense due to it. But at the same time there was happiness as well.

The next few weeks witnessed discussions in the village about possible division of Hindustan. All the people looked worried.

When such a discussion was taking place in Khan's house, Laxman provided them with another piece of sad and alarming news. The news was about a communal riot in an adjoining village. The riot took the lives of thirty people. It worried everyone.

The next two days witnessed some more killings in the adjoining village. The three families, as usual were having a discussion on the growing communal tension when suddenly they heard a loud noise. They came out from their houses and saw a group of people armed with guns and other kinds of lethal weapons. They were shouting anti - Muslim slogans and had already burnt two Muslim houses.

By their appearance, Babu could make out that they were Hindus. Babu could also make out that they had an intention to throw away the Muslims of the village.

They were shouting "Muslims, get out of India. This is the land of Hindus"

At this moment Babu alarmed Khan and advised him to stay in his house. He was sure that he being a Hindu, the rioters would not harm him. That night Khan could save himself only by a whisker. Otherwise the mobs killed the whole of Muslim community. Those who got spared were forced to go to the other side of the border-Pakistan.

The only Muslim family left in the village was Khan's family. Khan family lived in a lot of tension and hardship. More Muslim killings in the neighbouring villages further scared the family. So one day they decided to leave their beloved home in the village.

Tears came out from the eyes of Khan and his family. They felt a lot of grief. They were leaving their bosom friends. They were going to make new homes on the other side of border. Their eyes were full of tears on seeing the familiar landmarks. All these would remain but they would not be there.

It was not a magical year for them.

****

It was the year of 1965. Many years had passed by. The grandsons of two families of Alirampur had grown up. Some were Army officers. Khan's grandson was in Pakistani Army while that of Babu was serving Indian Army. This year witnessed a fierce war between India and Pakistan.

Their grandsons were posted on the war front. Khan's Grandson was assigned the duty of destroying Alirampur. At that moment he was unaware of the fact that he belonged to Alirampur.

Khan's grandson with his soldier friends reached Alirampur without much difficulty. One of them knew the area very well. Here they talked about their plans and expressed their feelings for Pakistan. Khan's grandson described his nation as the purest land on earth. He added that he did not mind sacrificing his life for his nation. But their plans did not work and they were soon captured by the Indian troops. At that moment, Ram Babu was also present on the spot.

It took some time for them to recognise each other. They hugged each other. But it was not the same person Babu had hugged. The other person had changed in many ways. He was no longer Indian, he was a Pakistani. He was looking desperate in handcuffs.

Even he was on the war front like his grandson.

Rambabu gave the boy a suspicious glance. He didnot know what to do. Whether welcome him with joy or slap him as he was now a foreigner who had come to destroy his own village. Baby's eyes were full of tears. At last he uttered:-

"We are meeting after a long time. But you and I are different. What an adverse meeting we had today. It would have been better if we had not met".

The boy didn't have any answer.

Hence, a good healthy relationship between the two families came to an end because of fanaticism and communalism.

THEY WERE NOT INDIANS OR PAKISTANIS, BUT WERE HINDUSTANIS.

62

Cock and Bull

John used to go for frequent evening walks in the park. One day he was seated on a bench upon getting tired. It was late evening. Lights were glittering like stars. It was a moonlit night. All the birds were making different sounds. Place looked like a painting.

John thought that he was the only person left in the park as most of his friends had left after walk. But it was not so. There were many others present over there. They did not come to park for walks or for a change like rich people. Park was their home. They were poor people.

A similar person came upto him. He was middle aged, tall, fat and was wearing an overcoat as winter was approaching. The man sat next to John and politely and softly said "Do you mind if I talk to You ?"

John agreed and the man started "I had come to this town for business work. I have finished and was supposed to go back today".

"Then what happened ?"John said suddenly without showing much of interest.

"And now you see, I have missed my evening flight. I have no where to go tonight".

"Why don't you go to a hotel ?"John advised.

"I was staying in the Hill View Hotel for a week. I can not stay there tonight as my booking was only till yesterday. When I returned to the hotel, I was told that the room was allotted to someone else and that no other room was vacant", explained the man.

"Why don't you go to some other hotel?" asked John.

"Yes I can go but I am scared that I may miss my flight again as I am careless". Today I missed the flight because I had forgotten my ticket in the hotel and when I came back to take it, I had already missed my flight", the man said angrily.

"I donot know what to do as I have spent all the money in paying hotel bills", said the man sadly.

"You seem to think that I have made a Cock and Bull story for you", said the man loudly and strongly this time.

Before John could say anything the man continued in his loud voice "No one believes me in this world and no one is ready to help me".

"I will believe you if you show your ticket to me" said John coolly and strongly.

"Ticket" said the man. "Oh !" The man looked into his pocket and said in a disgusting voice

"I guess I have left it in the taxi".

The man stood up and walked away slowly from John.

John felt that man was making a Cock and Bull story which did not work. He laughed softly at the man. He looked at his watch and was shocked to know that it was dinner time. He had wasted a lot of time in listening to the man's story. He stood up hastily when he saw a piece of paper fallen on the ground. He picked it up and found that it was not only a piece of paper but the proof of man's story.

John gave it a fleeting glance and started looking for the man. Luckily he found him at the exit gate of the park and loudly said "the true witness of your story" raising his hand and showing him the ticket. The man looked back with surprise and joy.

John apologised to the man and offered him his services. The man said" I shall be grateful to you if you can provide your house to me for a night".

John agreed and took him to his house. John got praise from the man and he thanked him for what he had done. John was glowed by the warmth of affection of the man. They had Dinner together. The man told John many stories about his friends full of gurgling laughter. By this time John was convinced that the man was a kind and good person. The man made a call to his family to tell that he was returning the next day.

Next morning John offered the man to join him for a walk in the park. But the man refused by saying that he was too tired and that he would have to go to the airport to buy a ticket. John did not force him and gave him the key of one of his cars to go to airport. John had lent some money to the man the previous night. John told the man that he would return in an hour's time.

John had a lovely time in the park as the weather was very good and soothing. After an hour he decided to return to his home. On his return the man had promised him to tell him some more humourous stories. John had become attached to the man. He was totally lost in these thoughts. He reached his house and rang the bell. He stood there for a long time as no one opened the door. He shouted the man's name but was answered by a silence which was unexpected. He became suspicious.

He thought of knocking at the back door. The door was found open. He entered like a mouse and could not believe what he saw. All the things were not there. He was shocked to see this and felt very sad. His hard earned money and his favourite car were not there. But he discovered a piece of paper on the marble- topped table. John picked it up. The following was written :

"Dear Mr. John. I thank you very much for giving me this opportunity to become rich".

The man was the culprit. Thus John had himself become a humourous character of his stories.

John was shocked and terrified. He was left with no clothes except the ones he was wearing. He had no money. He was depressed and was thinking about the ticket. He had many questions which had no answers.

The next morning when he was seated at the bench in the park, two other persons were talking in a loud voice.

"Do not make Cock and Bull stories" said one man.

"Believe me, I have lost my ticket on Monday under that bench", pointing towards the bench occupied by John.

This was the same bench where John was fooled by the man's Cock and Bull story.

John had found the answer to his question.

Notes

1. Sikkim Express, Gangtok, First Week Of February, 2021.
2. Sikkim Express, 17 January, 2021.
3. IndianBureaucracy.com, August 4, 2022.
4. IndianBureaucracy.com, July 11, 2022.
5. Sikkim Express, 23 March, 2022.
6. IndianCentury.in, April 26, 2022.
7. IndianBureaucracy.com, 3 August, 2021.
8. IndianBureaucracy.com, 3 October, 2021.
9. IndianBureaucracy.com, 7 September, 2021.
10. IndianBureaucracy.com, 24 December, 2021.
11. IndianBureaucracy.com, 26 October, 2021.
12. IndianBureaucracy.com, 22 December, 2021.
13. IndianBureaucracy.com, 31 August, 2021.
14. IndianBureaucracy.com, 13 June, 2022.
15. IndianBureaucracy.com, 21 September, 2021.
16. IndianBureaucracy.com, 15 November, 2021.
17. IndianBureaucracy.com, 2 August, 2021.
18. IndianBureaucracy.com, 20 March, 2022.
19. Sikkim Express, 8 June, 2022.
20. IndianBureaucracy.com, 2 July, 2022.
21. IndianBureaucracy.com, 10 September, 2021.
22. IndianBureaucracy.com, 7 August, 2021.
23. IndianBureaucracy.com, 17 August, 2021.

24. IndianBureaucracy.com, 25 August, 2021.
25. IndianCentury.in, 24 January, 2022.
26. IndianBureaucracy.com, 27 February, 2022.
27. IndianBureaucracy.com, 6 March, 2022.
28. IndianCentury.in, 24 March, 2022.
29. IndianBureaucracy.com, 8 April, 2022.
30. IndianBureaucracy.com, 14 August, 2022.
31. IndianBureaucracy.com, 13 May, 2022.
32. IndianCentury.in, 28 July, 2022.
33. Social Action, Vol. 59, No 4, October-December, 2009.
34. IndianBureaucracy.com, 17 February, 2022.
35. IndianBureaucracy.com, 24 February, 2022.
36. IndianBureaucracy.com, 21 July, 2022.
37. IndianBureaucracy.com, 15 August, 2021.
38. IndianCentury.in, 21 October, 2021.
39. IndianBureaucracy.com, 15 October, 2021.
40. IndianBureaucracy.com, 6 February, 2022.
41. IndianBureaucracy.com, July, 2021.
42. Indian Dominion, Delhi, March, 2013.
43. Sikkim Express, 22 March 2014.
44. Indian Mountaineer, IMF Journal, No. 44, 2008.
45. IndianBureaucracy.com, 8 August, 2021.
46. IndianBureaucracy.com, 21 April, 2022.
47. Outlook, Hindi, February, 2012
48. Akshar Parva, Delhi, January, 2013.
49. Grihswamini.e.magazine, August, 2020

FAR FROM THE
MADDING CROWD...
Sikkim
Small and beautiful

02/08/2006

Index

B

C

D

F

G

J

M

O

P

T

W

Y